To

CHRISTOPHER & GEORGINA

*This record of the environment
of their birth*

Israel

5 —

3.50
US

Leonard Becker.
1960.

NO ALTERNATIVE

D. R. ELSTON

No Alternative

ISRAEL OBSERVED

Ein Brera, Hebrew for
No Alternative, is the explanation usually given
by Israelis for their success against the
Arabs and their survival as
an independent State

HUTCHINSON OF LONDON

HUTCHINSON & CO. (Publishers) LTD
178-202 Great Portland Street, London, W.1

London Melbourne Sydney
Auckland Bombay Toronto
Johannesburg New York

First published 1960

This book has been set in Bembo type
face. It has been printed in Great Britain on
Antique Wove paper by Taylor Garnett
Evans & Co Ltd., Watford, Herts, and
bound by them

One

ONE had little to do with the Jews. They were sprawled over most of new Jerusalem and had their own garish city of Tel Aviv on the coast, too close to Jaffa. They had crude townlets of their own, like Baron Edmond de Rothschild's Zichron Jaacov, near Haifa, and Petah Tikva, another Rothschild Foundation upstart; and Rehovot, with the Weizmann Institute of Science putting on airs because there was nothing else like it between Rome and Tokyo. Besides, there were Jewish communal settlements all over the place: collective units where heaven knew what went on – free love it was said; and Marxism; and illegal training with illegal arms; and the hiding of illegal immigrants.

The Jews worked hard; one had to admit it. They had a culture of sorts. They were well organized – too well if it came to that, with their semi-autonomous Jewish Agency in that big, white, rather impressive building standing back from King George Avenue; and their local governing body called *Vaad Leumi*; and their wealthy National Fund, which would have bought up nearly all the land in Palestine if the British White Paper had not stepped in; and their American lobbyists.

The Englishman administering the Palestine Mandate rarely went into the Jewish quarters of Jerusalem; and, unless he were a policeman, was hardly ever seen in Tel Aviv or any of the small towns. As for the collective settlements, they were no place for him. There were District Commissioners, of course, in the administrative centres throughout the country, but there was hardly any inter-weaving of British and Jewish social life anywhere. If there had been, the distorted impression of the British as an occupation force, which later, when the war had ended, became more pronounced, might not have replaced the earlier impression of the British as liberators.

The Englishman in Jerusalem lived in quarters shared by certain well-to-do Arabs but almost free of Jews: the German Colony, founded by the Templars in a shady valley to the south; Upper Baka'a, next to it, with solid stone houses built by Arabs and Greeks; around Herod's Gate against the Old City walls; and, if a

7

bachelor, probably in rooms of that well-managed, cool, comfortable and oddly genteel institution known as the American Colony, on the Arab side of the dividing line between the new and the old city and close to the Anglican Cathedral.

He lived in these pleasant quarters and a car took him to the Secretariat in a wing of the big, heavy-looking King David Hotel, or to wherever his department might be, and took him back again; and scarcely a Jew did he see except some pushing official from the Agency, or one of his own Jewish colleagues appointed under terms of the Mandate requiring a certain number of Jews and Arabs in the public service of the country. But the Jews as a community were to the north and north-west, where all the lights were and the bright window-fronts and the cafés and the traffic; in the overcrowded, zealously Orthodox, Ottoman quarter known as Mea Shearim; and in the modern, well-built, tree-grown suburb of Rehavia, stretching westwards from King George Avenue and housing, for the most part, the Jewish professional and well-to-do classes.

In practice, the average Englishman in Jerusalem also saw less of the Arab than he might have done. But he did most of his shopping in Arab shops; his servants were Arab; he would often run out to have a look at some characteristic Arab town, like Hebron or Nablus; he supped with Arab notables, whose hospitality was more spectacular and interesting than that of the Jews; and from time to time he sauntered through the stone-paved, mat-roofed lanes of the Old City, stared at the Dome of the Rock or El Aksa Mosque; bought souvenirs in dusky, hole-in-the-wall shops; had skewered, tastily-grilled meats in some Arab restaurant; watched the nineteenth century animated lithograph of those who came and went through the Damascus Gate – green turbans, white turbans, red fezes, flowing *kefiyas* kept on the head by knotted black cords; long gowns of black or white or yellow; peasants in for the day; monks and mullahs.

For my part, at first I did what other Englishmen did and probably thought as other Englishmen thought. I had my cottage in Baka'a, was driven to my office in the old Convent of Gallicante south of the Zion Gate, went off now and then through the stony lanes of the Old City enchanted by everything I saw (and how enchanting it is, this walled Old City: the bent, robed men with their girdles and turbans; the clink of ear-rings on dark, straight women; the mischievous urchins with white teeth; the merchants

8

half asleep among their wares; the clanking cymbals of the water-sellers; the camels and the asses; the lanes sloping to the middle to form gutters; the gold and grey, and the green like green mould, of the walls on each side; the open sunny courts of the Dome of the Rock and the light perfection of El Aksa; the Greeks in and out of the Holy Sepulchre and the Armenians and the Franciscans in and out of it; and the way down through St. Stephen's Gate to Gethse-mane: – how enchanting it is!).

I attended parties given by other Englishmen or by one of the Nashashibis, who represented Arab nobility, or by that hardy promoter of Arab social life in Jerusalem, Madame Antonious, familiarly known as Katy, the widow of a remarkable Arab who wrote a book called *The Arab Awakening*.

The Arabs were difficult, of course; but one expected them to be. The Jews were the intruders, not the Arabs. And if at that time the Arab was less fervent than the Jew in support of the Allied cause against the German, that, too, could be explained easily enough. Besides, the Arab has a simple, perhaps primitive, ease of manners that is considered lovable by the Englishman, who is something of a lyricist and much prefers the Arab on his ass to the Jew in the driving seat of his tractor; the *fellahin* to the collective farmers; and people who come from deserts to people who come from the wrong quarters of East European cities. The Jew, to many Englishmen, was out of place in Palestine.

The German Jews were more presentable than the others. They knew they were different and tended to put on airs. They read their Goethe more reverently than any Aryan, played Bach on their pianos and Wagner on their gramophones and diligently talked German when most of the other Jews went about talking Hebrew.

I was interested in these differences and, having met a learned German Jew, Doctor Ernst Rosenbaum, asked him about them. Doctor Rosenbaum, like most German Jews of some substance in Jerusalem, lived in the Rehavia quarter. In Berlin he had been a statistician. Now he was old and a little tired. He had brought with him a fair sum of money from Germany and lived modestly on its return. He was writing a book about the influence of mathematics on the structure of society. It was a thoroughly German task to be at and there is little doubt that it eased these last, exiled years of the doctor's life.

He was small and gave the impression of being fat. His clothes,

9

dusted usually with cigar ash, were always rucked up so that the trouser legs and coat sleeves seemed too short for him, as if he had grown out of them. He was near-sighted and wore rimless glasses that shone like two small searchlights as he peered into one's face. He had a white moustache that drooped. But he was a kind, good, sad man whose Zionism could not be expected to drain away a nostalgia for the life he and his family had lived in Berlin long ago.

I said to Doctor Rosenbaum:

'Tell me, why do you German Jews remain so German when all the other Jews in Palestine are flaking off their origin and becoming Palestinian Jews – distinguishably so?'

He smiled pityingly. We were standing in front of a small grocery shop in Rehavia. Women with shopping baskets were going in and out, and there was a smell of freshly-opened packing cases. Doctor Rosenbaum watched the entrance to the shop as if he were looking there for the answer to my question. Then he turned to me. He peered so hard through those thick glasses that it multiplied the wrinkles about the corners of his eyes and gave the impression that he was amused.

'Are the others becoming Palestinian Jews?' he asked. 'I doubt it. I doubt it. Could it be that you don't know what a Pole or a Russian is like and so don't recognize the Pole or the Russian in these so-called Palestinians the way you recognize the German in us? Could that be it?'

'No, I don't think it's that. I think you isolate yourselves by continuing to speak German and making no effort, no real effort, to learn Hebrew. The others, the Poles and Ukrainians and so on, expand into the community as a whole by trying to make Hebrew their daily language.'

Doctor Rosenbaum nodded solemnly.

'Yes, yes, that's true. But you see, there is no particular point in their sticking to Polish or Russian or Turkish or whatever it may be. For us Germans it is different. German is the language of a great culture, a great literature. If we stopped speaking German we would simply stop thinking altogether except what to buy in that little shop, or what bus to take, or how to meet the rates and taxes.'

'What about the children of German Jews? They're learning Hebrew, and just a smattering of German picked up at home. Won't that create a barrier between you and your children?'

The doctor rubbed his nose.

'There is something in that,' he said mournfully. 'It worries us. We are meeting with it already. You see, most of us who come from Germany are politically Liberal. We are Zionists. But we are not in a hurry for a State. Our children are, because that is what they are taught at school and in their youth organizations. We do not want the British to go after the war. There are thirty million Arabs around us and our only defence against them is the British. But our children do not think like that. Their parents are to them a lost generation. And for that matter, so we are to ourselves – a lost generation.'

He wagged his finger at me, screwing up his eyes as he peered intently into my face.

'But do not be misled,' he said. 'We are contributing our share to this community. Look at the quality of the physicians, surgeons, legal men we have given to it. Ben Gurion and the other active leaders of the Jews of Palestine may be right in trying to build a community on the Spartan model. We German Jews prefer Athens to Sparta.'

'I see.'

Often, in those early days, that was about the only comment I could make. There was the war, of course, and that confused local issues, so that Jew and Arab and even Englishmen were guessing at what the accidents of peace might bring to their own particular problems in Palestine. The Jews, perhaps, except for those who had come out of Germany, like Doctor Rosenbaum, were the most realistic in their guesswork, and, as peace came nearer, intensified their preparations for war, or at any rate for a conflict bound to develop into violence.

But for those of us who were neither Jew nor Arab nor Englishman with his opinions shaped by policy, it was difficult to foresee the destiny of Palestine once the priorities of world war were removed; or to guess what would happen if either Jew or Arab became dominant. The Arabs, or such of them as one met at social gatherings, pretended the conviction that all Palestine would become subject to Arab rule soon after the war. But it was not a conviction one could take seriously. The Palestinian Arabs who at that time were regarded as the leaders of their people were not impressive. The most forceful of them all, Haj Amin el Husseini, former Mufti of Jerusalem, was then in Berlin conducting Hitler's Arab propaganda. In spite of that, the Husseini family was still powerful in Jerusalem and still actively nationalist. But their main contenders for leadership, the Nashashibis, who had more shrewdly calculated the probable outcome of the war, naturally were in better favour with the British Administration than the Husseinis.

I met Raguib Bey Nashashibi, the head of the family, at a party given by the Chief Secretary of the day, John Shaw. We were discussing general prospects and the difficulties of government in Middle East countries, and Raguib Bey said:

'When I am head of the government of an independent Palestine I shall close all schools above the elementary and forbid the entry of foreign newspapers into Palestine.'

'Whatever for?' I asked.

'Ach! All these people' – he waved his hand to embrace, I suppose, the *fellahin*, labourers and petty tradesmen of the country – 'all these people get ideas, silly ideas. They are made uncomfortable by education and newspapers. They lose their standards. They become lazy and rebellious.'

Once again I said:

'I see.'

But I do not suppose that Raguib Bey really meant anything of the kind. Probably it was a sincere expression of a nostalgia. Raguib Bey was likeable. He was broad, of medium height, had a guttural voice and a complexion darker than that of most town Arabs. He was more Turk than Arab, and looked rich – richly composed, that is, as if behind him were many years of good eating, opulent divans to rest upon, deferential servants to attend him. He walked with short steps as if little used to walking, and when he stood still his posture was one of complete relaxation. I could not help thinking that under his loose-fitting, well-made clothes his flesh, as he stood, rested roll upon roll and, as it were, cushioned him.

But he belonged to the old, Ottoman order. It was not surprising that the nationalist Arab hotheads of Jerusalem, Hebron and Nablus looked to the Husseinis rather than the Nashashibis for leadership. Raguib Bey's only chance, as that of most Palestinian Arab moderates, lay in the fact that Adolf Hitler, patron of the red-bearded Haj Amin el Husseini, was on the way to humiliating military defeat on all fronts. Rommel had been beaten at Alamein and the German army, which a year ago had been expected to come up from Egypt into Palestine, was on the run. If the Germans had occupied Egypt and moved up through Sinai into Palestine that, by Arab reckoning, would have been the end of the Jews and a merry dispensation if only for that.

As it was, the Jews had begun to puff themselves out. They considered themselves to be allies of the winning side. Under British initiative and guidance at the time of the Rommel scare, they had formed guerrilla units and sabotage bands to be used against any German army that might enter Palestine. Jewish commando and reconnaissance units had been used by the British against the Vichy French in Lebanon. British aircraft had been dropping Jewish saboteurs and trouble-makers behind the German lines in Eastern Europe. Now a Jewish Brigade was about to be set up and put into action in North Africa or Italy or wherever the British might want them.

All the Arab could do at that time was wait and see. No one can more easily be stirred to hysteria and no one more readily droops into passivity. Now he was passive. Legal Jewish immigration had as good as come to an end thanks to the White Paper issued and enacted by the British Government on the eve of war. Jewish land tenure had been restricted by the same instrument. All in all, there was nothing much the Arab could do and, on the whole, he likes it when there is nothing much he can do except dream his way through life in the vague expectation of ecstasy one day, here or in the hereafter.

Besides, the Jews were buying Arab farm produce at high prices. On the sly they were also buying Arab lands at high prices. Arab and Jew would get around the White Paper decrees by introducing a third person, who might be a Greek or even, as in one or two cases, an Englishman, to whom the Arab would sell his land, and who would then complete the agreed transaction by selling to the Jew. And meanwhile public services were progressing and making things a little easier for everyone: that was thanks mainly to Jewish pressure.

One way and another, therefore, the Holy Land from the summer of 1943 until the end of the war enjoyed something like prosperity and peace. It was an amiable land. Jew and Arab left each other alone and both were friendly to the British. It was a pleasant, comfortable station to be at and I felt myself in luck. Jerusalem is, of course, a city of vivid enchantment at all times. In those days its slow-moving racial streams meandered and mixed along broad, modern avenues; in shady suburbs; down the narrow stony lanes of the Old City; in the sunny courtyards of the Haram-esh-Sherif and round about the bundled cupolas and dark chapels of the Holy Sepulchre; along the cool road by the gilt and blue of the Armenian Cathedral; within the compound of the bulbous Russian Church on rising ground in the new city. Arabs, Jews, Syrians, Bedouin from Transjordan, slender Druse tribesmen, Franciscans and Benedictines, Greeks and Armenians, shuffled along the polished stones of the Old City lanes, waited at bus stops in the modern, new city, mingled like the upshot of seed cast idly on fertile ground. Such was Jerusalem among its stark hills and under its blue sky; after which, as Ronald Storrs wrote, there is no promotion. But a bowl of scorpions it had been called by a much earlier observer and the scorpions were beginning to stir.

2

At that time there were upwards of 100,000 Jews in Jerusalem. As I have said, the Englishman had not much to do with them. Their paths crossed ours seldom except in the process of official business. Probably they were none the worse for that, although some of them resented what was thought to be the social indifference of the British. Of course, there were formal parties given by the High Commissioner or the Chief Secretary or some head of Department, at which prominent Jews as well as prominent Arabs were entertained. I have seen Mr. Shertok, then head of the Jewish Agency's Political Department (and later, with his name Hebraized to Sharett, Foreign Minister in the Government of Israel), in fluent Turkish conversation with a Nashashibi, the Chief Secretary standing by a trifle wistfully and perhaps with some faint hope that Jew and Arab would one day fall into the habit of friendliness and collaboration. One day they will. There was no sign of it then and there has been none since.

I once asked a British medical officer in Jerusalem to give me his opinion why there was so little informal social contact between Jew and Englishman, and he replied:

'Well, for one thing they know so much more than we do.'

As he said that he smiled, but his tongue was not in his cheek.

'It's embarrassing. Take me, for example. I'm a well-qualified, reasonably good physician. But those fellows at the Hadassah

14

Hospital are nearly all of them high-class specialists. Many of these Jewish medical men led their field in Berlin or Vienna or wherever it may have been. In a way, they're medically too big for a country like this.

'That's one thing. There's another on the same level. What decent Englishman wants to go to parties and talk about Kafka – is that the fellow's name? Or sit upright in a ponderously-furnished sitting-room listening to someone playing Bach on the piano? I mean, that sort of thing is all right now and then. But me, if I want to hear music I switch on the wireless and listen comfortably, and probably read *The Lancet* or some book or other while I'm listening. If I want music socially I prefer to pay for a seat in a concert hall. They've got a damn good orchestra here and there's always one of these international johnnies, like Heifetz or Rubenstein, to make it the kind of occasion one shouldn't miss. Maybe I'm not as cultured as I should be. But most of the Jews are over-cultured. You know, "Whenever I hear the word Kultur . . ." – old Göring reaching for his gun. Understandable, in a way.'

He really meant what he was saying, and I felt a certain sympathy for his views. Many Jews were indeed over-cultured: at any rate they seemed so against the Palestine background.

'Thirdly,' went on this medical officer, '– and I wouldn't be a bit surprised if this were at the back of it all – it's difficult in this country, especially with the Jews, to keep social relationships free of politics. We have to move damn carefully. There's a war on and I suppose we've simply got to play up to the Arabs a bit. That seems to be the policy, anyway. Finally, my dear fellow, as you will see for yourself after you've been here a while, the Jews can be as nice as pie, of course, but they are a bit pushing, a bit over-whelming don't you think? One isn't quite used to them. Not so many of them all at once.'

Again there was nothing I could say but:

'I see.'

But in fact I was not seeing at all well and resolved to move a little more among the Jews and try to discover what that tireless people were about.

It seemed to me that the easy way to begin was to start dropping in at Max Hesse's restaurant and bar, which I had been told was the best place of its kind in town. At any rate, that seemed the way an unimportant member of the British official community, who was answerable not to the Mandatory Administration or the Colonial Office but to a hush-hush chief poised in Cairo, should begin. I, too, was supposed to be hush-hush.

My little organization was lodged in the abandoned Convent of St. Pierre en Gallicante. We prepared and transmitted wireless broadcasts, some open, some secret, in German, Polish, Czech, Hungarian and the languages of the Balkans. My British staff numbered about fifteen. The rest, just over one hundred, were members of East European and Balkan resistance movements, most of them Jews. We had brought many of them out of their countries of origin to Istanbul by the secret means we had, and they included Titoists, Greek E.A.M. supporters, members of the Bulgarian Fatherland Front, a strong German team and some Poles, Rumanians and Albanians. Our transmitters were outside the Arab village of Beit Jala, near Bethlehem.

The main purpose of the broadcasts was to hearten the resisting peoples of Eastern Europe and to provide direct contact, by code, with organized resistance movements and with our own agents. We were a happy, eager group of men and women, winning the war in the only fashion we knew, and thoroughly enjoying the cloak-and-dagger attributes of the organization. In fact, we were hush-hush only in the sense that everybody, from the Arab urchins to the Jewish taxi-driver, called us by that name. Our existence and our purpose were as well known to the people of Jerusalem as the Palestine Broadcasting Service. You cannot be particularly hush-hush with a mixed staff of over 120, and with three conspicuous shortwave transmitters, in a city where each one of our seven different languages was the mother-tongue of some section of the community. But we took ourselves and our isolation from the rest of Jerusalem seriously. So did many of the Mandatory Government officials. Secrecy, if it has the proper sanction, can be invested with an impressive authority even when everybody knows what it is all about.

Anyway, no one in Jerusalem could question the propriety of my taking a drink and a meal at Max Hesse's. My chief wireless engineer, Major Nevit Massey, agreed to go with me. He was young, he was a handsome Scot and he dearly liked showing off his excellent knees below the London Scottish kilt. He was also a good engineer, a reckless car driver and a superb scrounger. When we badly needed an additional and powerful short-wave trans-

16

mitter, Nevit hovered about Haifa port watching the ships come in and unload until one day a magnificent transmitter destined to finish by road its journey from Liverpool to Teheran, was carefully swung out from a ship's hold and put down on Haifa quay. Under Nevit Massey's guidance it found its way, instead, to Beit Jala. Oddly enough, the authorities concerned were persuaded without much difficulty to accept the diversion as a fair enough fortune of war.

And so, on a summer's night, we went to Hesse's. Hesse's is a smallish place up a smallish street off Princess Mary Avenue, in the busy eastern sector of the new city. The smallish street is hardly more than a lane, with some fair-sized buildings at the Princess Mary end and at the other end the rather bleak and neglected Moslem cemetery of Mamillah.

Max Hesse greeted us at the door. He greeted us with the courtesy and ease appropriate to a former chief steward of the Hamburg-America Line.

'Hullo Max,' said Nevit. 'This is my Big Chief.'

'Welcome, sir. Any friend of the Major's is welcome.'

'If he spends enough,' added Nevit.

Max Hesse spread out his hands.

'But of course. Those who come to my place come to spend. And I think you will agree, Major, they get value for money.'

Max Hesse was short and plump. He had a large face with full lips and troubled eyes. When he was not looking anxious he was looking defiant, as if ready to argue pointedly with anyone who should think his drinks too expensive or his food less than superb. His drinks were not too expensive as prices went in those days and his food, although not superb and tending to monotony, was good, plentiful, and tastefully served.

He liked the British because a good half of his clients were British: not Secretariat British, but Army people. The bar was always full of young officers from sunset until closing time. The Army, of course, in all circumstances has fewer inhibitions than the civil authorities. When to all intents and purposes it is an Army of Occupation, it is apt to form its own judgements and ignore the advice of the civil authorities. That was so in Palestine towards the end of the war and even more so after the war when, the Jews having become troublesome, curfews and armed searches became a matter of routine.

Besides, young officers, and for that matter young other ranks, billeted in populated areas and far from their own homes, have a right to feminine company. Arab girls, even of the Christian community, were hard to come by, and there had been occasions when British soldiers had had to be rescued by their comrades from the wrath of Arab elders bent on preserving the pitiless integrity of their womenfolk. Armenian and Greek girls, attractive as they were, offered little: they were shy of being seen with British soldiers except in the presence of chaperones. But the young Jewish women were thoroughly progressive in their outlook and, at the persuasion of neat uniforms and good, open British faces, let any rancour they might have felt towards the White Paper become impersonal.

The Jewish girls were, for the most part, charming. Their intelligence was of high order. They dressed well and were not prudish. It would have been ungracious of the British Army to let pass the opportunities they gave. Later, after a bad round of Jewish terrorism, the G.O.C. of the day issued an offensively-worded order to the troops requiring non-fraternization and calling upon the British soldier to hit the Jew 'where it hurts him most – his pocket'. Sad days followed that order. British soldiers went about with yearning or boredom in their eyes, and pretty Jewish girls, who should have been out having a good time, stayed at home. And Max Hesse's bar and restaurant were half empty. Soon afterwards, the incautious G.O.C. was transferred.

But all that was after the war. Now there was truce. And at Max Hesse's I met and talked with Army officers, Jewish lawyers, university professors, businessmen, newspaper reporters, even an occasional member of a collective settlement up for a brief visit; and in some cases the encounter led to invitations to Jewish homes, so that presently I began to feel the glimmer of an understanding of these people, who, paradoxical as it may sound, seemed to me to have become less consciously Jewish now that they were a thoroughly Jewish community with a measure of autonomy, than they had been when, like Doctor Rosenbaum, they had considered themselves good Europeans. The first fruits of something like territorial nationhood were evident in a desire to expand from Jewishness into the wide realms of a people working not from an exclusive historical or spiritual heritage but from the uplands of a civilization common to all progressive peoples. They were not rejecting their Jewishness. They were taking it for granted. It was no longer used as a spiritual refuge from the blows of their enemies. Enemies, in future, would have to reckon with the Jews as with anyone else: on a battlefield if necessary.

But as far as I could see there was little arrogance: no wish to be defiant for the sake of defiance: a justifiable pride in what the National Home had done and an almost touching anxiety to have other people see what had been done and declare it good. 'Look at the land we have reclaimed. Look at our farms and herds. Look at our factories. Look at our scientific institutions, our university, our schools. Don't you think we have justified ourselves out here?' And if you mentioned the Arab, they would ask you to show a single Arab who was worse off than he had been before the Jews came. 'But I can show you Arab village after Arab village that is prosperous because of us.' And if you said, then, that the Arab might prefer to be master in his own land even if it meant less prosperity and lower standards, they would answer as Doctor Weizmann did: 'Which is the greater good? – Another independent Arab State and another dispersal of the Jews, or a solution of the age-old Jewish problem in a manner that need give no hurt to the Arab?'

3

They were a surprising people. I found myself getting to know a community the like of which I had never before encountered. There was Hannah, for example. I met her at Hesse's. She was worth meeting. Nevit Massey brought her in one evening and introduced us. Hannah was small and dark, and had brown eyes with flecks of green around the pupils. Her voice was quiet, low-pitched, oddly resolute. Small, girlish, and young as she was – perhaps eighteen or nineteen – she seemed to be as wise and learned as Hypatia. She had graduated with the highest honours and brightest prospects from the Hebrew University, but had come from a *kibbutz*, or communal settlement, and to my surprise intended going back to it.

'Won't you find it rather dull there?' I asked.

'Dull?' She smiled. She had a smile that curled up at the edges, giving an expression of irony. I almost felt that I should apologize for my question.

'No, it's never dull in a *kibbutz*. There's too much to do and too much to look forward to. Besides, the *kibbutz* is a kind of family affair. Everyone is concerned with everyone else's business. It is impossible to be dull. A *kibbutz* is like a self-contained little colony. It's on the move all the time. Doesn't stand still.'

It was time for me to say: 'I see'; and leave it at that. But I did not. Rashly I said:

'But all this learning you got at the university. What will you do with it?'

'Enjoy my life all the more for having it. And probably turn out to be a better *kibbutznik* because of it. Anyway, I suppose that was the purpose behind sending me to the university.'

It was then that I said: 'I see'; and shifted to another topic.

I saw more of Hannah as time went on; and shall tell more of her. She was typical of the new kind of Jewish girl who, so to speak, had come out of the Balfour Declaration. There had been colonies of Jews in Palestine long before the Declaration: east Europeans for the most part, many of them settled in the country with the assistance of Baron Edmond de Rothschild's Foundation set up for that purpose. But they had remained Jews. They had clung to their Jewish ways and their Jewish isolation and their minority outlook. The effect of the Balfour Declaration and its creative intention was to cast the Jew into a new mould.

Hannah looked Jewish: more so than many of the new generation of Palestine Jews, who seem to have reverted – if that is the right word – to fair hair, blue eyes and noses which, if not snub are far removed from the common idea of what Semitic noses should be like. Hannah reminded me of the Hittite prisoners carved in relief on the walls of Karnak; but she had, also, a curiously Egyptian appearance. Her eyes had the disconcerting repose and knowingness of Anubis. Her figure was good: a hard-packed, firmly-held figure. The hands were not delicate. They were well-enough shaped but had been formed by the pressure of mule-harness, pruning-knives, and automatic rifles used stealthily in night training. Her feet, by the calculations of a society shoemaker, were big, They had already covered much ground.

Her manners and perhaps her morals were as light as thistle-down. She was not one of those preposterous people often called 'nature's children'; but right and wrong she defined in accordance with her own instinct and intelligence rather than by any book of rules. One day I was discussing with Hannah the kind of man she might marry. In her low pleasant voice she said, as if it were the most reasonable thing in the world:

'I would never marry a man until I had seen what he was like next morning. The important thing is not to know whether a man is good in bed or not, but whether he is good when he gets up in the morning.'

Alas! As shall be seen, Hannah was never given the opportunity to put her theory into practice: at any rate, not as far as a decision on marriage.

Two

And so it was that I began to know something of the Jews of Palestine. Jews I had known before that, of course: who has not known Jews? I had met them and taken them for granted in England. I had known many of them in Germany.

In 1931 I had spent some months at a certain Badische hotel which was popular among Jews, and which, of course, received Jews gladly. In those days the National Socialists were already noisy and oddly compelling even to many decent and apparently intelligent Germans. But the owner of the hotel in the Badische hills was bitterly opposed to Hitler's anti-Semitism, which could affect the fortunes of his hotel, and was always quick to express the indignation it worked up inside him. Four years later the Jews had been told that they were not welcome in his resort and hotel, and it was not long before the hotel was chosen officially as the place where Nazi leaders of second rank should take rest after the wearing glorifications of the Nürnberg Rally. I do not know how many of this hotel proprietor's former Jewish guests ended up at Dachau or Bergen-Belsen, or whether any of them found the way to Palestine.

The Jews I had known in England I had known as Englishmen rather than as Jews. Whitechapel was not on my beat, and its denizens I saw only from a distance, as they descended from buses to the Leicester Square or Piccadilly pavements on Saturday evenings. One met the English Jews more or less as one met any other English people. Because they bore the name Cohen, or Nathan, or Samuel, one realized vaguely that they were Jews, but their instincts, habits and outlook were thoroughly British. The anti-Semitism one met with was usually of an idle, almost impersonal kind, which I had never interpreted as racialism, certainly not of the kind that found such despicable expression in Germany, and not even of the kind that seems to flourish in the United States. I was to discover later, however, when the war had ended and about one hundred Jewish members of my Jerusalem staff were no longer needed by the organization I was working for, that even the genteel anti-Semitism of the Englishman who detested the methods of Hitler could be effective.

A great deal of what must be called the anti-Semitism of the Englishman is a matter of habit rather than of conviction. One gets into the habit of saying: 'I'll bet that's a bloody Jew', when a flashy car nearly runs one down on the Oxford Road. It is a habit of small harm in itself and of no hostile intention; but gradually, as I had found from my own experience, it creates the assumption, which goes unquestioned because it seems not to lead to anything, that the Jew is somehow a lesser and more vulgar member of society, and is tolerated only because tolerance is a virtue to be encouraged in oneself and the community of which one is a privileged member.

The presence of this kind of anti-Semitism in Gentile countries has never been dealt with seriously. A few attempts have been made to point out where the Jew himself is at fault, as in Hilaire Belloc's *The Jew*. But there is no helpful analysis known to me of a problem not settled by the defeat of the Nazis in war or by the setting up of the State of Israel. That most authoritative of Israel's leaders, Mr. David Ben Gurion, is always pointing out to Jewry beyond Israel that anti-Semitism, even in the most civilized of Gentile communities, is latent when not active and that the only solution for the Jew is to settle in Israel.

It is not easy to see how Israel, within its present boundaries, could absorb even the half of Diaspora Jewry, but the point Ben Gurion is trying to make probably needs to be made. In essence it may not be far removed from the argument Arthur Koestler put out soon after the establishment of the State: that Jews who wanted to stay Jews should become Israelis; with the rest giving up their Jewishness and becoming thoroughly assimilated into the Gentile community of their choice. The trouble is that assimilation can never mean anything much for the Jew as long as he keeps his Jewish name. The only kind of assimilation likely to be of real help to the Jew is the kind that would hide his racial origin.

I suppose Diaspora Jews are themselves in some part responsible for the anti-Semitism that plagues their race. A good many of them are odd, to say the least. And because of their oddness there is something very like anti-Semitism even among Israelis of the new generation. The young Israeli feels what is not far short of amused contempt for the American and British Zionists who from time to time visit Israel and go about their sightseeing a trifle noisily.

The young Israeli is not deriding the Jew. He is deriding qualities which the Diaspora seems to have given the Jew, and especially the American Jew: the unseemly qualities, as he sees them, of people who have not grown with their incomes, and who prefer the fleshpots of Egypt to the hardships of a free, independent and self-respecting Jewish State. And, of course, the young Israeli is apt to resent his economic dependence on world Zionism. In many ways he feels towards Diaspora Zionists something of what the young Australian or Canadian used to feel towards citizens of the Mother Country. It is a characteristic of colonialism, deriving in part from the fact that the Israeli is, indeed, a colonizer, partly from the European origin of most of the native-born Israelis and their parents, who think it proper to be contemptuous of that origin, and, as I have said, partly from economic dependence on world Zionism, which from time to time, in the persons of American or other Jews who have given generously to Israel, makes a conspicuous tour of inspection to see how the money has been spent. In fact, most of these visiting Zionists are eager, warm-hearted people, who have what is little short of adoration for the Israelis. Perhaps they are too maternal towards what they consider to be their own offspring: a trifle too Yiddish for the Israeli.

Doctor Nahum Goldman, an American citizen and the acknowledged leader of world Zionism, said to me in Tel Aviv long ago, part in fun but part in all seriousness:

'What Israelis are inclined to forget is that their chief Metropolis is New York, not Tel Aviv or Jerusalem. Every Zionist in some fashion or another is a citizen of the State of Israel and should be represented in the State's institutions. He contributes heavily to them.'

The idea of any such representation is something Mr. Ben Gurion cannot swallow. It has long been a source of conflict between him and Doctor Goldman. Ben Gurion's attitude is that if Doctor Goldman wants to take part in the government of Israel, let him become an Israeli and head the list of his own political party, the Progressives. That is another odd example of Israel–Diaspora overlapping: active membership abroad and particularly in America, of political parties represented in Israel's parliament, the Knesset. The Progressive Party, headed in Israel by the jurist, Doctor Rosen, who has been Minister of Justice in successive administrations, pays great heed to the Diaspora's Progressive Party, which is led

24

by Doctor Goldman. Much of the strength of the Progressive Party in Israel, which has only four representatives in a Knesset of 120, comes from the fact that the party is powerfully represented in world Zionism. Israel's General Zionist Party, now in opposition, likewise is influenced by the judgements of the General Zionist Party in America, which is headed by Rabbi Silver of Cleveland. Mr. Ben Gurion's party, *Mapai*, which also has strong representation in America, listens to no one except Mr. Ben Gurion.

When all is said, however, it is the Jew of Palestine who has done most to bring about Jewish national freedom. His was the effective force and courage that gave hope and the promise of security to millions of Jews in Europe and North Africa who were homeless and insecure.

That fact is not sufficiently realized. It has been obscured by an exaggerated emphasis on the funds raised by world Zionism and on the influence of Jewish lobbyists in the United States. To some extent also it was obscured by the distorting shadow of terrorism, which crept sombrely over a whole land and a whole people and concealed forces greater than its own. It was the Jew who farmed his own lands, built his own roads, worked his own iron furnaces, ran his own schools, shepherded his own sheep, sailed his own ships, who made the National Home and then the State a reality, and by doing so fulfilled the mission of Zionism. That mission was to provide the substance of freedom for all Jews who needed it. It was the true purpose of his own presence in Palestine.

Except for the German Jews, who had come because they had been violently rejected by the land of their adoption and preference, most of the half million Jews in Palestine when war broke out had come to that country, not so much to make a living as to establish conditions in which the Jew could rebuild himself and his nation in freedom. The organization of illegal immigration became, therefore, almost a sacred duty; the evasion of the White Paper a patriotic compulsion. The half million or so Jews in the country in 1945 were the commandos of the Jewish race. Of them, Ben Gurion and his immediate followers, and the members of the communal settlements, moderate Left and extreme Left alike, were the *élite*. They stuck to the purpose whatever the hindrance might be, and that purpose was to find a way into Palestine for every Jew who wanted to come, whether a displaced person in the camps of Germany or a frightened bootmaker of Tunis; whether he had money or none; whether he would make a good pioneer and a profitable member of society or not; whether he was well or sick, young or old. All this may have been contrary to the promulgated edicts of the Mandatory Government, but it was splendid. Never in history has there been a more steadfast and fearless effort by a small people to save and restore to self-respect their whole, numerous race.

In 1939 Ben Gurion had said that the Jews of Palestine would fight the war as if there were no White Paper, and the White Paper as if there were no war. They did. But when, in 1945, the war ended in victory for the Allies and the opening of the gates of Nazi concentration camps, the White Paper remained, by the Jews' calculations, an enemy to be fought against harder than ever.

2

It was a big day for Palestine, the ending of the war. British and American and Russian flags, and the blue flag of the Jews with the emblem of David upon it, went up all over Jerusalem, Tel Aviv, Petah Tikva, Rehovot, and all the Jewish towns and settlements. Crowds of rejoicing Jews cascaded into the open spaces of city, town and village. They sang and they danced. For one reason or another the Jews of Palestine love to get into the streets and dance to the music of pipes and violins the peasant dances brought with them from Eastern Europe and Russia. They are merry dances. The music is not merry. It is a combination of Slavic lament and Oriental narrative song and has a liturgical quality. What has become the national anthem, known as *Hatikvah*, is a melodious and impressive song, however, and it was sung that night in a hundred places a hundred times. For the victory of the Allies was the victory of the Jews: at any rate the end of a frenzied hate that had brought to death some six million European Jews. Now the great national task of rescuing and rehabilitating the survivors could begin in earnest.

Arthur Koestler was in Jerusalem at about that time, his face screwed up characteristically, as if the sun were always in his eyes, his head bent forward in resentful thought, his short legs striding angrily.

'The war's over,' he said. 'Something should be done about it.'
'What?'

'I don't know, damned if I do. That's the trouble. Nobody knows.'

But he had strong views on what Britain should do in Palestine.

He was not a conventional Zionist and seemed slightly contemptuous of those who were. He admired the Jews of Palestine, especially the communal settlers, and he liked the idea of a small people struggling against the policies of a big people. He liked a conspiracy and was sympathetic to what is commonly called activism. He referred to the Arabs as 'our cousins' and was always stressing the relationship between the two Semitic peoples, but with how much sincerity I could never judge.

'If these Jews have to fight the Arabs they'll do so and beat them,' he said on one occasion. 'And if they have to fight the British they'll do so and beat them.' He thought the British would be thrown out of Egypt within a few years and, after that, out of Iraq and even Transjordan. 'Britain should let the Jews come to Palestine as fast as ships can be found to carry them,' he said. 'A Jewish Palestine is their only chance of keeping some hold on the Middle East. You'll never be able to enforce the White Paper. If you try, the terrorist movement will become a national movement and that will be the end of Britain in Palestine.'

I thought he was going too far and told him so. But Arthur Koestler thinks hard, even laboriously. He thinks with the intentness of a mathematician. He writes the way he thinks, almost painfully, and always reminded me of a conscientious child working over an examination paper with a stubbed pencil. He tends to be cocksure but his deductions usually are sound. As events proved, they were sound on this occasion. We were kicked out of Egypt. We were compelled to withdraw from Palestine in something like humiliation. We were dismissed from Transjordan. And, to everybody's surprise, we were hurled from Iraq. I have no notion what would have happened in Palestine if, instead of putting our faith in the White Paper, we had preserved our faith in the Balfour Declaration and its logic; but there is good reason to suppose that something on the Commonwealth pattern could have been devised and every reason to believe that, at the very least, our relationship with Jewish Palestine would have been warm and co-operative.

The Arabs took the end of the war reposefully. They sipped their coffee, smoked their *nargilehs*, went about the business of life with their customary dignity. Some of them pondered. The defeat of

Hitler meant the defeat of Haj Amin el Husseini and, for the moment, of Palestine Arab nationalism. Not many Palestine Arabs cared much on that score. Very few of them understood nationalism except as something to get intoxicated on when an agitator met them some Friday noon in the courtyard of a mosque and stirred them with visions of what they would gain when the British left and what they would lose if the Jews stayed.

But if Hitler's defeat meant the defeat of the Husseinis, did it also mean the victory of the Jews? No Arab was quite sure of that; and if a problem is unclear, why bother about it? Anyway, the British would remain, and to the common people that was no bad thing. The British would see that the Jews toed the White Paper line. They would spend money and provide work. One day, perhaps, the Arabs would be able to get at the Jews and loot their rich towns and take over their lands; but for the moment there was nothing the ordinary Arab could do and nothing that he particularly wanted to do. Even the politically-minded Arabs were quiet. A young and intelligent Arab friend of mine probably expressed the opinion of many of his people when he said to me:

'There is nothing we can do for a few years except stick to our claim to the whole of Palestine. The Jews will do the rest. You watch. There will be illegal immigration, acts of terrorism against the British. And in the long run you will have to act harshly. Then our turn will come to make life difficult for you. And you will decide to give up the Mandate and hand the country over to us. You dare not do otherwise. You cannot afford to have the whole Arab League against you.'

'Suppose that happens, what will you do with the Jews?'

He laughed.

'Don't believe all this nonsense you hear about our wanting to drive the Jews into the sea. The Jews in Arab countries have always been better treated than those in European countries. Look at the money they make – the banks and big trading concerns in Cairo and Baghdad and Beirut. We shall treat them well, too. But they will stay a minority and be subject to our laws.'

3

For me, the end of the war meant the end of my Palestine tour of duty. By the spring of 1946 we were ready to wind up the organization and to hand over most of our equipment and some of our staff to Sha'ak el Adna, a broadcasting service set up by the War Office with the object of keeping the Arabs of the Middle East friendly to Britain. It had plenty of money and used the best Arab entertainers and Koran readers available in the region, and it distributed wireless sets to cafés and other Arab meeting-places all over the Middle East. It provided what was easily the best Arabic wireless programmes in the area. But its propaganda merits were few. It was restricted by the inhibitions of its British controllers. Subtlety and suggestion, however adroit, touch the Arab neither in heart nor head. He responds only to the vigorous drums and cymbals that heat his blood and fire his imagination.

The closing down of our organization was simple enough except for one thing: I had about a hundred Jews, many of whom were without immigration papers, and some of whom wanted to go back to where they had come from. It was a fair supposition that those who elected to remain in Palestine would get their papers sooner or later. Their main difficulty was to know how to make a livelihood until certificates had been issued. But those who wished to return to their countries of origin were another matter. Most of them were members of resistance movements which, with the coming of the Russian armies, had turned themselves into Communist parties and, with the support of the Soviet, were giving short shrift to their political rivals. By the reckoning of our Administrative Headquarters in Cairo, the members of my staff who were associated with what had once been useful resistance movements had become dangerous: they were not only unwanted Jews, but revolutionary Communists as well. For troublesome people of that kind we had a detention camp in Kenya. According to the military officer who was responsible for the weeding out of political undesirables, it was a good camp. He said to me one evening:

'It looks easy to escape from. The way out is by fording a shallow river. Sometimes they try. But that's the end of them. The river's full of crocodiles.'

It is not surprising that there should have been a good deal of distress and even panic among my Jewish staff. In the countries they had come from they had worked loyally, and sometimes at risk to their lives, in the Allied cause. They had found their way out, or been brought out by us, to Istanbul, and, after passing through the Aleppo screening camp had been put to work in the organization of which I was a member. They had worked diligently, even ardently. Now, if politically harmless they were being dismissed with a month's pay and considerable doubt about what was likely to happen to them; and, if politically suspect, were faced with the prospect of Kenya. I decided to go to Cairo to plead their cause with the Administration.

It was a wasted journey. The courteous, friendly officer in charge of our Administration could not understand why I was making so much fuss about a handful of Jews. At the end of an argument that lasted pretty nearly a whole morning, he said:

'My dear fellow, those Jews of yours are lucky they didn't end up at Bergen-Belsen or Dachau.'

I returned to Jerusalem and shamefacedly reported the failure of my intercession. Several of the staff, who had been members of the Greek E.A.M., disappeared. I gathered that they had crossed the frontier into Lebanon and would try to get from Beirut to Athens. Several Poles and Bulgarians, and one Titoist, also disappeared. The rest settled down in Jerusalem or Tel Aviv to await the dispensations of fortune. Since then I have run into only one of them, a Bulgarian who earns his living by carving olive-wood souvenirs and selling them to tourists.

For myself, it seemed high time to get out of official 'hush-hush' environment and back into my trade of newspaper correspondent. I resigned. But the Jewish problem and the Palestine question generally had got under my skin and I decided to watch events and study their causes and perhaps, with luck, after six months or so be assigned to cover Palestine for a newspaper. That is what happened. Illegal immigration, and above all terrorism, soon made Palestine 'newsworthy'.

Three

ERRORISM is a wretched thing. The terrorist risks his life and is never free from fear of arrest and the ultimate penalty. He is not a coward. But he is coldly inhuman. In what he believes to be the cause of humanity, he becomes inhuman. A chill vanity possesses him and he puts himself apart even from those in whose name he acts and for whom, indeed, he has only contempt. His methods ensure his corruption as a human being among his fellows. He declares his own particular war without identifying himself as the belligerent, so that for most of the time he remains indistinguishable from the peaceful citizens about him. His enemy is plainly visible: a soldier taking a glass of beer in a café; a policeman on the corner; an official bending over his files. The terrorist creeps up in the dark ready to pitch his grenade. He disguises himself as a milkman and his deadly explosives as a canister of milk. He shoots from a curtained window and a minute later stands among the gaping crowd on the pavement.

I have known terrorists. I knew one in Jerusalem. He was a young boy whose mother was my landlady at one time. He was a Pole. His father and other members of his family had been killed by the Germans. He, a sister and his mother had escaped from Poland and come down through Yugoslavia into Italy along the secret way organized by hardy men sent by the Jewish Agency into Europe during the war. At a small, remote cove on the eastern Italian coast, which they reached soon after the war had ended, they had waited for five months until, one night, a ship of sorts showed up darkly outside the cove. Judah and his mother and sister, with about 300 others, were packed hurriedly into the little ship, which steamed off at dawn. It sailed around and around, slowly getting near to the coast of Palestine.

The sea was rough. There was always the chance of a British warship coming down upon them, and that would mean a Cyprus detention camp. There was not enough food, not enough space. Everybody was sick. Children died, and with heavy things tied around their small bodies were cast into the sea. And the women

31

cried and the men stood up and looked and looked, day after day, towards where, by their inexpert calculations, the waves lapped against the shores of the Promised Land. I have often wondered what force it is that compels such people to go on endlessly, through one misery after another, their few belongings dwindling, their limbs aching, their hopes unassured: fleeing from human beings like themselves; from prejudice, from political systems, from hatred, and from war. But the force is there. And it is that force rather than the orderly progress of society that preserves the race.

And so one night, with the Rabbis chanting and all the religious ones blubbering and swaying in a kind of ecstasy, there, under the clear starlit sky, was the line of waves breaking on the shore; and the blur of dunes; and behind that, hills: perhaps the range of Carmel? Or the foothills of Judaea? Excitedly, the tears rolling down their cheeks, they watched the land coming nearer, and they prayed. Would British soldiers be there to carry them off to Haifa and put them into transports that would take them to Cyprus and one more detention camp?

They were not. Only the illegal Jewish militia, *Haganah*, were there, men from the settlements who, in a little boat, took out the seaward end of a kind of rope bridge. Hand over hand, and getting soaking wet, the *Haganah* men helping with the children and the old and the sick, the immigrants were landed on the sacred shore, and many of them lay flat on the ground and wept.

That was how Judah reached Palestine.

I have never heard by what means he became a terrorist. He was seventeen when he landed on the shores of Palestine. He was taken to a settlement and later moved, with his mother and sister, to Jerusalem. His mother, helped by the Jewish Agency, opened a small shop where she sold sweets, lemonade and cigarettes. Judah was accepted in a *yeshiva*, or seminary for the study of the *Torah*. He was a quiet, pale, lonely young man. He was friendly enough in a remote way when we met. But it was almost impossible to get him to talk about anything. If it rained and I said to him: 'Lots of rain, Judah,' he would nod his head: the obvious fact hardly called for any other response. But even if I said: 'There is a good film at the Zion Cinema, Judah,' he would only shrug his shoulders. They were not wide shoulders. He was rather thin and, on the whole, poorly developed; and he wore glasses. But he was able to stay out all night on whatever might be his mission and next day go to the *yeshiva* where, his mother told me proudly, he was considered to be a promising student.

His mother was a dumpy little woman. Long ago she had been made too tired to be able to think anything out. It did not occur to her that Judah had become a terrorist. His unexplained absences were his own business. Perhaps somewhere in her mind was a suspicion, a fear; but when had she been without fear? One day she said to me:

'Judah is a good boy. You must not think him unsociable. For over a year we were hiding at a place in Poland near the Czecho-slovak frontier, and all that time he had no one to talk to except me and his sister. There was not much to talk about. We just stayed inside and waited.'

I said I understood, and that I supposed he had got out of the habit of talking.

'That is right, sir.'

It was only in 1947, after he had been arrested and sent to the fortress prison of Athlit, that I learned of Judah's association with the organized terrorists.

2

I suppose terrorists are pretty much the same the world over. I have found them to be quiet, unobtrusive men as a rule, except, of course in their profession; but it has been the quiet and unobtrusive-ness of men who are not modest, but put themselves above the average. Menahim Begin, top leader of the biggest terrorist organization in Palestine, was no exception in those days. After the setting up of the State, when he became leader of a recognized political party, he opened out, set aside his quiet and unobtrusive-ness and became a noisy politician. In the years between 1945 and 1948 he organized the terrorist movement, known as the *Irgun Zvai Leumi*, familiarly the I.Z.L., or *Ezel*. It was responsible for ambush, murder and sabotage, and its proudest and most dastardly act was the blowing up, one summer's noon of 1946, of the south wing of the King David Hotel, which housed the Mandatory Administration's Secretariat. Ninety-one innocent persons were killed, forty-five injured.

Menahim Begin is a small man, not so slim as he may once have been. He is gracious enough in manner, eloquent in speech, courteous and good-humoured in argument. He has little charm. His brown eyes have no expression of fervour. He is quick, almost bird-like in movement, and in conversation his words come easily, but with the tone and gestures of sincerity. There is little about him to suggest leadership, although now and then, when rubbed by emotion, he gives off a spark of fire. Normally he looks like what he pretended to be in the years of terrorism: an import-export agent of no special distinction or prosperity.

On one occasion as we sat together in the restaurant of the Knesset, Begin said:

'Of course terrorism has to be cruel. War is cruel. If an enemy tries to occupy your country you go to war against him. We Jews could not go to war in the conventional, professional way you went to war against the Germans. So we did it in the only way that was open to us. But it was war all the same. It was the kind of war the resistance movements in Europe fought against the Germans. No difference at all. You called us terrorists. But that was only a manner of speaking.'

One could have argued, of course. Perhaps one should have argued. But argument is idle with people like Menahim Begin. Terrorists do not change their point of view. The terrorist reaches a conclusion and never moves from it. Those who think differently are lesser men and their arguments mere childishness. The terrorist leader would never think of questioning his own judgement.

3

My first experience of an act of terrorism came on a spring day of 1946.

The spring in Jerusalem is a gentle season. The city glows softly, as if its stones were transparent and candlelight shone from inside. There it lies on its high Judaean hills, the new, Jewish quarters rising westwards, the Old City of the Arabs behind its stone walls, multiple-breasted with domes and cupolas, and straining upwards with iron-balconied minarets and tall church towers; and behind it the Mount of Olives and Mount Scopus pale against the sky, lifted up from the long ridge concealing the rift of Jordan.

It is a beautiful city; and as you walk through it on a quiet April evening your thoughts are quiet, too, and perhaps far away, the mind not alert.

'*But what was that?*'

One evening, long ago, I began climbing an Anatolian hill just outside Brusa. All at once I felt ill. There was a tree beside the path and I put out my hand to rest against it. But the tree moved, literally moved, about two metres. I turned and stumbled back. At the hotel I soon learned what was the matter. There had been an earthquake. Now, as I approached the Jaffa Road from Princess Mary Avenue in Jerusalem, I had the same odd feeling as I had had on that Anatolian hill-side. I had come almost opposite the Russian Compound. Well inside the compound is a big, copper-domed Russian church; and just where the compound begins, fronting the Jaffa Road, was the C.I.D. building: it sprawled backwards, with long, top-floor balconies.

Now it was sprawling forwards into the Jaffa Road, dust rising, sheets of flame cutting through the dust. I kept on walking. Somewhere deep in my consciousness I had become aware of a big sound, not a detonation but a groaning, retching sound, a wrenching of walls from foundations. This was followed by an explosion, probably the second within a few minutes. It happened almost twenty yards from where I was walking. I was almost opposite the C.I.D. building when its front collapsed. It collapsed softly, amid dust and smoke, the groaning, wrenching sound a few seconds behind. A blue tongue of flame cut through the dust. I noticed that the street had emptied except for shadowy figures crouching close to the fallen, smoky masonry. The crouching figures held sten-guns. They would fire a few rounds and then, bending low, would move backwards in my direction; then down on their knees again to fire two or three more volleys. Heavy firing was coming also from the other side of the wreckage. The men moving from that side were crouching, too, and then running a few yards and crouching again.

All at once I realized that the terrorists, the men with their backs to me, were making for a gap in the buildings on my side of the Jaffa Road. The gap led to open ground on the far side of which was the wall of an old Arab cemetery and, just below it, Max Hesse's restaurant and bar. By this time my consciousness had rid itself of the soft numbness of a spring evening in Jerusalem. It had become alerted to danger. I had to get to that gap before the terrorists got there, and then to sprint down to Hesse's. Otherwise I might easily be caught between the fire of the two sides, the terrorists as they backed and the police as they advanced.

I leapt for the gap and reached it just as the first terrorist got to the pavement. He yelled something at me in Hebrew. I dashed through the gap, over the stony waste-ground, and down to Max Hesse's. I was able to straighten myself and put on an air more or less of nonchalance as I opened the door and entered the bar. But I need not have bothered. By that time the shooting had come to the waste-ground and close to Hesse's. The few people in the bar were standing as far from the windows as they could get. Some were lying on the floor. The barman was crouching low behind his bar. Max Hesse himself, his jowls hanging lower than ever, his eyelids drawn resentfully half over his eyes, and his mouth sulkily drooping, stood at the end of the bar, close to the door leading to the kitchen.

Gershon Agronsky, Editor of the *Palestine Post*, sat alone at a far table out of harm's way. He looked troubled as he sat there playing with a pencil. Agronsky hated terrorism. His newspaper sometimes had been accused of fermenting it. He hated it because he was a good Jew and good Jews hate violence, hate hurting. I believe that to be true: at any rate it is my experience and the experience of others. Many years earlier, when I was sent to Germany on a fairly long assignment, my London doctor, a thorough-going Englishman and fervent Anglican, said to me:

'If you need medical attention in Germany pick a Jewish doctor. The Jew never hurts if he can help it. And if you are in pain, never insults you by telling you to bear it like a man.'

Agronsky sat there playing with his pencil and looking up at the ceiling as if he were praying. He was not praying. He was thinking out the next day's leading article. He wrote good leaders: a trifle rich, but forthright and readable.

Occasional bullets came through the bar windows, and we all stared wonderingly, perhaps a little fearfully, at the splintered glass. But gradually the battle in the wasteland moved to the Mamillah Arab cemetery. Presently the shooting was heard from far away, and after about an hour it had ceased altogether. Some of those in the bar hurried out, including Gershon Agronsky. It was a sensible thing to do. Curfew would be down upon us in a few minutes and it might be difficult to get through the streets. I remained in the bar. I needed a couple of whiskies and soda. I drank them and felt better. Then I climbed to the restaurant and had dinner.

Four

THE official Jewish militia was known in those days as the *Haganah*. It was armed. Its members went through hard, professional training. And it was, of course, illegal. But so cleverly did it acquire and conceal its arms, so secretly conduct its training, that neither the British C.I.D. officers nor the Army, which must have numbered some 40,000 to 50,000 men, were able to check its growth. Occasionally a military search at one of the settlements would yield a small store of rifles, sten-guns and grenades. Now and then a body of *Haganah* men at their training exercises would be come upon by a unit of the army, and those who were too slow in getting away would be arrested and charged with the illegal possession of arms. It was a crime for which the death sentence could be imposed but rarely was unless the culprit were shown to be a member of one of the terrorist groups.

Haganah was not a concentrated force that could be tracked down. Its units and its arms were scattered over the length and breadth of Palestine. Every able-bodied man of every Jewish settlement whether collective, co-operative or of the conventional village type, from Dan to Beersheba and from the Mediterranean to the Dead Sea, was enrolled in it. Apparently something of the kind had existed in the far-off days among Jews living within the Russian Pale. Its effective development began, however, during the Arab rebellion of 1929, when Jewish self-defence was encouraged by the British Administration and the Jews of threatened settlements were trained in night fighting by a British Army officer, Captain Orde Wingate, later General Wingate. Orde Wingate was a Scot whose remarkable personality drew much of its forcefulness from the Old Testament. There was nothing namby-pamby about his Christian faith. He believed in God as he believed in the earth under his feet. He believed in the Prophecies as he believed in the states-manship of Winston Churchill. And he believed in the Jews, who owe to him, and proudly admit the debt, the source of their astonishing skill at night fighting, and of a mobility that makes their operations in the field incalculable to the enemy.

The *élite* and most highly-trained arm of *Haganah* was the *Palmach*, a striking-force of young, eager men recruited for the most part from the Left-wing collective settlements put down and maintained by *Mapam*, the United Workers Party, which in those days was made up of idealists rather than ideologists. But an executive member of the Jewish Agency directly responsible at that time for the maintenance of *Haganah* was a certain Doctor Sneh, who was a representative of the Right-wing General Zionists. (After the setting up of the State he moved left to *Mapam*, and later he went as far as Communism.) The real head of this militia, however, and its inspiration, was David Ben Gurion.

I shall never forget Ben Gurion's efforts to evade questions on the subject of *Haganah* that were put to him by Sir John Singleton, Chairman of the Anglo-American Commission of Inquiry, at a hearing in the Jerusalem Y.M.C.A.'s theatre in the summer of 1946. Sir John Singleton was a slim, neatly-dressed, patient and rather schoolmasterish examiner, who added to the dry severity of his voice and the authority of his thin, intelligent-looking face a quality of the imperative, by stretching out his arm and pointing a long, slender finger at the witness.

'Mr. Ben Gurion, do you admit the existence of a Jewish armed force known as *Haganah*?'

Ben Gurion marches up and down, his long white hair ruffled, his face red and shining, his arms waving; and as he answers there is almost petulance in his voice:

'*Haganah* means defence. Defence – that's what the word *Haganah* means. Nothing else.'

'You have said that before Mr. Ben Gurion. But you are not answering my question. I shall repeat it. Is *Haganah* an armed body of men and do you admit its existence as such? Please answer that.'

Ben Gurion again waves his arms and marches up and down. Obviously he is impatient and cross. He acts as if he were trying to make a stupid child understand a simple equation.

'I tell you *Haganah* means defence. Defence. It is the Hebrew word for defence.'

And so it went on for about twenty minutes. In the end, Sir John Singleton gave it up. He realized that he could get nothing out of Ben Gurion, who, I suppose, was one of the most unsatisfactory of all the witnesses called before the Anglo-American Committee of Inquiry.

It was, of course, natural that he should evade questions about *Haganah*. If he had admitted the existence of an armed Jewish militia of which he was the pertinent leader, he would have admitted to what had become one of the most serious misdemeanours in the Mandatory Administration's long list of crimes against order and security. *Haganah*, to him, was the one reliable safeguard of the Jews of Palestine and at the same time provided the most effective means of organizing and carrying out illegal immigration. It is improbable that, even if he had admitted to Sir John Singleton the existence of *Haganah* as an armed force, anything much could have been done by the governing authorities to liquidate it. But it was a risk he could not be expected to take with what was, after all, his darling achievement.

He is a difficult man, as the Committee of Inquiry soon found out. He can be as obstinate as a spoiled child. But there can be no doubt of the value of that obstinacy to the Jewish cause throughout the years of conflict in Palestine. He is a curious little man, short, a trifle podgy, but somehow dignified in spite of his unimpressive physique. His white hair fluffs in Lloyd-Georgian style around a bald crown stained by the sun. His cheeks are as rosy as an apple-woman's. The expression of his light brown eyes can be humorous or angry or indifferent at will, but it is humour that has marked the corners, not anger or indifference. He has a high-pitched monotonous voice and is very far from being an orator. He dresses carelessly. All in all, from looking at him or listening to him one would not suspect outstanding leadership: certainly not the kind of exhilarating, steadfast and courageous leadership he has given to the Jews of Palestine.

Once, as I sat opposite him in a small, dingy office of the Prime Minister's Department in Jerusalem, he said to me:

'The State has been here all the time, you know – from 1918 onwards at the very least. It was just a question of filling up its corners with more people and formulating it in the conventional design. We did not fight in 1948 to establish the State. We fought to defend it.'

'Would you say that the State was brought about, in the real sense, by U.N.?'

'No, I would not. U.N. gave it international sanction and then ran away. We brought it about ourselves.'

Ben Gurion's *Haganah* was in no sense a terrorist body. Its original purpose was to provide trained and armed units capable of defending outlying settlements that might come under Arab attack. Although after 1930 the likelihood of sporadic Arab attack became remote, there was always the risk of another rebellion. When Hitler governed in Berlin and the hideous persecution of Jews began, *Haganah* became the training-ground for young men to be sent to Europe to organize escape routes. When the Germans occupied Czechoslovakia and entered Poland, the need for such young men became even more urgent. Then, of course, there was the British White Paper, which, if continued in force after the war, might call for some more effective challenge than political agitation.

Finally, there was an internal problem. The Right-wing parties within the Jewish Agency Executive were thought to be behind the big and growing terrorist organization, *Irgun Zvai Leumi*, and the Left-wing parties under the leadership of Ben Gurion's *Mapai*, or Labour Party, needed *Haganah* if they were to hold their own in the struggle for supremacy within the Jewish community. Conditions throughout the period from 1945 to 1948 were such that more and more young people were becoming impressed by the conspicuous activities of the I.Z.L. Whilst terrorism horrified the older generation of Jews, including Ben Gurion, it had an appeal, in the 'resistance movement' sense, to many Jewish youth and especially to those who had been brought illegally into the country and had carried with them a certain hard fanaticism.

Haganah, therefore, was tempted every now and then to take the centre of the grisly Palestinian stage. When it did so, there was no deliberate killing. Instead, bridges were dynamited, lengths of railway torn out, radar installations, which were used to detect incoming illegal immigrant ships, blown to pieces. Sabotage it was and sabotage enough to justify the Mandatory Administration in outlawing *Haganah*, and the British Army in carrying out searches for arms and explosives. But Ben Gurion's organization was too clever for both. *Haganah* grew and grew and so did its arms stores. When, in 1948, the British quit Palestine and the Arabs moved in to take over, there must have been 10,000 trained and partially armed Jews to defend the new State.

It was often claimed by the Mandatory and Home Governments that the Jewish community in Palestine not only connived in *Haganah*'s sabotage and the murderous activities of the terrorist organizations, I.Z.L. and the so-called Stern Gang (a small band of anarchists associated with no political party or national movement), but were accessories to both. On that assumption, the authorities imposed harsh restrictions and, on occasion, collective penalties. Large areas were put under curfew. Onerous and often humiliating searches were conducted by the Army. As might have been anticipated, and probably was, the searches rarely uncovered anything except, perhaps, a wretched immigrant without papers. Wholesale arrests were made. Curfew-breakers, most of them innocent of intent, were bundled into makeshift detention places and put through crudely performed interrogation.

I never heard of any worthwhile yield from these measures, which irritated the population and delighted the terrorists. The harsher our response to acts of terrorism, the greater, by the reckoning of the terrorists, their success; and, of course, the more recruits the terrorist organizations received. I got the impression that curfew, house to house searches, the dragging of a whole Jewish quarter into the street at midnight to be screened, and wholesale arrests, were done because the authorities felt they had to assert themselves in some conspicuous fashion after an act of terrorism. There was a punitive object as well, of course. The argument that the community as a whole did nothing to help law and order and gave concealment to the terrorists was an exaggeration. It was difficult to see what the community, as an aggregate of individuals who wanted only to be left in peace, could do. It may be true that some of the people did help terrorists to hide or get away. It is not easy to take an armed terrorist and hand him over to the police or army; nor does it pay an ordinary householder with a wife and children to give the authorities information about where a terrorist is hiding. Terrorists, in short, are dangerous people to handle; they usually create as big a problem for those whose good they pretend to serve as for those whose ill they brutally contrive.

But the community as represented by the Jewish Agency Executive, which was controlled by Mr. Ben Gurion and his followers, and which, through *Haganah*, now and then learned of terrorist

41

plans, in its fashion did help law and order. On several occasions it jumped in and put a stop to I.Z.L. operations before those operations could be got going; and on several other occasions it warned the authorities of an impending terrorist act. Naturally, it did nothing to reveal the names and lodgings of terrorists. It could not be expected to act as that kind of informer. It did try hard, however, to bring Menahim Begin's organization as nearly as possible into line with its own policies, and to put it under some kind of discipline. From time to time these efforts had some success, and for a short period *Haganah* and I.Z.L. would work together: at such times there would be no killings, no treacherous flinging of grenades, no hostage kidnapping. But I.Z.L. was unwilling to lose its identity or give up its claim to be the leading 'resistance movement' among Palestine Jews. Besides, the men who were financially behind Menahim Begin were loth to give up, or see weakened, an instrument that might come in handy one day if and when the struggle between Right and Left for political dominance within an independent or autonomous Jewish State, should begin. When that struggle did begin, years later, Mr. Ben Gurion made short work of I.Z.L., which today is a constitutional political group with extreme ideas but conventional manners.

The average British soldier disliked carrying out curfew, search and arrest. He felt it to be humiliating to stride into someone else's flat or house at midnight, wake the children, force the parents to dress and descend, as happened in the heart of Jerusalem on one occasion, to a large pit excavated for building purposes, and to wait there for hours while one by one upwards of 800 people were brought from the pit to the adjacent roped-off street to show their papers and answer questions put to them by a weary but courageously good-humoured sergeant at an orderly-room table set on the pavement. A few senior officers delighted to put the Jews to inconvenience and embarrassment, whether because they thought Jews deserved no better, or from a natural resentment provoked by terrorist violence, I could never guess and preferred not to know.

The Jews, for their part, bore no malice towards the British soldier who forced them out of bed and put them through the indignities of search and interrogation. Occasionally, during an arms search in one or other of the settlements, women settlers whose menfolk had been caged for the period of the search would throw pots and pans at the soldiers who set about prising open doors, digging holes all over the place, hunting in lofts and under floors and down bricked water-wells for the arms stores that usually eluded them. But pots and pans did nothing but bruise; and the army paid only humorous attention to them, which, of course, exasperated the sturdy amazons still more.

3

Curfew, search, detention camp and so on, nowadays are a pitiful response of Government to the hostility of the governed. Terrorism has to be got at and if possible put an end to. But never yet has it been got at effectively through measures aimed at the whole people. Palestine and Cyprus both have shown that the traditional devices of the harassed authorities serve no good purpose and sooner or later worsen affairs to such an extent that authority is forced to surrender, or to resort to still harsher repressive acts, which are humiliating to its own people and give rise to sharp world criticism.

It is, of course, easier to point out the failure of repressive acts than to suggest measures likely to end rebellion while preserving the reasonable authority of the Government rebelled against. Perhaps in present-day conditions there is no way a Government can preserve reasonable authority over a community that actively repudiates such authority. However that may be, repression is not a way. And for my part I am convinced that a solution to the Palestine question could have been found if Britain had shown foresight and courage enough to deal with it on its own merits and not within the framework of an Arab policy that was already beginning to wear paperthin. The bulk of the Jews did not want to sever their association with Britain, and, I believe, would have been willing to take something less than sovereign independence if Britain had offered it. I believe, too, that Arab Palestine could have been brought into a general settlement if we had shown firmness instead of something very like panic.

In any event, it became clear in those days that the Jews had three clear-cut alternatives: continued White Paper Administration; Arab control of the whole of Palestine; and independence, whether as a homogeneous State in a part of Palestine or, as certain Jews under the leadership of Doctor Judah Magnus advocated, a bi-national

43

Jewish-Arab State in the whole country. Continued White Paper government was intolerable to a people who saw the National Home as a means of gathering together all Jews, from all the world, who were, or might be, subject to persecution simply because they were Jews. Predominantly Arab government of Palestine would mean, in effect, the return of the Jews to minority status and all that that implied to their race. There was left independence. And it was not long before every Jew in Palestine except a few frightened Germans resolved upon independence as the only solution.

Five

THE Government in London could no longer leave matters to the 'man on the spot', so often and so unfairly quoted in the House of Commons by the Foreign Secretary, Mr. Ernest Bevin. Instead, His Majesty's Government and the Government of the United States – the latter because, with the largest Jewish community in the world, it had a proper, not merely electoral, interest in Jewish affairs – agreed to form a joint Committee of Inquiry to study the Palestine problem and report back to both Governments.

The Anglo-American Committee arrived in Jerusalem in the spring of 1946. It was not a particularly impressive committee. It would have been difficult for any twelve men sitting in a row to look impressive against the dramatic backdrop of Palestine in 1946.

The Committee's chairman was the Englishman, Sir John Singleton. He was a pleasant-spoken, neat, tightly-buttoned man, who presided at meetings of the Committee and at the frequent hearings it gave, with the chill impartiality appropriate to his place on the King's Bench and doubtless to his place on the Committee of Inquiry. He had a function to perform and it was plain that he would perform it judiciously, without sentiment, without favour, without prejudice. His senior American colleague was James Macdonald – tall, slim, distinguished-looking; a man with an academic career behind him and a fairly close association with President Truman and the Democratic Party to sustain him.

On the American side, too, was a judge – Judge Hutchinson of Texas, as kindly and warm-hearted a man as could be found anywhere; ready to let his heart counsel his mind. 'Policy,' he said to me before leaving Palestine, 'must fail if it is without compassion.' I asked him whether policy, once framed and promulgated, could acquire compassion. 'If not,' he said, 'it's bad policy.'

On the British side we had Reginald Manningham-Buller, who looked like a man with that name and talked like it. He was – and of course is – a lawyer of distinction. The Americans had a lawyer of distinction, too – Bartley Crumm, who picked up and gobbled evidence with the dexterity and satisfaction of a bird picking worms out of upturned earth. Early in the hearings one knew where Bartley Crumm's sympathies lay. He made no attempt to hide them. Among the British members of the Committee Richard Crossman made little effort to hide his pro-Jewish sympathies. I had been tenuously associated with Dick Crossman in the early days of the war, had admired his sharp wit and appreciated his intelligence. In Palestine he was quick to comprehend the Jewish case, not alone from the viewpoint of the Jews' need, but also from the striking evidence of what had been done already in Palestine by that country's half million Jews.

The Committee called witness after witness – officials of the Administration, Jews and Arabs. Long shall I remember the appearance before it, in the Jerusalem Y.M.C.A.'s theatre, of Doctor Chaim Weizmann.

He was ailing and half blind, but brought with him a moving dignity.

I sat immediately behind him as he spoke. His broad back, the sun-tanned baldness of his large head, the slow, almost weary gesturing with his shoulders and arms, were curiously expressive: they seemed to me expressive of a powerful and melancholy personality, as of a man who had ventured into greatness and now, with the promise of victory for the cause he served, was disappointed by what he foresaw. He was a big man physically and looked bigger than ever as he sat hunched in a chair too small for him. He spoke slowly, in a tired, pleasant voice with only a slight accent; and his words were simple, at times almost Elizabethan, spoken as by a man who had said these things over and over again before one inquiry after the other. But the quiet fervour of his pleading came through. The sincerity and appeal of his words beat gently upon the consciences of the audience in that hushed hall. He was not interrupted. He neither raised his voice nor lowered it. The Committee sat silently through it all, rather like a pew of churchwardens listening respectfully to a sermon of the visiting Bishop. And when it was over Sir John Singleton said:

'Thank you, Doctor Weizmann.'

The Committee went here and there, looked at this and looked at that, heard this one and that, studied documents galore: the 1936 Peel Commission's Report (a brilliant paper), a careful Jewish Agency analysis of the country's absorptive capacity, contradicted

46

by an equally careful analysis prepared by the Administration; an impressive account of the extent to which the Arabs had benefited from Jewish settlement, and an impressive account of the hardships the Arabs would suffer if Jewish immigration were allowed on a big scale. A fat volume containing the reports it had submitted to the Committee was published afterwards by the Jewish Agency. Like the Peel Commission's Report it is essential reading for anyone who would know the full background to the Palestine problem as it stood between 1918 and 1948, and the basis of Israel's 'viability' as a sovereign State.

But nothing came of the Anglo-American Committee of Inquiry. Its main recommendation was that 100,000 Jews then in Displaced Persons' Camps should be admitted to Palestine. The Prime Minister, then plain Mr. Attlee, would have none of that. Heaven knows what he had expected to come from the Committee he and President Truman had sent to Palestine. The most urgent of the bitter Palestine urgencies of that day was the question of the homeless Jews left over from Hitler's crazed hatred of Jews. The National Home had been proposed by a British Government, and given international sanction, in order to provide refuge for just such people. What, then, did Mr. Attlee expect would follow his rejection of the Committee's manifestly just and proper recommendation? I do not know. I only know what did follow. At about that time I ran into Doctor Dov Joseph, a prominent Jerusalem lawyer who had come from Canada and was one of the leading members of the Jewish Agency Executive. He trembled as he spoke of Mr. Attlee's curious attitude:

'The Rabbis will come out with the Scrolls of the Law and lead our people to rebellion,' he said. Doctor Joseph, shrewd lawyer as he was, could be emotional in that fashion if he liked. No Rabbi came out with the Scrolls of the Law. There were a few bearded and black-hatted processions but they amounted to nothing. What happened and what could have been expected was foretold to me by Moshé Shertok (Sharett), head of the Jewish Agency's Political Department:

'Don't think the terrorist organizations are disappointed,' he said. 'They are delighted. The Committee's recommendations didn't go half far enough for them. Now they will start killing and burning and blowing up more vigorously than ever and will probably double their membership. And *Haganah* won't dare to

47

stop them. Besides, American Jewry will step up its lobbying until President Truman is forced to intervene again. And they will step up their donations, too, which means that illegal immigration will be intensified. Even the Arabs know that.'

Some of the Arabs did know it.

There came to Jerusalem in the autumn of 1946 a certain Egyptian professor from the Farouk University as it was then called. I had known him in Cairo in between his periods in prison, which were the outcome of his political opinions and his courage in expressing them. He wanted Palestine for the Arabs but he recognized the plain fact that the Jews were there to stay and would have to be given some form of autonomy along the coast area even if the country as a whole should be given over to an independent Arab people. He thought Mr. Attlee's refusal to allow the entry of the 100,000 a mistake.

'That many will come in anyway, illegally if not legally,' he said. 'But if they were allowed to come legally, we Arabs would still be well in the majority and would have an unanswerable argument against letting in any more Jews. As it is, the Jews will now demand more and more and in the end we shall have to go to war against them or let them take over the whole country.'

2

So it ran from 1946 to 1947, through winter, spring and summer, with the drift of British policy and the crazed arrogance of terrorism running into each other every few weeks with an impact of horror. The Government fought terrorism and fought the *Haganah* as well. The *Haganah* fought both terrorism and the Government. The terrorists fought whatever stood in the way of their madness. The Royal Navy held up immigrant ships on the high seas and brought them into Haifa. The Army herded the immigrants from their miserable hulks into transports that would carry them to Cyprus detention camps. Agricultural settlements were surrounded by British soldiers and, against almost hysterical opposition from the settlers, searched for immigrants whose ships had slipped through the blockade. Lorry loads of explosives were driven by apparently authorized drivers into British army camps and there blown up. Terrorists were tried and hanged. British Army officers, a British judge, and a British official of the Secretariat, were kidnapped. Roads were mined.

1946 had been pitiful enough. In the spring of that year the Anglo-American Committee on Palestine, created at the initiative of the British Prime Minister, issued its report, based on the impressive evidence it had collected during its sojourn in the country. Whatever may have been the general merits of the Report, it had emphasized the justice of President Truman's plan for the immediate entry into Palestine of 100,000 Jews from the European displaced persons' camps. Mr. Attlee and Mr. Bevin refused to heed the recommendation and, quite naturally, the Jews took the matter into their own hands and began loading to the very crow's nest unseaworthy ships with men, women and children spirited from Germany and eastern Europe and collected for the most part along Italy's Adriatic coast. Some of the ships were stopped. Some got through. In the process of stopping, transhipping, and searching for the immigrants who got through, one piteous spectacle after another was enacted before the eyes of the embittered Jews of Palestine, and given world-wide publicity by a corps of newspaper men to whom Palestine had become the predominant 'story'.

The worst of these incidents concerned 4,500 hapless refugees from Germany who, in July 1947, while making for the Palestine coast, were intercepted by the Royal Navy and brought to Haifa. There they were transferred into two British transports and turned back upon their tracks. The Jewish Agency people responsible for illegal immigration may have organized this conspicuous effort at smuggling Jews into Palestine knowing full well that the ship, called the *Exodus 1947*, at best had only one chance in ten of getting through. They may have done so in the hope of dramatizing still further the plight of European Jews and the remarkable efforts of their Palestine brethren to bring them 'home'. They may have done so hoping that such a large number as 4,500 persons in a single ship would put before the British Government a problem that could only be solved by letting the unfortunate wretches land, giving them immigration certificates and leaving it to the Jewish Agency to take responsibility for caring for them and settling them.

If that was what the Jews hoped, Mr. Bevin proved too much for them. Not surprisingly, he regarded the *Exodus 1947* as a challenge. He was not the man to let a challenge of that kind pass. If he had let the 4,500 land at Haifa, goodness knows what would have happened to his precious Arab policy. And there was no room in Cyprus for the 4,500. B y the Foreign Secretary's calculations, their proper place was back in the D.P. camps they had come from. It was not a calculation he came to on his own, but it was appropriate to his mood of that time, which seemed to be directed by determination not to let the Jews 'get the better' of him. Anyway, back went the 4,500 of the *Exodus 1947* to Hamburg and the displaced persons' camps. For some days almost every Jew of Palestine was ready to become a terrorist in one form or another. Certainly the *Haganah* was hard put to it to keep its young men from transferring their allegiance to the exultant terrorist organizations. Equally, from the world point of view, Mr. Ernest Bevin's tactics had been crude; for there could hardly have been a single newspaper reader who was not moved to heartfelt sympathy for the disillusioned 4,500 and to something like deep understanding of what the Palestine Jews were doing, call their actions illegal or not.

And on a Tuesday of that merciless July three young Jews were hanged, who had taken part in an attack on Acre Prison. That was the day the 4,500 refugees of the *Exodus 1947* refused the offer of the French authorities to let them land on French soil. The next day, two British sergeants were vengefully killed by *Irgun Zvai Leumi*. That was Wednesday. Nobody except the terrorists knew of the killing then. But the next day, at the first soft coming of the dawn, their bodies were found hanging from trees in a glade near the seaside town of Nathanya, which, until a day or two before, had been under martial law.

As the night of that day fell, a posse of British soldiers dashed through the crowded streets of Tel Aviv shooting up people travelling in buses, tossing bombs into cafés, and generally behaving like lunatics. Of course, they had been provoked. There was provocation and counter-provocation, violence and counter-violence, unending. The Jews may have been getting out of hand, but so was British policy. That night passed fearfully and when the day came the two military victims of terrorism at its brutal worst, and the five civilian victims of military revenge and indiscipline, were buried. The funeral of the Jews was interrupted by a charging armoured vehicle, and the mourning procession degenerated into a riot. That afternoon there was more shooting and more deaths. And then came the Sabbath.

The Jewish Sabbath begins on Friday evening with the coming

of the first pale star. At the star's signal, short men in black hats stride through the streets with a toy trumpet held between beard and whiskers. With the assurance of men on God's mission, they toot their little trumpets from street to street and lane to lane to tell all who live there that now is the Sabbath of the Lord their God, in which all work shall cease, no fire be lit, no light made to shine, no trading done, no vehicle propelled; and happily, no bomb be set, no violence done. It is a good day for pondering.

On this July Sabbath, a good deal of quiet pondering was done by the leaders of the Jewish community – the *Yishuv* as it is called in Hebrew. The hanging of the two British sergeants had indeed shocked the *Yishuv*. On the Thursday of the following week the political and military leaders of *Haganah* met in conference at Tel Aviv and sat up all night working out plans to combat terrorism. These plans were approved next day at a meeting of representatives of every constitutional body of the Jewish National Home. Political moderates and intransigents, members of all political groups from Left to Right, sat with the Executive of the Jewish Agency, approved the *Haganah* plans and talked about what they should do next.

The outcome of it all was the first attempt at some kind of co-operative effort by Government and the Jewish Community since the blowing up of the King David Hotel in July of 1946. The High Commissioner, Sir Alan Cunningham, had pressed for mutual effort against the opposition of the Army and, it was said at the time, of the Home Government. But the Police chiefs were on his side and in the end he got his way. Shortly afterwards British troops were withdrawn from the main centres of terrorist activity, that is from the towns of Tel Aviv, Petah Tikva and Ramat Gan, and responsibility for security in those areas was transferred to Jewish Civic Guards, who were, in fact, *Haganah* units.

While all this was going on, the United Nations Special Committee of Inquiry had been in Palestine listening and looking and shaping an opinion. It was a sound body of men. When it arrived it gave the impression of a group of arbiters with the open minds of judicial investigators, but also with the blank minds of men who had no notion of the causes and condition of the problem.

But sitting there day after day at the horseshoe table of the Y.M.C.A. auditorium, directly opposite the King David Hotel, the Committee let no one mistake its purpose. It was there to find out what was wrong in Palestine and what should be done about it. It

saw little of the Arabs except their schoolrooms and the parlours of
close-lipped nervous mayors. The Arab Higher Committee and
those Arab bodies which dared not run counter to the Higher
Committee, were boycotting the U.N. investigators. In numbers of
witnesses and the talk they did, the Jews, of course, made up for the
absence of the Arabs. Day after day they talked and talked and
talked, as well they might; for the issue was independence or no
independence, a State or not a State, the revival of Israel after two
thousand years of suspension or the extinction of a hope prayed and
sung in the synagogues and ghettos of alien lands ever since the
dispersion, and now, thanks to people like Theodor Herzl, Chaim
Weizmann, Arthur Balfour, David Ben-Gurion and over half a
million Jews of the National Home diligently proving to themselves
and the world that they could follow a plough and build a road and
not merely be traders and bankers – thanks to all these people and
the fact that the United Nations had become 'siezed of' the Palestine
Question, a hope that had begun to fuse itself into incredible
substance.

The Special Committee of Inquiry sat at its horseshoe table in
Jerusalem, looked at Tel Aviv, Petah Tikvah and Haifa, visited
collective settlements, stared at the Arabs and tried to talk with them
in private, heard the Government tartly refuse to delay the execution
of death sentences passed on three Jews. The hearings, and a back-
breaking schedule of tours that covered almost every acre of
Palestine, took place to the raucous accompaniment of terrorism and
the countering action of Government and *Haganah*, until the
observant bystander could pick no reliable prospect out of the
confusion; and began to feel that even if the Committee should
recommend a form of independence for the Jews on the one side and
for the Arabs on the other, nothing would come of it but bloodshed.

I sat one evening with an Arab friend of mine talking of the
chances over Turkish coffee and Jewish cognac. He said:

'You know, we Arabs are fated to make mistakes. It's a kind of
destiny. As nations, we live in rather backward conditions, but those
of us who are educated dream of a renascence in terms of Haroun al
Rashid. Between the fact and the dream there is too much hard,
plodding thought and work needed and we don't seem much good
at that. We expected the British Government, and now we expect
U.N., to give us substance of the dream, which somehow we have
convinced ourselves lies in Arab sovereignty over the whole of

Palestine. It doesn't of course. Still, we don't want anything short of that – and so in the long run we'll get nothing.'

3

The U.N. Commission, its inquiries done, sent in a majority report recommending partition of Palestine between Jews and Arabs and the setting up of an independent Jewish State and an independent Arab State in the area allotted to each. In many ways the recommendation looked preposterously complicated and unreal. Boundaries leapt over boundaries and the city of Jerusalem was to become a City of God, all alone among its hills, a *corpus separatum* bound formally neither to Arab nor Jew but in some fashion made the responsibility of the pious world. However, the proposal for economic unity between the two divisions of Palestine, if it had been accepted by the Arabs as well as the Jews, might have made the rest of the plan workable. In it was the seed of a Federal or Bi-National State; at the very least of a co-operative arrangement beneficial to both sides.

The United States Government firmly backed the majority recommendations, which the Jews had thankfully accepted and the Arabs had angrily rejected. On November 11th these recommendations were carried into a resolution and approved at a special session of the U.N. General Assembly. And there was a State for the Jews if they wanted it, and a State for the Arabs if they wanted it. The Jews did. The Arabs did not.

4

Memorable was that night in Jerusalem, that starlit night of 29th November 1947 when, thousands and thousands of miles away, the Resolution partitioning Palestine between Arab and Jew and giving sovereignty to each, was put to the vote of the General Assembly of the United Nations. Jerusalem was as still as a waxen model in a glass case. There were hardly any Jews on the street. Across the way, on the other side of the walls, the Arabs played with their beads, talked softly. Now and than a British armoured patrol car came by.

But almost every Jew in the city sat or stood by his or another's wireless set.

The reception from New York was clear. One by one the representatives of the member-States of U.N., was asked by the Chairman of the Assembly, on that occasion the head of the Australian delegation, to state whether or not he approved the Resolution recommending the gift of sovereignty to Jew and Arab separately in Palestine.

How long it took! How ominous the silences! How exciting to these listening Jews, far away, the affirmative vote of a nation whose attitude had seemed doubtful!

'Yes.'

'Yes.'

'No.'

'Yes.'

'No.'

'No.'

The sounds coming through the loudspeaker from the distant Assembly had a quality of strain; as if tension were there, too. On that night, where was there not tension? Jews were gathered about their receiving sets in Palestine, in Germany, in Moscow, in Teheran, in Algiers, in Casablanca, in Baghdad, in Cairo and Beirut. The Arabs were as tense as the Jews but from different causes.

'Yes.'

'Yes.'

The Resolution needed a two-thirds majority. Would it get it? Half-way through the voting it began to look like it. France had said *Yes*: so had Belgium, and the Netherlands: and one by one – most important of all among the so-called block votes – Latin America was saying *Yes*. The votes in favour mounted steadily beyond the votes against. Then it was over. The count was made and there was a burst of excited cheering in the Assembly when the Chairman announced that thirty-three nations had given assent to the setting up of a sovereign Jewish State and a sovereign Arab State in Palestine; thirteen nations had refused their assent; ten had abstained from voting. The Resolution had been given the necessary two-thirds majority.

It was a miracle in a way: an act of greatness whatever the motives and devices, and whatever might be the immediate consequences: the most human thing that any congress of nations had ever brought about. The United Kingdom, under the guidance of the Labour Party, abstained. It stood apart disdainfully, and, as it proved, most unwisely.

That night, when the count in the General Assembly became known, Jewish Jerusalem came alive as if its people, laughing and singing and crying, had been plucked from their houses by some invisible hand and tossed into the streets and public squares to spin and dance and sing happily the night through. Laugh, sing, spin, and dance they did. And what made it more joyful was to see British army patrols stop their cars, shout hurrahs and festoon their vehicles with young Jewish boys and girls who were driven triumphantly through the dense crowds to the heart of the celebrations in the big forecourt of the Jewish Agency building in King George Avenue. The building was floodlit. When not another soul could be squeezed into the forecourt, out on to the long balcony came Mrs. Golda Myerson, that matronly, housewifely deputy of Mr. Shertok (who was in New York receiving eager congratulations). She had Dov Joseph with her, and other members of the Executive. Ben Gurion was in Tel Aviv.

Mrs. Myerson said a few words that nobody could hear. She dabbed her eyes. Then the crowd began to sing *Hatikvah*, the national anthem. And all around me people cried.

I went into the Old City, where the Arabs were. A few lights gleamed from behind curtains or slatted shutters. Here and there low voices were heard. One or two coffee houses were still open and had customers drinking coffee and smoking hubble-bubbles and playing tric-trac. Here and there under a street lamp three or four people stood together talking. But it was already late and most of the Old City was asleep. At the *Haram esh Sherif* there were lights in what had been the reception room of the Grand Mufti, Haj Amin el Husseini, and I suppose that those who guided the affairs of the Arabs were seated there or marching softly up and down the big room with its carpets and low, carved tables, its handsomely-decorated brass trays and its old-fashioned photographs on the walls. I fancied they were sitting there or marching up and down, debating what should be the immediate response of the Palestine Arabs.

Whether in Haj Amin's reception room or elsewhere, the Arab leaders did in fact decide that night upon direct action. They called a three-day strike throughout the whole country, to begin on December 3rd.

Arab resistance to the U.N. recommendations was natural. But there was a big difference between the motives of the Palestine Arab and those of the Arab or Moslem Governments supporting his claim. When considering both it is as well to keep in mind that the resistance of the Arabs was an official resistance in the first place. It became a popular movement thanks mainly to agitators representing factions ambitious of power or governments desirous of putting Palestine to their own uses. The Husseinis of Palestine wanted rulership. Amir Abdullah wanted Palestine as a means of lifting his own petty kingdom to the level of his neighbours. Cairo was concerned to prevent just that, and Baghdad to prevent the Egyptians from pushing out their influence beyond Sinai. Damascus had little notion of what it wanted but was determined to get its share of the pickings. The Governments of the countries adjacent to Palestine cared very little about the welfare of the Palestine Arab.

The Palestine Arab, of course, was as much opposed to the setting up of a Jewish State in Palestine as anyone else. But if the so-called Higher Committee, dominated by the Husseinis, had not been persuaded that Farouk's army and the armies of the two Hashemites, Faisul of Iraq and Abdullah of Jordan, as well as contingents from Saudi Arabia and Syria, could bring the Jews to their knees in a matter of days; and if the Arab peasant, worker, and tradesman had not been fooled by the same gay assumption, from which followed the exciting prospect of getting at wealthy Tel Aviv and Rehavia and all the towns and settlements and everything they contained from Biedermayer bedsteads to pots and pans, from wireless sets to electric toasters, and from pedigree cattle to flocks of woolly sheep: – if it had not been for these misjudgements and the crazy fantasies that grew up about them, I doubt whether popular resistance by the Palestine Arab to the Partition terms would have survived the initial strikes and rioting of the first few days.

On December 3rd, the first day of the Arab strike, brickbats hurtled and knives flashed from one end of Palestine to the other. The Tel Aviv-Jaffa border and the crowded areas in Jerusalem between the western gates of the Old City and the main streets of the New, were choked with ragged, howling mobs out to kill, smash, burn and loot. I have never seen such concentrated and idiotic fury. These distorted faces, these flailing arms, these gaping mouths from which poured a mad orchestration of inhuman sounds, had no more bearing on nationalism that the wailing and shrieking of a madhouse. I saw the crowd, whipped up by agitators, come jostling up Mamillah Road to its junction with Princess Mary Avenue. Nobody tried to stop the rioters. They had already set ablaze a group of Jewish warehouses at the rear of Mamillah Road and known as the Commercial Centre. British police were in Princess Mary Avenue and against the entrance to Julian's Way, which is a continuation of the avenue. They made no effort to send the rioters packing: merely blocked their way into Princess Mary Avenue and Julian's Way. *Haganah* had some men on the spot who tried to protect Jewish lives and property. They were not hindered by the police. A local journalist was grabbed by the rioters and stabbed. Smoke from burning houses blew over the scene. The smoke added to the uncanniness. Through it the eyes of the yelling mob glowed red. The groans of the injured rose up to join the din.

That kind of thing went on for three days. The Tel Aviv border up against Jaffa became charred. Jewish vehicles passing along the highway through Ramle were ambushed and burned and those inside who were unable to escape were burned with the vehicle. When the strike was over, the mobs went back to whatever may have been their customary routine, and the attack on the Jews gradually worked itself into some kind of organized pattern. So-called national guards, hastily recruited and armed by the Arab Higher Committee, blocked certain main streets in Jerusalem including Julian's Way, which led from the centre of the Jewish town to the King David Hotel and the Mandatory Administration's Secretariat. They patrolled the road leading up to Mount Scopus, where the Hebrew University and the big Hadassah Hospital were situated; and when a group of doctors, nurses and technicians tried to get through to the hospital with supplies, their convoy of ambulances was set upon and burned out and every soul it carried burned with it. Armed Arab bands lined the steep-sided gulch of Bab el Wad through which the main road from Tel Aviv to Jerusalem ran. Jews travelled along that road only in convoy. After scores had been killed and the wreckage of some twenty or thirty buses and trucks which had been fitted with makeshift armour had been left against the roadside, even that had to be given up. Jerusalem was isolated and its stores began to run out.

And all this was well before Britain's surrender of the Mandate. We no longer hindered the *Haganah* or searched for arms and we had let the Jews take over the policing of Tel Aviv. But with something like 50,000 troops in the country we did nothing to protect the Jews, or even to keep the main streets of Jerusalem clear of barricades and armed Arabs, or the main roads to the coast open. We had withdrawn into our own heavily barbed-wired zones, from the houses of which Jews had been ejected, and there we sat while Palestine fell into anarchy and shaped itself for war. We continued to wave the White Paper about. Immigrant ships attempting to get what amounted to Jewish reinforcements on to the shores of Palestine, were boarded by the Navy and their passengers taken off to Cyprus. But we left the land frontiers of the country open to any band of armed irregulars that might wish to enter from Syria, Jordan or Egypt to attack Jews. I have myself seen an official British log-book reporting the passage over the frontier into Palestine of armed Syrian and Iraqi irregulars coming to join the northern force under the command of the notorious Fawzi Kaukje, one of the rebel leaders of the 'thirties. We did nothing to stop them. We did nothing to bring back some order to Palestine. We snubbed the U.N. Commission which was supposed to ease the transition from Mandatory to National administration. We let the country go to pieces and we did so deliberately. We were not handing Palestine over to the authority of U.N. Having failed to settle the Jewish problem as it affected Palestine, we were leaving it to be settled by the Arabs from the adjacent countries, whose armies we had equipped and in some cases trained. Such was the considered policy of Her Majesty's Principal Secretary of State for Foreign Affairs, Mr. Ernest Bevin, and of his Labour colleagues. It must be admitted that these lordly Socialists were in this matter under the thumb of stick-in-the-mud Army strategists and petulant Foreign Office officials who could not rid themselves of their dream-like notions of what the Arab League was like.

It is probable that many senior British authorities, including Mr. Attlee and Mr. Bevin and the sadly harassed Colonial Secretary, genuinely thought the Jews deserved no better than they were about to get and that it was high time someone put a match to the Balfour Declaration, which had been a nuisance from the start. But why so many of them were able to convince themselves that the Arab armies were enormously superior to anything the Jews might be able to do in defence, and would settle the whole matter before even U.N. could hitch up its skirts and run to the rescue of the Jews, I cannot guess.

To be sure, the Arabs had all the armaments they needed. We had supplied them ourselves. To be sure, they could put ten times as many thoroughly trained and highly equipped men into the field as the Jews could. The Jews for their part were short of the most elementary armaments and had at best from 10,000 to 12,000 reasonably well-trained men and a group of garrison-type settlements where, however, the settlers had nothing better than rifles and grenades to fight with and would not have known how to use more effective weapons. The Jews had no artillery better than a mortar; no tanks; no air force; no naval vessels. Studied on paper, the Jewish chances, I suppose, did look pretty poor. But Britain, with its long and intimate association with the Middle East, surely could have done better than base its calculations on simple arithmetic.

To begin with the Jew had to fight or die. There could be no retreat for him. Physically and mentally he was well ahead of the Egyptian, Iraqi and Syrian rank and file. His ingenuity had been shown over and over again and his moral stamina was something to be reckoned with. He could use an automatic rifle to better effect than the Egyptian soldier could use a Bren gun, and a grenade to better effect than the Egyptian his twenty-five pounder. Besides, the Jew had scientists and skilled technicians and up-to-date workshops in which, given a little time, he could produce weapons of his own, as indeed he did. And given that little time, he could call upon the help of Jews abroad and get reinforcements, arms, aircraft and pilots; as indeed he did. In deceiving ourselves we deceived the Arabs and did to them as to our own good name and international fortune, a disservice for which we, and they, are still paying.

Six

So came the night of 14th–15th May 1948.

I had made up my mind to stay in Jerusalem and by next morning was, I think, the only non-Jewish Englishman left inside the new city. It was no heroic decision on my part. Here was I, among a people under siege and curiously confident of their being able to stand up to its rigours and privations. It was not an intelligent confidence. They had no right to it. It was rather a kind of quiet faith, which, in the manner of faith, was contagious. I felt it, too, and from a mournful calculation of the odds, had been carried by that contagion to a level of assurance: these people could not lose, however few their fighting men – and if Jerusalem had two hundred trained men that was all – and however mean their arms – they had rifles, but too few; twenty to thirty machine-guns; a store of grenades. The fortitude and good humour around me, as that night fell, in its way was exalting. There was fear. Of course there was fear of what might happen once the British had turned their backs. Until then, Britain had not provided much of a shield but at least the Arab Legion, with its guns poised along the ridge of Scopus and out towards Ramallah and south-westwards against Bethlehem, had hesitated to go into action as long as the British were in the city. As for the Egyptian army, it was still far away in the southern Negev, on the first lap from Sinai, with one column ready to move in the direction of Tel Aviv and the other to turn east into the Hebron hills and up towards Bethlehem. There had to be fear among the Jews of Jerusalem on that ominous night.

It was a clear night. There was a moon, too. When the moon shines on Jerusalem the city becomes like a thing of alabaster: beautiful when there is peace and all is well: ghostly, and fearful, when the alabaster hides armed men waiting for the dawn; and, unseen along the outline of the eastern ridge, are primed guns; and the army of a majestic Power, brought there to protect the people, Jew and Arab, is lining up surreptitiously in dusky squares ready to march out and away into the hills and down through Tulkarm to the coast road and so to the waiting ships at Haifa. Every shadow-bedded lane, every darkened wall, hid armed men – Jews here, Arabs there – waiting tensely until the British, at dawn, should have got into the hills and the race for the evacuated and dominating positions could begin: the railway station and the adjacent suburb of Deir Abu Tor jutting out like a bluff; the King David Hotel looking straight upon the Old City's western walls; the lofty buildings of Mamillah Road commanding the way to and from the Jaffa Gate; Barclay's Bank on the high ground looking down towards the Damascus Gate; the big General Post Office in Jaffa Road; the broadcasting station back from Queen Mellisande's Way; the old Syrian Orphanage, which could lodge five hundred men and massive stores.

How oddly quiet was the night. There were occasional volleys of machine-gun fire from high roof-tops but they only made the quiet palpable. There had been little to eat for supper. Food had been scarce since the main road was severed by the Arabs in March. Children would cry for more but there was none to be had. On this night the children had gone off to bed without crying, as if even they were conscious of something more urgent and possessive than the need for food.

One could hear, from the fenced zones, the shuffling of soldiers' feet, the soft plash of rifle-straps fitted to shoulders, the settling of packs on to bent backs; now and then an indistinct command: all done as if in whispered conspiracy behind closed doors. There was no singing, no marching song as they strode softly off through the city, up by Sheikh Jarra, out to the long, winding road down through the hills. There was the sound of lorries, armoured cars, the groan of tanks. And yet it was quiet in the city.

The smooth, vehicular sounds drew away, leaving only the rhythmic shuffle of feet, now fading, now coming again. There was some muttering of words, a cough. Once there was whistling for a few moments but that ended quickly. And then all at once there was no sound at all. Everything fell into the stillness of an empty house on a hill-side, where no cat prowls, no dog rattles its chain. At that moment there could have been hardly a soul in Jerusalem except little children, who did not lie awake, intently listening, or stand by an unshuttered window in a darkened room, intently peering.

An hour passed. The stars went out and a pale light drifted in, like smoke. Then a yellow wash spread over the eastern hills, where the Arabs were, and it was dawn. The city came alive. It was as if thousands of synchronized alarm clocks had begun to jangle. Out of the still dark lanes and deep shadows sprang men firing automatic rifles, flinging grenades. The race to occupy the city's commanding positions, which Britain had just abandoned, began. And as dawn gave way to full light it was evident that the Jews were beating the Arabs to all the high points and useful buildings west of the Old City walls.

That was not surprising. Most of the Government buildings and Army stations were in the new, mainly Jewish city. There were fewer *Haganah* men than National Guards but they moved faster and straighter; and once the Jews had got into position on the high ground commanding the streets and lanes between the Jewish and Arab quarters there was not much chance of the Arabs getting westwards. They took over, and held for a day or two, the convent of Notre Dame, high above the Damascus Gate; but many of the westward positions they had held while the British were still in nominal control, they had been compelled to give up on that morning.

By nine o'clock the battle had as good as ended. In the Jewish city shops were opened, water-carts came by, street-sweepers appeared. Women, lacking the customary fuel for cooking, built wood fires in their gardens, or on the pavement, and brewed coffee if they were lucky enough to have coffee, heated water for washing the children if they were lucky enough to have water, prepared milk for the babies from milk-powder if they were lucky enough to have milk-powder.

Throughout the morning a few shells were lobbed into the streets of the new city from somewhere along Mount Scopus, but no great harm was done. The stone houses of Jerusalem are like fortresses. The shell from a twenty-five pounder can chip out a lump of stone. Machine-gun fire pocks the wall: no more than that. But a shell or a bullet can kill a man or a woman or a child walking in the street and one had to go out into the streets and fossick about among the shops; or stand on the pavement in a queue with buckets as the water was doled out; and children had to be led to schools set up in basements with the entrances sandbagged. Besides, the street-sweepers had to sweep; the doctors had to get to their hospitals and their patients; lawyers and clerks to their offices. There was always the chance of getting caught in the street and many people were so caught. The mother of Judah, the terrorist, crossing the road on some errand was caught that way. When I heard it, I wondered sadly if Judah had survived. When I last had heard of him he was a prisoner at Athlit. And I wondered what had become of his sister, Carmella, who had lived in a back street of Tel Aviv against the boundary of Jaffa. Theirs had been a luckless coming to the Promised Land.

That first day after Britain's stealthy going was not particularly eventful. The Arabs could take their time. They had not been able to stop the Jews from occupying all the strategic positions in the western half of the city. But they were confident. They had reason to be. Their regular army, the thoroughly equipped and well-trained Arab Legion under the command of the British General, Glubb Pasha, was moving up steadily and occupying the commanding ridges to the east, the north and the south. It was not a big army – 5,000; but it had everything that goes with modern armies. The handful of trained men in New Jerusalem was a pitiful counter-balance.

The Jews were cut off from the main body of *Haganah*, which was disposed in Galilee, where Fawzi Kaukje's irregulars were operating, and around Haifa, Lydda and Ramle. The Jews in Jerusalem could turn out what young men they had and make a show of them, but for the most part they had to rely on paunchy tradesmen, lawyers and clerks, who had not enough rifles to go round but went out on guard duty for a few hours each day and night and in between served behind the counters of their shops, worked at their desks, and snatched what sleep they could. After a week or two certain weapons and ammunition were got to the Jews by a Piper Cub aircraft for which a landing-strip had been made by cutting down an olive grove and levelling a short stretch of the wady in which stood the Greek Monastery of the Cross. I, and others, had been in the habit of picking mallow from the slopes of this wady. Boiled, it makes a good food. But by the time the Piper Cubs started coming the mallow had begun to wither under the hot sun.

2

The night of that first day of formal siege fell without much ado. There was intermittent shooting from the Old City, which was in darkness. Intermittently, shooting was returned. Occasionally a volley could be heard from over against Deir Abu Tor, beyond the railway station. There was no gunfire. The electric power station worked in fits and starts and when it worked the street lamps came on, garishly. A few cafés and one of the well-known restaurants remained open and served what they had.

Walking in the streets I met Jaacov, a quiet-voiced young *Haganah* officer, he invited me to his house in Rehavia and I gladly accepted the invitation.

'Why aren't you away from all this?' he asked. 'Like all the other newspaper men.'

I said I did not know: partly a desire to see how matters would work out; and partly, perhaps, a kind of inertia.

'Here I was, not really believing that the Army and the Secretariat would move out like that, before anyone else – U.N. or something – could come in and take over for the time being. Then, when I knew our people had abandoned ship I felt inquisitive to know whether the damn thing would go on floating and where it would float to. Besides, here is a people under siege. They're as quiet as mice on the whole but it's exhilarating to watch them. Let's say I'm here because it's an experience.'

Jaacov's wife, Poriah, one of those fair-haired, fair-complexioned Jewesses common in Palestine, from whom most of the characteristic physiognomy of the Semite seems to have vanished, was ironing when we entered the house.

'Goodness knows how long the electricity will last,' she said. 'I've been waiting for this opportunity for days.'

They lived on the ground floor of the house. Ted Lurie, who assisted Gershon Agronsky as editor of the *Palestine Post*, had the floor above. Tziela, his wife, came down to us on that evening, sat herself at the piano and played Bach. And there we were, Jaacov and I drinking from his hoarded bottle of local brandy, diluted with a few drops of water from the morning's dole; Poriah ironing for all she was worth; her baby daughter, Shoshana, crawling about the floor in search of adventure; and Tziela strumming away at the piano. It was good to have the electric light shining from table-lamps, instead of flickering candles, which, charming as they may be when their purpose is decorative, are troublesome and inadequate when they become a necessity. The table lamps shone. The brandy was friendly and lightly, pleasantly intoxicating. There was an

64

atmosphere of almost tender relaxation, which Poriah's determined ironing, and Tziela's equally determined strumming, and little Shoshana's intent search for mischief, deepened.

'Any news?' I asked Jaacov. He was stationed at *Haganah*'s headquarters in the city and might be expected to know what was going on.

'No. No news. Nothing much has happened about here. We had a few killed up near Sheikh Jarra. And we got where we wanted to get this morning. All the main points this side of the wall are ours. There won't be much now for a day or two.'

'And along the coast.'

'Don't know,' he replied. 'Won't know until the morning.'

Jaacov lit one of his precious cigarettes. Then, as if expressing an afterthought, he said:

'Of course, the State was proclaimed today. I don't know whether you would call that news. The Provisional Council met in Tel Aviv – at the Museum I think – and Ben Gurion read the proclamation of independence. We're back to being Israelites again. The State's to be called Israel.'

I smiled.

'So you don't know whether I would call that news, Jaacov,' I said. 'How I wish there were a cable office around the corner.'

Jaacov said:

'What did you expect? After all, the ceremony in the Museum at Tel Aviv was only a formality.'

I thought for a moment and it was indeed as if the State had been there all along. Now, so to speak, it had come out to be looked at and photographed.

At that moment Tziela clapped her hands, got up from the piano, and joined us.

'You're crazy,' she said, looking at me. 'Why didn't you get out with the rest?'

'Too damn lazy,' I replied. 'And besides, what's the matter with this?'

'Matter? You try scrubbing floors, washing children's clothes and things, making coffee and flushing lavatories all from a pail of water twice a week. And what's more, try feeding two kids on a tin of sardines and some half-rotten potatoes. You ask what's wrong. Everything's wrong.'

But Tziela laughed as she spoke. Like almost every other Jew in the city she was quietly uplifted. The children were a worry, of course. They would become a bigger worry later on. Besieged cities are no place for children.

On that first night of the declared siege and of the State of Israel, we had bread and tinned tongue and afterwards a cup of coffee, with sugar in it. That was thanks to Jaacov's *Haganah* rations, which had included a packet of English cigarettes. The cigarettes had been a parting gift from a British Officers' Mess. There had been many little gestures of that kind during the previous night. Not all the British Army had been anti-Zionists: far from it; and many officers who were not pro-Zionist either, had felt sympathy for the beleaguered Jews, and a good deal of admiration; even some confidence in their ability to do better than the Arabs. Up to field rank, most officers I had talked with during the past two or three weeks gave the Jews a sporting chance. It was above that level that one met with the notion that the Jews, in the phrase of Field Marshal Lord Montgomery, had 'bought it'.

We took out coffee on the darkened balcony, which looked south and east. The moon was high. When the moon lights it, the sky of Jerusalem is enchanting. It has a liquid quality, as if it were an upturned lagoon, the stars not glittering but poised like illuminated water-lilies; and the moon like its own reflection in the quiet water. Here, underneath, the Holy City stood still. There was an occasional shot but one hardly noticed it. Tracer-bullets scratched the sky but the scratch healed at once.

We stayed there on the balcony, talking idly, until it became time to go to bed. Tziela had already gone upstairs. I took my leave of Jaacov and Poriah and sauntered through the streets for about an hour. I was a newspaper correspondent after all, and although I had no means of communicating with my paper, and therefore no need to write despatches, the habit of years was strong. Besides, it is good to investigate what looks like becoming a big story, take notes, write it up in one's mind, and then put the notebook away knowing full well that one cannot reach a cable office or put through a telephone call: stories without 'deadline' are lost stories, and lost stories have much to be said for them.

But all was quiet: the streets, the houses, all were quiet and dark. Now and then I passed someone else walking, on what mission I had no idea. Once I came close to what looked like a platoon of armed men going south. I had noticed flares bursting in that area, lighting up the houses that jutted out over the valley. I came to the office of the *Palestine Post*, which was close enough to the Arab lines to be uncomfortable.

I turned about and began walking homewards. It is not a comfortable thing to do, to walk alone at about one in the morning through the dark and deserted streets of a besieged city. A few bullets came whizzing by the corner of Zion Square. There was a burst of firing from one of the northern quarters. A dog limped up the middle of Ben Yehuda Street, one of the main shopping thoroughfares; and when I turned into King George Avenue I was met by the howling of cats from behind some packing-cases. Jerusalem's homeless and often hungry dogs and cats had multiplied rapidly once the Arabs from the western quarters had begun moving, bag and baggage, into the overcrowded walled city.

The electric power had failed. There was a glow of candlelight and oil-lamps from some of the windows of the Jewish Agency building. But all was quiet. New Jerusalem waited. What it waited for I could only guess at. Perhaps an artillery barrage from Scopus: an air bombardment: an assault by the Legion with tens of thousands of screaming Arabs behind: relief from the coast.

It was about two o'clock when I reached my apartment overlooking the airstrip. I lit candles, crawled into bed and fell asleep at once.

Seven

NEXT day, eavesdropping against a parked motor car with its wireless set tuned to an English-language broadcast, I overheard the announcer tell of President Truman's *de facto* recognition of the day-old State. That swift and surprising action by the head of the United States Government and people brought a touch of reality to events in Palestine which, I had felt, were steadily withdrawing into an aloof circle of fancy.

Twenty-four hours ago and thirty miles away, Israel, the place where King David ruled and Jesus was crucified and Titus marched vengefully, that place of long ago and of tender words spoken and sung in church and of the crucifix above my bed and the coloured text on the wall – that place had come again into being. Perhaps in Tel Aviv it was all plain and reasonable. Here in the besieged Holy City, Ben Gurion's State of Israel was as remote as King David's. More so; Biblical Israel had history on its side. The Israel of 15th May 1948 had only a declaration and a few men with guns to defend it. And there was no looking out from besieged Jerusalem to see what was happening on the other side, where this rash adventure, the State of Israel, stood with the morning sun in its eyes.

One way and another it was as if one lay sleepless in the dark, imagining strange things. But Presidents of the United States are not given to imagining things. If President Truman said there was a State of Israel *de facto*, then there must surely be a State of Israel.

I went on my way. From the house on the corner came the sound of one of Chopin's *études* played haltingly, searchingly, on a piano. That was little Miriam, with the dark, sombre eyes and the long pigtails. She did her piano practice every morning as regularly as the street-sweepers did their sweeping and Mrs. Judah Magnus, growing old, took her ten minutes' walk under the trees.

2

In Jerusalem at that time there was very little difference between one day and another. Electric power failures were many, sometimes for days and nights at a time. One had to expect that, what with all the gunfire and the shortage of skilled technicians. Only occasionally were our wireless sets of much use; and for news of what was going on outside we had to rely on rumour and the sparse news gathered from where it could be gathered by the *Palestine Post*. In the quiet hours I walked; and sometimes in the unquiet hours, just as the others did, to collect a loaf of bread to which I had become entitled, or merely to observe others. I visited people I knew and I talked a great deal with Jaacov and Poriah, who lived only half a street away from my house; and Poriah would say:

'The stars are bright. Let's sit on the balcony and look at the stars.'

Then things got bad. The Egyptians joined up with the Legion in the Hebron-Bethlehem sector and shells began falling all over the place. Soon after dark Poriah would take Shoshanna down to the sandbagged basement and there they would stay.

Often, in the morning, I met with Gershon Agronsky, neatly dressed, carrying his walking-stick, walking the thirty minutes' walk to his office, deliberately striding out and swinging his stick as if nothing in the world were the matter; shell-fire no worse an affliction than the summer flies; short rations so much the better for everyone's health. It was a pose, of course; but a good one. Now and then he grew tired of it. One morning he said to me, almost petulantly:

'Why doesn't Glubb attack?'

'Why should he? He's got the city tied up. He must have a pretty fair idea of what your effective strength is and if he has he can't be worrying much about an attack on the Old City from this side. From what Jaacov tells me Glubb has most of his forces in the Latrun area and your fellows can't dislodge him. As long as he is in position there, the highway up to Bab el Wad is his and there is no chance of *Haganah* getting a relief force through to Jerusalem. Isn't that the way it is?'

'I suppose it is. But he had better not be too sure about no attack coming from this side.'

In fact, an attack did take place some days later, which I shall tell of in its place; and, in fact, relief for Jerusalem was on its laborious way. We did not know it then, but men were working like mad, day and night, just across the hills from Latrun and south of the main highway controlled by the Legion. They were putting down a road,

69

up the hills and down again and as straight as it could go, with complete disregard of gradients. They were building it from south of Ramle and carrying it to the highway at the dark gorge of Bab el Wad. From there on, the main road had been under the control of the Jews following their capture of the dominant Castel height before the departure of the British from Jerusalem. In the battle for that height the Arab Commander, Abdul Kader Husseini, a kinsman of Haj Amin, had been killed.

Latrun, with its Trappist monastery and vineyards; Ramle with its big tower left over from the Crusades; Lydda with its airfield and its tale of St. George and the dragon; Beersheba smelling of leather harness; Haifa, the Emek and Galilee: these were far-away battles told fitfully to us in Jerusalem. The city knew vaguely that its relief depended on the far-away battles; and as a dreamlike matter of course was confident. But for the time being Jerusalem was a battle on its own. Shells fell indiscriminately. Machine-gun fire chipped away bits of stone. One of the shells went through a window of the makeshift hospital in Strauss Street, killed a few people, smashed instruments. Every morning, outside my door, were two or three spent cartridges. Rebecca would gather them and place them in a bowl and set them on the small table in the living-room.

Rebecca was a Yemenite woman of about twenty-two. She had fine, almost Hindu features and black straight hair, and her complexion was much darker than that of most Jews. She came every morning to sweep and dust, and do a little washing if there was water. She swept, dusted, washed, hardly ever saying a word. Even when shells were falling fifty yards away, she did not look up or show interest. To get to my apartment she had to walk through the town from the Mea Shearim quarter in the north-east, and I said to her several times:

'Rebecca, would it not be sensible to stay at home with your children?'

'No. I do not mind.'

'Aren't you afraid for the children, all alone?'

'Yes. My neighbour watches them for me. I am afraid all the time. If the Arabs break through they will come first to Mea Shearim and my children will be killed. What can I do?'

But one morning towards the end of the second week of the siege Rebecca did not come to sweep and dust. I never saw her again. I began doing the sweeping and dusting myself, and every morning I gathered the spent cartridges outside the door.

From my roof I could watch the Egyptian shelling of the settlement of Ramat Rachel, which, on high ground a mile or so this side of Bethlehem guarded the road from Hebron to Jerusalem. The settlement's houses were blown to pieces, but some thirty men, dug in around the settlement, kept the Egyptians away. It was incredible that thirty men with rifles, two machine-guns and a stock of grenades, should be able, even from the superior height they occupied, to repulse a fully-equipped force of at least two companies. But they did. After that the Egyptians did nothing but swivel their batteries. I could watch their shells bouncing in a straight line down the one street of a small suburb west of the Monastery of the Cross. Up down, up down, went the smoke and the dust.

3

It is hard to tell what would have happened in Jerusalem if the truce had been long delayed. Food, water, arms, ammunition were running short. There was no source of reinforcement. Hospitals were crammed with emergency cases: casualties among the *Haganah* units – machine-gun victims as a rule; civilian casualties – victims of gunfire; the seriously ill. Children were falling sick with a new and strange enteric. To make matters worse, much of Jerusalem's medical equipment and supplies was out of reach in the Hadassah laboratories and store-rooms on Mount Scopus.

It cannot be said that there was acute hunger. There always seemed to be a little of something to hand round: rice, noodles, a few old potatoes, now and then a loaf of bread and perhaps once a week some tinned meat or fish and a packet of milk-powder. Where it came from I cannot tell. Obviously, every house and shop of the abandoned Arab quarters of Katamon, Baka'a, the German Colony and Deir Abu Tor, had been ransacked and their contents stored for distribution among the besieged Jews. Water, which long ago had ceased to flow after the Arabs had destroyed the pipe-lines from the reservoir some twenty miles to the west, came from house cisterns built to gather rain-water. The cisterns had been sealed up by the Jewish authorities in the city, and the seals were broken only

to fill water-carts which afterwards distributed the ration of one or
two pails to each family about twice a week.

The organization of the besieged community – about 120,000 –
was impressive. The chief authority was Doctor Dov Joseph, who
had been given by the Jewish Agency Executive and then by the
first provisional Government what amounted to a governor's
warrant. For some years he had been practising law in Jerusalem and
serving as a member of the Agency's Executive. He is not a particularly impressive person to look at or listen to. One would not
expect him to perform remarkable deeds. But his and his staff's
handling of what must surely be one of the rarest, most delicate,
complicated, despairing, and significant tasks anyone can be called
upon to perform – the maintenance of morale in a city under prolonged siege and without means of relief short of victory for armies
operating at the other end of the country – was exceptional. It was
exceptional both for the range of its organization and for the
manner of its application. There was no fuss; there were no heroics;
no unnecessary restrictions. The siege of Jerusalem under the
guidance of Dov Joseph and the city's military commander,
Colonel David Shaltiel, was borne steadfastly and uncomplainingly
and in the realization that there was much to be thankful for.

4

One day a small body of Yigal Alon's *Palmach* fighters turned up
in Jerusalem: lean, tanned, eager-looking boys, none of whom could
have been more than twenty. They had wormed their way up
through the Judaean hills. Jaacov had warned me of their coming.

'They've come up to do a job and do it quickly,' he had said.
'They haven't much time.'

I watched them tumble into their Jerusalem billet, the Rehavia
High School, in the early morning; and thought to myself that that
was where most of them belonged – in school, not on a battlefield.

After dusk of that same day they moved down towards Deir
Abu Tor and when it was quite dark scrambled into the valley and
then, carrying their mortars and rope ladders and cases of grenades,
up the other side, behind the Bishop Gobat school, past the Church
of the Dormition and the flat-roofed *coenaculum*, to the shadows of

the Zion Gate. The assault on the gate began soon after midnight. From Jaacov's and Poriah's balcony we watched the flares and heard the exploding mortar-bombs, the so-called *Davidkes* (Little Davids), made in a Tel Aviv workshop. Entrance was quickly forced, the defenders withdrew, and by dawn the *Palmach* were in occupation of the old Jewish quarter inside the walls.

As Jaacov had said, the *Palmach* were in a hurry. They departed as recklessly as they had come. The Zion quarter was sealed off from the rest of the Old City and looked relatively easy to defend. A section of the Jerusalem *Haganah* was left in charge of the captured positions and *Palmach* made off westwards into the hills towards some other daring venture. The Arabs then counter-attacked and reoccupied the quarter. No further attempt on the walled city was made until, on the eve of the truce, a body of *Irgun Zvai Leumi* warriors forced the undefended Jaffa Gate, moved through deserted lanes and then ran up against a strong group of the Arab Legion, which had little difficulty in forcing a withdrawal.

5

And then there was Hannah, that splendid person with the up-turned smile, the eyes of Anubis, the keen quiet intelligence of someone born to assay shrewdly the hard metal of human life. She was serving with the *Haganah* and in the second week of the siege had been brought to Jerusalem by a Piper Cub and allotted to some special duty.

I saw something of her at that time. She wore a kind of uniform – khaki shirt and grey trousers, and had cut her black hair. She came now and then to my apartment overlooking the Monastery of the Cross: always reposeful; tired from lack of sleep; oddly girlish in spite of the uniform and a steady preoccupation with sten-guns, grenades and night-watches – almost pathetically girlish, as if, willy-nilly, the feminine in her were asserting its rights against the harshness, danger and crudity of soldiering.

'When all this is over,' she said to me on her first visit to the apartment, 'I'm going to get into a warm bath and keep changing it for more warm water and stay there for days and days and days. And when I get out of the bath I'm going to wear frilly things and make love to every reasonably decent-looking young man who will let me make love to him. And I'm not going to be frightened any more.'

I laughed.

'You frightened!'

She looked intently at me from those brown, green-flecked Egyptian eyes. There was an expression at her lips that might have been contempt.

'Yes,' she said, 'frightened as hell. Creeping in the darkness down from Deir Abu Tor and listening for the sound of Arabs. Spending whole nights in an empty house above the Damascus Gate watching for movement on the walls. I hate it. And then next day trying to teach silly little girls how to toss a grenade and hold a gun. And have them come to me with all their griefs about their boy-friends, or a brother down at Latrun, or quarrels with their parents.'

She smiled.

'I want to go home. That's it, I suppose. But you must not take any real notice of what I'm saying. I wouldn't miss all this for anything. It's only. . . . Do you know? I have a feeling that I won't come through it. And that would be a pity.'

She said it lightly. But whether it was the tense atmosphere of the city under siege, or the curiously antique, almost prophetic atmosphere that seemed to go with Hannah, I do not know; but I was moved by her remark. We said no more and she went off to her duties, leaving me the last inch of a rare cigarette that we had been smoking together, two puffs to Hannah, two to me.

And then came that Friday at the beginning of June. We had gone together to the building behind King George Avenue, in which was *Haganah* Headquarters. There had been a good deal of gunfire from Scopus during the day. Mortar-bombs had been lobbed into the Old City by the Jews. There were gusts of smoke along the southern ridge towards Bethlehem. It was hot. I sat on the steps of the building and waited for Hannah to come back from a briefing which, she had told me, was likely to be, for her, of some importance. She returned after about thirty minutes, smiling that knowledgeable smile of hers. The sun was already low and we walked up and down King George Avenue for an hour or two, saying little. Then we met Gershon Agronsky, neat as usual, swinging his cherry-wood walking-stick as usual, affecting his 'business-as-usual' manner and pretending to be merely sad at the waste of lives and the foolishness of war: not frightened.

'Come,' he said. '*Haganah* found a case of whisky in one of the derelict German Colony houses. They've given me a bottle. Let's open it. I've been wanting an excuse.'

It seemed to me to be an excellent idea. I had no notion of what Hannah's briefing had been about but I guessed that it had to do with some enterprise to be carried out that night. The day was already moving towards dusk and a couple of whiskies and soda before she set out to wherever it was she had to set out to, could do her no harm. Besides, I had not tasted whisky for many a long day.

We walked on, Gersohn's stick gesturing like a baton. When we came to the office of the *Palestine Post* he pointed, with the indifference of one who was used to such things and thought nothing of them, to a place in the wall where a stone had been dislodged by shell-fire. We went to his comfortably furnished room and each of us had two generous whiskies and water. There was no soda to be had in Jerusalem. Gershon Agronsky, screwing up his face in real delight at the taste of the whisky, said:

'God bless the things that tempt us to sin, like alcohol and . . .' He turned and bowed to Hannah ' . . . pretty women.' He liked saying things like that.

'God bless sin. Period,' said Hannah, who liked saying things like that. As for me, I savoured the whisky, longed vainly for a cigarette and, once the bottle had been put away, felt glad to be moving off again with Hannah.

We walked into Zion Square.

'This is where I leave you,' said Hannah. 'Good-bye.' I stood watching her as she strode, without looking back, up Jaffa Road. Then she turned off into a small side street.

It was Jaacov who told me all about it next morning. Not that there was much to tell. It had been a minor operation. But three of the *Haganah* had been killed. The bodies had been brought to Schneller's, the old Syrian Orphanage, which had been turned into a kind of *Haganah* barracks. A bullet had gone through Hannah's throat.

Eight

THROUGHOUT this confused, heartbreaking, and yet uplifting period, one felt acutely the presence of David Ben Gurion over the whole land. He was referred to by everyone as B.G. The children in their sandbagged basement schools would say to each other:

'You wait until B.G. comes. Then it will be all right.'

Poriah would say to little Shoshanna:

'Hush, darling. B.G. will come soon and then you can have as much to eat as you can swallow.'

One got into the habit of saying: 'I wonder how B.G.'s getting on at Latrun'; when it was really a question of how *Haganah* was getting on at Latrun, or its commander in that sector, the American, General Marcus, who had come to help the Israelis. That was sad, too: General Marcus was killed by one of his own nervous sentries, who, in the dark, mistook him for one of the Arab Legion.

Ben Gurion was a politician and, since the 15th May, Prime Minister. He was not a soldier and had no military command. But one felt that it was he who led the people into battle. One felt it was he, rather than young Moshé Dayan with the black patch over his blind eye, who dashed through Ramle in a tumble-down jeep and with a handful of *Haganah* men behind him, frightened the unit of Arab Legionaries away, and had the whole town in his possession after about an hour. One felt it was he, rather than the boyish General Yigal Alon, who had sent the Syrians and Fawzi Kaukje packing. All this was a trifle unfair to the brilliant, youthful commanders operating in the field; but those commanders themselves would not have contested the implication. The feeling most of them had for B.G. was little short of adoration. They were in constant and personal touch with the 'Old Man'.

I cannot tell whether this small, rosy-cheeked, white-haired man with the womanish voice and wearing a broad belt because his back ached will be counted among the great men of his time. I only know that he served his people greatly. He has been called obstinate, and I suppose he is: forthright, uncompromising, steadfast he has always been. Obstacles could not for long sustain their hindrance against his determination. If his wings were spread to fly south, fly south he did, however the wind might blow. He had fought the White Paper until that wretched document lay in shreds and its authors were confounded. He fought five Arab armies and the hostility of Great Britain until the Arab ran and a British Government stood shamed. Against the pleadings of Weizmann and the political caution of Shertok (Sharett) and the timidity of some of his own public, he declared sovereign independence and set about defending it with the military odds at ten to one against.

And in the morning, downstairs he would come at his small, white house in Tel Aviv, wearing an old dressing-gown, and would eat his breakfast in the kitchen with Paula, his wife, who once upon a time had been a nurse in a New York hospital; and Paula would say to him:

'It's hot today, B.G. You'll sweat in the office and you know how bad that is for your back. See that you change your shirt at lunch time.'

Like many great and visionary leaders there is a quality of the feminine about Ben Gurion. He can be as gentle as a woman and as waspish. Although coldly shrewd in his decisions, his sense of mission has the emotional intensity of a woman bent on saving a loved one from the fires of hell. He sees this quality in himself as being in the true line of the Biblical Prophets, and one gets the impression that his profoundest desire is to grow immensely old, and in some fashion legendary; and from an austere retreat to set down in the Hebrew he fervently loves, and for the comfort and guidance of his people, the wisdom of his years and far-sightedness. But age as a physical affliction distresses him. Standing one morning with his military aide at the window of his office in the Prime Minister's Department, he noticed two or three bent men, probably in their seventies, walking along the pavement below. He turned and said:

'Old age like that has no dignity, no usefulness. It's pitiful.'

Perhaps that was why he had only young men about him. Nearly all his advisers and most of the men he had picked out to build up and command *Haganah* were under thirty-five. He always gave the impression of being more at ease with men half his age than with those of his own generation; perhaps because young men answered promptly to his own daring, as he did to theirs.

Ben Gurion is not a publicist. He is shy of the photographer's lamp and suspicious of the newspaper-man's notebook. He addresses gatherings when he has to and as a rule is mercifully brief. But for the most part he leaves it to his lieutenants to raise proud standards and be the centre-piece of national occasions. His white hair flutters, of course, with the flags of Independence Day; for that day is peculiarly his. I doubt whether there would have been a State of Israel today if Ben Gurion had not been there to prepare for the opportunity he foresaw and to seize it uncompromisingly when it came.

As I have already said, there were many in those days who, whilst longing for freedom and ready to go on politically badgering the British Government, were afraid of sovereign independence. Doctor Chaim Weizmann was one of these. He was, in Mr. Attlee's words, a 'gradualist'. About a year before the State was founded he said to me, in the library of his handsome Rehovot villa:

'We Jews never pronounce the name of God. In the same way and for much the same reason we should never pronounce the word State. If sovereignty is to come to us, it should come of itself, so to speak, when we have deserved it.'

That was not Ben Gurion's way.

Ben Gurion's chief deputy on the eve of independence was another who hesitated before the immense responsibility of sovereignty; or at any rate felt that it could wait a little, at least until it was assured of the full backing of the United States Government, which, about that time, had put forward a proposal for a trusteeship over Palestine to be exercised by U.N. This was Moshé Shertok, who led the Jewish Agency's political department and afterwards, with his name hebraized to Sharett, became the State's first Foreign Minister.

He was not, as Weizmann was, a 'gradualist'; but he was not a visionary either, as B.G. was. He was a politician who counted the cost meticulously and preferred to be on the safe side. When the British left Jerusalem, Sharett was in the United States and probably subject to advice from Washington. However that may have been, he is said to have cautioned Ben Gurion against the hasty declaration of independence and to have hurried back to Tel Aviv in an attempt to delay that event. He was unsuccessful. He then accepted Ben Gurion's decision and loyally upheld it; and, as Foreign Minister of the Provisional Government and the constitutional administrations that followed, did much to earn for the new State the respect and even admiration of those governments with which it had diplomatic dealings.

Sharett was the 'talker' of the Palestine Jewish leadership. He could talk his listener's head off without showing the slightest fatigue or the simplest deviation from logic. He was a good debater. No subject ever found Sharett wanting in argument. But he was apt to go on and on in a quick, toneless voice, so that in the end one often found oneself, as in the old tag, to be of the same opinion still. Sharett and Ben Gurion are alike in nothing; but in this, the method of persuasion, are more unlike than in almost anything else. Ben Gurion knows what he wants and believes it wiser to get what he wants than to prove endlessly his right to it.

Nine

ARAB invasion had failed. That had become clear by the first days of June. The concerted plan of the Jordanian-Iraqi forces from the east, the Egyptians from the south and the Syrians from the north, to occupy Haifa, Jerusalem and Tel Aviv before the end of May had misfired. They had been operating with aircraft, artillery and tanks in areas defended, in the main, by farmers dug in around their settlements along the planned line of advance. At the same time relatively small *Palmach*, or Jewish Commando units, kept up an astonishingly mobile offensive, which had the invading Arabs in a state of nerves and convinced their leaders, including General Glubb Pasha, Commander of the Arab Legion, that the Jewish forces were several times as numerous as they were in fact.

By the 3rd of June Ben Gurion was able to report to the Provisional State Council: 'We cannot say that the danger has passed . . . there are still grounds for anxiety . . . the invading States have failed signally . . . Israel's armies now hold a bigger continuous area than they did three weeks ago . . .'

And so a truce was arranged by U.N. and came into force on June 11th, almost exactly a month after the Arab armies had entered Palestine with the intention of bringing about a harsh and final reckoning with the Jews. Both sides were glad of the truce, the Arabs because they had no notion what to do next or how otherwise to save their faces, the Jews because they had been stretched to the limit and needed a breathing-space in which to get more arms and ammunition.

In Jerusalem the truce discovered the Old City securely in Arab hands and the New securely in Jewish hands. Tank traps and huge, coiled dragons of barbed-wire divided the two. The first day of truce coincided with the completion of the madcap relief highway built through the hills south of the Legion-held Latrun sector of the main road. Relief was assured, truce or no truce. The road, known after a famous predecessor as the Burma Road, had been the work of hundreds of men toiling night and day in the first summer heat, lacking the customary engines of road-building and subject to gunfire from behind Latrun. Along its rough surface came, on that night of truce, a long, triumphant convoy of fresh food, the first of such supplies to reach Jerusalem for nearly three months. Crowds gathered to cheer the truck-drivers and the convoy's escort and to sniff the half-forgotten odours of fresh potatoes, tomatoes, lettuce, juicy meat; and stare in wonderment at sacks of flour, crates of eggs, great canisters of fresh milk, cases of medical supplies.

A little old woman wearing a black straw hat with a posy of daisies stood beside me, glowing. Her face was transfigured as she watched.

2

With the truce and the opening of the relief road I moved to Tel Aviv. There were cabling facilities in that city and besides, the Provisional Government was there, and so would be the diplomatic missions following upon the recognition of the State.

I shall long remember my passage from Jerusalem to Tel Aviv. There was no normal transport and the road was still reckoned as dangerous. The *Haganah* Commander in Jerusalem (formerly a member of the French Foreign Legion) gave me a rickety army jeep and a robust, merry driver named Itzhaak. Itzhaak stood about six feet two inches tall and was as broad and hard built as a slab of Jerusalem stone. He had come to Palestine as a boy from Russia. Most of the Russian Jews were big, open-faced, enterprising, independent in thought and action, and gaily good humoured. Itzhaak was one of these. He was a builder by trade.

'But I like soldiering better,' he said, grinning over his broad, rather flat face. 'There is much joy in being more clever than the enemy. I like much when my commander says: "The Arabs on that hill-top.We want that hill-top." Then I say to myself: Tonight I and my comrades will go out and chase the Arabs away and tomorrow I shall be on that hill-top and maybe one day my son – ah! You should see my son – his is twelve, big, strong, happy boy – maybe one day he will grow grape vines on that hill-side. See?'

I said I saw.

Itzhaak drove like mad. When we got through the dark defile of Bab el Wad and turned south to the Burma Road, he ran the jeep on two wheels along the side of the steep hill, shouting merrily at me:

'I give you sensation, Sair!'

He did.

When, after about ten minutes (which should have been twenty), he turned west, running parallel with the Arab-held Latrun sector of the main road, Itzhaak drew up.

'Come,' he said, 'let us look at Glubb Pasha's Arab Legion.'

I had no fervent wish to look at Glubb Pasha's Arab Legion, which might resent being looked at. The truce was only one day old and it would be easy to revert to the habit of picking off inquisitive observers. Besides, there were companies of Iraqi and Syrian irregulars roaming the countryside to whom the truce meant nothing and for whom a pot-shot at intruders from the Jewish side was something to bring off whenever the blessed opportunity presented itself.

But I could hardly show my caution, which was brother to fear, in the presence of Itzhaak, who looked upon the venture as good and proper fun. His eyes glittered with a kind of mischievous expectation as we climbed to the top of the low ridge looking down to Latrun. He was carrying a gun, and I said to him:

'Hadn't you better hide that gun of yours? At least swing it over your shoulders instead of carrying it like that. You look as if you want to shoot someone with the damned thing.'

Itzhaak laughed and patted his gun. Then, in a spirit of generosity he pushed the gun towards me.

'Here, you take it, Sair,' he said. 'Make you feel good.'

I took the wretched thing, one of those new-fangled, short-barrelled things of the sten-gun type, slung it over my shoulder and hoped that no prying Arab on the Latrun side would notice it; or for that matter notice me.

At the top of the ridge we lay flat and peered down to where the road swung around the grounds of the monastery. A group of Arab Legionaries stood around immediately below us. One of them was an officer. He looked like an Englishman. If he were, he was required under the terms of the truce to take prolonged leave of absence. As we watched, he seemed to be giving instructions. After a few minutes he moved off, using a khaki handkerchief to wipe the sweat from the back of his neck. Beyond the Arab Legion group a few men in *ghalibiyehs* were moving idly through a vineyard. There were coils of barbed wire everywhere, without much apparent purpose.

Then, suddenly, from somewhere east of our position, we heard the crack of rifles. Bullets whizzed over us. They were high and, at worst, intended to frighten us. Itzhaak laughed loudly:

'Very bad shots, very bad.' he said.

'O.K. But good enough shots for me,' I replied. 'Next time they will aim lower.'

'You think? Maybe. Maybe they good shots if they try. Eh? Perhaps better we go back.'

'Certainly better we go back.'

We retraced our steps, but this time crawling on our stomachs until well below the crest of the ridge. Then we stood up and strode down to the jeep. I handed Itzhaak his gun and was glad to be quit of it. He threw it up and caught it again, laughing loudly:

'We good friends,' he cried out.

We set off again along the Burma Road, the emergency character of which was evident in its surfacing and in the steep gradients it followed to get over hills with speed rather than with the safety and comfort of easier slopes that would have added a few hundreds of delaying yards. At one point Itzhaak felt it necessary to halt the jeep, get out, and show me his skill with a revolver. It looked as if it were a favourite spot for such exhibitions. Shattered bottles were all over the place. That done, we got back into the jeep; but after about another twenty minutes Itzhaak turned off the road in order to illustrate to me how a jeep could take a goat-track with the agility of the goats themselves.

At last we rejoined the main highway near the town of Ramle, which was already filling up with newly-arrived Bulgarian Jews: good, quiet, hard-working types – perhaps the best of the new-comers then streaming into the State of Israel.

From Ramle it was an easy and unexceptional run to Tel Aviv. There was scarcely any sign of the Israel army. Arab villages along the way were in ruin. Not an Arab could be seen. The villages had been destroyed after their abandonment. Their rubble was a piteous monument to the wanton absurdity of a war forced upon a simple people by leaders who, from their elaborate palaces in Cairo, Amman, Baghdad and Damascus, made promises they could not fulfil, issued proclamations that meant nothing, and cared very little what happened to the unfortunate Arabs of Palestine.

And so, like a Moroccan horseman drawing up his steed from the gallop to the ceremonial standstill, Itzhaak drew up his stained and rattle-trap jeep before the entrance to Tel Aviv's Kaete Dan Hotel, which in those far-off, modest days before the coming of its elaborate successor, the Dan Hotel, was considered to be a hostelry of rare distinction. It certainly had distinction for me: hot baths as often as I wanted them; as much food and drink as I could take; quiet nights with a bedside lamp that went on and off at the touch of a switch; and by day thronged, cheerful streets to walk along and smart shop-window displays to stare at. There was no evidence of battle and not much of any military activity and nothing to remind one of the remarkable event of a month ago, when the independent State of Israel was proclaimed. There was conspicuous gaiety in the city, perhaps the outcome of released tension; and, of course, the Kaete Dan Hotel was crammed with British, American and French newspaper-men, including, again, Arthur Koestler, who was there for the *Manchester Guardian* and had acquired for his use an old jeep, which he drove with the same concentrated and brow-furrowing effort that he wrote.

3

Tel Aviv is a pale, yellowish, angular city: plain walls; ugly, boxlike balconies with rusted iron railings; flat roofs, often with a small pent-house on them; streets running parallel with the shore and, therefore, denied the summer dispensation of sea-breezes. But the city is conspicuously, almost crudely, alive. It is alive from the moment you enter it at the southern end, against the outskirts of Jaffa, where your ears are deafened by the din of a hundred work-shops and the grinding of truck-gears, until you emerge from crowded shopping-streets to the tall apartment houses of the northern quarter, through which traffic streams coastwards to Haifa.

It has become unfashionable among many Israelis to express a liking for Tel Aviv. For one thing, the city is wretchedly hot in midsummer. It is a damp heat. Sitting at a typewriter one is harassed by sweat-dripping fingers, which glaze the keys and smudge the cable-form. The heat of the day is absorbed into the sponge-like night and sleep becomes a hazard. The cool places are the cafés and hotel terraces along the sea-front, where Tel Aviv ladies who have servants to attend to their household meet to gossip over coffee or ice-cream. And that, too, is held against Tel Aviv, which by the reckoning of the dour citizens of Jerusalem, the trade-unionists of Haifa, and the pioneers of the settlements, has too many idle rich. And, of course, in 1948 Tel Aviv was sniffed at by the people of Jerusalem and even of Haifa because it had come through the war without a scratch, or almost without a scratch. What had happened for a few weeks up against the Jaffa border hardly counted. The city had no real wounds to show, as Jerusalem and Haifa had; no medals to boast; no privations to talk about.

To be sure, Tel Aviv is crude. It cannot fairly be judged by the antique design and cathedral-town atmosphere of Jerusalem, or by the ascending far-seeing Haifa, which has Carmel magnificently at its back and the swinging Bay of Acre before it. In 1948, Tel Aviv looked cruder than it does now, mainly for want of paint and a building or two of style. Probably, by certain standards that tend to be stuffy, it behaved crudely. It did a great deal of dancing. It had big, modern cinema-halls. Almost every second frontage along the three main streets – Ben Yehuda, Allenby and Dizengoff – was a café. There were pavement tables with pretty cloths on them and there, true enough, sat people who, perhaps, should have been working instead of gossiping and laughing and tinkling ice in tall glasses. The city kept late hours. It was up and about among its neon lights long after Jerusalem and Haifa were tucked away in bed. It even had night clubs, forbidden in Jerusalem and too extravagant for Haifa. And it had a set of wealthy industrialists who supported and financed political movements which opposed Ben Gurion's *Mapai*. That, of course, was something of a heresy.

For myself, however, I liked Tel Aviv. It had three metropolitan-style daily newspapers. It had two theatres, one of them a handsome, pillared affair built for *Habimah*, which was a kind of Jewish national theatre in Europe long before there was anything like a National Home, much less a State, in Palestine. The Palestine Orchestra, later to be called the Israel Philharmonic Orchestra and ranking among the world's best, gave frequent concerts in Tel Aviv, its home, and during the winter season had guest conductors and soloists of the highest international level. There were a dozen good restaurants and as many good cafés.

But aside from all this, Tel Aviv represented the new, plunging, eager Israel far more than did Jerusalem, or for that matter any other of the Jewish towns. It was built amid the enthusiasms of the first years of the National Home and was Jewish from the first brick to the last. Why that particular site was chosen I know not. Its yellow dunes against a long beach without promise of anything resembling good harbourage had never borne town or village in historical memory. And right alongside it was Jaffa, a busy Arab town that might not be easy to live with. But whatever the motive for building where they did, those colonists of the early 'twenties let nothing hinder them. Up went Tel Aviv on the astonished dunes, street by street, block of masonry by block of masonry, with insufficient regard for town-planning and not much for achitectual niceties; until, within a matter of ten years, it had become the biggest and most populous town in Palestine. It was an act of faith and fervour that did more than is generally supposed towards giving the substance of nationhood to the National Home. I have often thought that the Israel of today could do without Jerusalem. It could not do without Tel Aviv.

The new immigrants who, already in 1948, had begun to pack Tel Aviv, had arrived for the most part without a penny and with little more than the clothes they were wearing when they stumbled down the ships' gangways at Haifa. Initially, most of them were given help by one or other of the Zionist institutions. But it was not long before they found means of helping themselves. They peddled, opened kiosks, turned to unskilled labour in the workshops: found something to do, somewhere, and in their fashion pioneered as effectively as did the *élite* of the settlements, the foundrymen and cement workers of Haifa, and the doctors, professors, and lawyers of Jerusalem.

Their lot was much harder than the lot of those others. I employed a housekeeper who had come from Tunisia. She bore the un-Jewish name of Madeleine. Her husband, who had been a master-shoemaker in Sfax, now pushed a builder's barrow for eight hours a day. They had six children of school age and every penny they could raise went to seeing that the children should have medical attention, schooling, and clothes of a standard that would have been out of the question in Sfax even for the children of a master-cobb er. Madeleine and her husband saw the new land as the promise of happiness for their two sons and four daughters. For themselves, Israel offered security in the physical sense and they were grateful for that. But Madeleine would sometimes stare wistfully into nothing as she thought back upon their little home in Sfax.

'It had five rooms. I had a piano in the front room.'

The piano had become the symbol of Madeleine's nostalgia. She could not play a piano. But the piano in Sfax had given tone and pride in her house. Guests would come and admire it. She would never again have a piano in her front room: indeed, probably she would never again have a front room. The three rooms they had now were three crowded bedrooms, with a kitchen of sorts fitted up on a balcony. No matter. It was a sadness to think about the piano. But no matter. The children would grow healthily in Israel. They would not be jeered at or have anything to fear at school. They would be properly educated and perhaps – who could tell? – one day would become doctors or lawyers or something grand like that. It was worth going without the piano in the front room. It was worth her husband's giving up his shoemaking; although, said Madeleine, he had made shoes 'as good as anything you could buy even in Tunis. Frenchmen used to wear his shoes and once upon a time an American officer bought a pair. Brown ones they were.'

Tel Aviv merges into the Arab town of Jaffa. But already in April 1948 the Arab population of Jaffa had fled, the well-to-do to Cairo or Beirut, the others southwards in the direction of Gaza. From the start of the year Jaffa had been troublesome. Every wall along the southern boundary of Tel Aviv is pocked with bullet-marks. Then, on a day in April, Menahim Begin's I.Z.L. organization decided to attack and occupy Jaffa. They did so against the wishes of *Haganah*, which, in return for the right to police the whole of the Tel Aviv area, had promised the British to resist any temptation to occupy Jaffa as long as the Mandatory Administration was in nominal control of the country. I.Z.L. paid small heed to promises given by *Haganah*. With a great deal of noise it broke through to Jaffa town. The Arabs who were left, perhaps remembering the hideous I.Z.L. killing at Deir Yassin, outside Jerusalem, put up little resistance. They fled along the southward roads or made off in small boats. I.Z.L. made drunk by an easy victory and what looked like a rich prize, turned to looting; but, at that, *Haganah* moved in and took over.

Gradually, Jaffa filled up again, mainly with released detainees from Cyprus and new immigrants from Rumania and Morocco. It became a suburb of the rapidly-expanding city of Tel Aviv, and, in time, brought to the State of Israel social problems that had been unknown in the National Home.

Ten

I REMAINED in Tel Aviv. A young member of one of the collective settlement of the Emek Valley had just inherited a comfortable flat in a house near the seashore. By rights, I suppose, his legacy should have gone to the collective treasury of the settlement. Instead, the young man rented the flat to me and shortly afterwards, so frail are ideals, he gave up the life of a pioneer with a mission and settled himself in Tel Aviv. With the flat went Madeleine, the housekeeper, and a six-months-old golden spaniel known as Kleffie, which is a variant of the Hebrew word *kelef*, meaning dog.

Kleffie and I would set off each morning for the Public Relations Office in what was once an hotel and is now the French Embassy, a low, roomy building with a garden in which tall palm-trees grew. There I and some twenty to thirty other newspaper-men would be told at a briefing what the Government wanted us to be told. We were told it by Moshé Perlman, a London Jew with experience as a British Army P.R. Officer. His briefings were adroit. Moshé could draw himself up from a door-jamb by his finger-tips. His briefings, although they left much unsaid, were as fair as these things go. There were other sources, of course, and one moved about as much as one could, using eyes and ears. I had the good fortune to be in friendly relationship with two senior Govermnent people who were helpful.

Very soon it became evident that the State of Israel foresaw a resumption of battle and was preparing for it. Shiploads of arms were coming in from Czechoslovakia. An air force of sorts was being hastily put together. Volunteer pilots with war experience were arriving from America and South Africa. As far as Government and Zionist institutions could manage it, priority on immigrant ships was given to young men and women fit and willing to serve in the army. The terms of the truce had forbidden member nations of U.N. to supply any of the belligerents with arms or men. But there were ways around that, and Israel found most of them.

The truce moved peaceably enough through the rest of that hot

June. When July came, with the grass in the fields gone yellow and the birds gathering open-beaked at irrigation taps, the footbeats of returning war could be heard. Tel Aviv became more subdued. Torn sandbags, which had spilled most of their contents, were replaced. New tape was affixed to window panes. Army traffic along the roads was heavy. At night one heard the grind of half-tracks and occasionally what sounded like a tank. Israel's army was still pretty poorly equipped by modern standards but at least it had twice as many weapons as before, and better ones, and certain heavy armaments of which it had had none before. Most of the re-inforcements brought in after the truce began were still only half trained. But all in all the Israel army was a far better fighting instrument at the end of June than it had been at the beginning. That fact, which must have been foreseen in Cairo, Amman, and Damascus, and possibly in London, spelled the end of any dreams of conquest still nudging the half-awakened Arabs.

War broke out afresh on the 9th July. It took the Israelis exactly ten days to overrun pretty well the whole of Western Galilee and to improve their positions along the central and south fronts. Ramle, on the main Jaffa-Jerusalem highway, was occupied. So were the town and airfield of Lydda. The Security Council then came together and ordered a cease-fire, threatening sanctions if the order were ignored. Count Folke Bernadotte, who had been appointed U.N. Mediator and had set up his headquarters on the dulcet island of Rhodes, dashed about among the belligerent governments. On 18th July, firing ceased.

From the beginning of the second truce onwards through August and September the big question was whether Count Bernadotte's new version of partition, which, contrary to the U.N. plan of 29th November 1947, would have given Jerusalem and that apple of David Ben Gurion's eye, the spacious, sandy triangle of the Negev, to Transjordan, and Western Galilee to Israel, could win world support. Not surprisingly, the new plan was favoured by the British Government, which, if it could maintain land communi-cation via the Negev between its Egyptian, Transjordan and Iraqi garrisons, was now willing to cut its other Palestine losses and make the best it could of a bad job. Count Bernadotte's proposals were known in general outline to most people soon after they had been communicated to the governments concerned in June. But they were not published until September 17th.

On September 18th the Count was driving with some of his advisers through a tranquil quarter of Jewish Jerusalem. Standing at a street corner was a man with a gun. He was a member of the small, fanatic, anarchistic Stern Gang. As the car came by he leapt out into the road and fired at Count Bernadotte, who fell back in his seat, dead. The terrorist disappeared.

There was still no knowing what would become of the Mediator's proposals, which the British and U.S. Governments were supporting and which were expected to go before the Political Committee of the U.N. General Assembly almost at once. But, with the original U.N. Partition Resolution still in force the Israelis could hardly be expected to resist the temptation to influence events. Possession, if not nine points of the law, was impressive evidence of right in the confusion of that time and place. On the pretext that the Egyptians, by hindering the Israeli provisioning of settlements cut off in the Gaza district, had broken the truce, Israel attacked. In seven days its forces occupied Beersheba, cleared the southern Negev and penned the bulk of the Egyptian army into a narrow coastal strip between Gaza and el Arish on the Sinai border. Left behind was the sturdy Egyptian garrison holding out in the Faluja pocket north of Beersheba.

U.N. again stepped in with a threat of sanctions. There followed something like tranquillity until the Egyptians in December decided to break out from Gaza and go to the relief of the Faluja garrison. The Israelis held the advance and then, towards the end of December, turned on the Egyptians and forced them into Sinai and back upon Gaza and would have rolled them all the way to the banks of the Suez Canal if they had dared. There was no knowing what would happen if the Egyptians should invoke the Anglo-Egyptian Treaty and so bring about British armed intervention. As it was, four British Spitfires together with Egyptian aircraft came nosing over the Israeli lines one day and all four were shot down by Israeli fighters. It is said that the Spitfires had gone on their mission after receiving orders from London to do so. But the British Government never could be drawn to give any explanation of this astonishing event. On 8th January the Egyptians asked the Israelis for a cease-fire and were given it. On the same date Abdullah of Transjordan invoked the Anglo-Transjordan Treaty and asked for protection against the Israelis. A British force was then landed at Abdullah's Red Sea port of Aqaba, a few hundred yards from where the

victorious Israelis were paddling their tired feet in the waters of
the gulf.

2

By the end of the year Israel had had enough of fighting, enough
of blood-letting; and the Arabs had been beaten to a standstill. Both
were ready for a tranquillizing agreement of one kind or another.
Israel held all the territory allotted her under the 1947 U.N.
Partition Plan and had added about one-third to it. It was not much
use asking her to evacuate any of it. On 30th January the Attlee
Government, which had made a miserable job of justifying its
Palestine policy to an angry Opposition, recognized the State of
Israel *de facto*. On February 24th, under the guidance of that
persuasive negro, Doctor Ralph Bunche, who had succeeded Count
Bernadotte as U.N. Mediator, began the negotiations that led to a
series of armistice agreements, which remain to this day the sole
and unsatisfactory instruments determining relations between Israel
and her neighbours.

It was all over by then.

How came it that a people numbering less than 700,000 had
defeated the combined forces of a group of States numbering over
30 million souls? The 700,000, when attacked, were confined to
Jerusalem, Tel Aviv and a sliver of territory between that city and
Haifa. They had settlements in what had been predominantly Arab
areas in the Jordan Valley, Galilee and, sparsely, the western Negev.
The Arabs had an almost inexhaustible hinterland as well as an
almost inexhaustible manpower. They had armies equipped with
heavy armaments, supported by up-to-date air units and, in the case
of Egypt, by a navy of sorts. Israel, when the invasion began, had
only light weapons and mortars: no field guns, hardly any heavy
machine-guns, no air force, no armoured vehicles or tanks except
for two cumbrous monsters sold to *Haganah* by a couple of scallywags from a British tank unit. Small wonder that Azzam Pasha,
Secretary General of the Arab League, and on the whole no fire-
brand, felt able to say on May 15th: 'This will be a war of extermination, a momentous event that will rank with the Mongolian
massacres and the destruction of the Crusaders.'

How then did it happen the way it did?

If you had asked that question of any ordinary Israeli he would have shrugged his shoulders, as like as not, and replied: '*Ain Brera—* no alternative. We had to win or perish.' If you had asked Glubb Pasha, Commander of Abdullah's Arab Legion, he would have attributed defeat to the hopeless conflict of aims among the several Arab commands and at the several Arab courts. Often one heard expressed by Israelis the opinion that the Arabs had failed because, excepting the Arab Legion and one or two instances among the Egyptians, their officer class was indifferent to the welfare of the bedraggled ranks it was supposed to lead.

However, taking all possible excuses into account, the Arabs, if only by weight of numbers and armament, should have been able to break the back of the main Jewish defences in a matter of days. I have sought for an historical parallel that might help to explain the incredible success of the Jews, but it is not easy to find one that is appropriate. The only one that comes to my mind is the defeat of the Habsburgs by the Swiss.

David Ben Gurion makes an odd William Tell. But, as in Switzerland a trained and well-equipped conventional army had to give way before a resolute civil population formed haphazardly into a national militia, so in Palestine trained and conventional columns fighting for no better reason than reluctant obediance to orders, could make no headway against a people every adult of which was ready, if need by, to take up a rifle and a grenade and go out to fight. Every time a unit of the *Haganah* went into action it knew that behind it stood what was in effect a massive line of reserves. In that sense it could be said that the Arab armies were outnumbered. Out of the Jewish population of over 600,000 as good as none was ready to capitulate. They were ill-trained and their lack of training sometimes made itself felt. The Jews' failure to dislodge the Arab Legion from its position at Latrun and so break through to the relief of Jerusalem, probably was due to the fact that most of the attackers had come straight from immigrant ships, factories and offices without having had so much as twenty-four hours' military training. Even so, they were able to bar the Legion's passage seawards and keep it from occupying a single square inch of the territory allotted to Israel by U.N.

Out of the 600,000 there may have been between ten and twelve thousand well-trained men, who were here, there and everywhere, so that for much of the time the Arab commanders had not the slightest idea of what was in front or behind them or on their flanks. And as luck would have it the young State that had been invaded on the very first day of its existence as a State, had at hand a group of clever tacticians. The Chief of Staff, General Dori, now Principal of the Haifa Institute of Technology, was brilliantly served by a Chief of Operations – later Chief of Staff in succession to Dori – who was an archaeologist by profession and knew, almost inch by inch, the territory over which the invaders moved. That was Ygael Yadin, son of Professor Sukennik of the Hebrew University. Ygael Yadin knew the land physically and historically. Thanks to this odd injection of history and archaeology into the Jews' operational reckonings, the enemy several times, and once decisively, found himself set upon from quarters where no enemy could be expected in logic or by military reasoning to appear. Knowledge of the tactics and communications of the Hasmoneans in their revolt against the Seleucid Empire in the second century B.C. on one occasion provided the outline and direction of an operation that drove the Egyptians from one of their most powerful positions.

The fortress-like unity of over 600,000 Jews who had to win the war or perish was, I repeat, a main factor bringing about the humiliating defeat of a superior enemy. Over against this massive unity were four Arab armies acting independently, each suspicious of the other, none of them backed by anything better than the ambitions of its rulers. The Jews had conspicuous leadership, the Arabs had none. Where the Jewish commanders were resourceful, daring and in some instances tactically brilliant, most of the Arab commanders showed little skill and less daring. Between the Jewish leader in the field and his men there was no social distinction. Instead, there was comradeship. Nothing of that kind existed between the Arab officer and the men under him.

But when all is said and done I am tempted to agree with those Israelis who say they won because they had to – there was no alternative; even as the State continues to survive as an independent entity because it has to – there is no alternative.

3

Armistice negotiations began with Egypt. They were held on the Greek island of Rhodes and were conducted under the supervision of Doctor Ralph Bunche. The negotiations were concluded

93

and the agreement was signed on February 24th. Lebanon came next, signing on March 23rd. Jordan put its signature to an agreement with Israel on April 3rd, and the negotiations at Rhodes ended on July 20th with the signing of the Israel-Syrian Armistice Agreement. Iraq was not brought to Rhodes and no armistice agreement was ever worked out between that country and Israel, which was mainly concerned to have some contractual cessation of hostilities and acceptance of frontiers by the Arab States directly against its borders.

The Armistice Agreements are dangerously less than the Peace Treaties they were designed to lead up to. But they are better than nothing. Their successful negotiation was something of a triumph for the tact and wisdom of Doctor Bunche as well as striking evidence of the impression Israeli arms had made on the Arabs. Bunche, doubtful of the likelihood of Peace Treaties within any foreseeable time, tried hard to formulate the intermediate agreements in such manner that they might be expected to work well until bitterness had died out and something like realism had replaced illusion in the Arab capitals. But it is most unlikely that he expected the Armistice Agreements to remain in force for ten years and more. He intended them to be a stepping-stone to peace treaties. If they have proved to be a barrier to peace, behind which the Arab States take refuge until such time as they may once again feel capable of destroying Israel, that was not Doctor Bunche's fault. His armistice agreements have lasted for eleven years. An elaborate U.N. agency, seated in that conspicuous and Gothic Government House built by the first British High Commissioner, Sir Herbert Samuel, now Viscount Samuel, and stealthily abandoned by the last, General Sir Alan Cunningham, has supervised the performance of the agreements throughout those eleven uncertain years and, for the most part, has done magnificently well. If U.N. has justified itself in nothing else, it has done so in the fact that the frontiers drawn up by Doctor Bunche at Rhodes still keep the two sides apart, and that the terms then laid down still have positive validity, however often the one side or the other may transgress against them.

Bunche gave the impression of being a simple fellow. He had few negroid features and could easily have been mistaken for an Arab. His manner was quiet and easy. He lolled comfortably in a chair; stayed up late at night; would not be denied his hot bath in the morning. He was as easy with the Jew as with the Arab and gave the impression of being intensely interested in anything either of them had to say. He spoke in the soft, musical voice of his race, and when he laughed everyone about had to laugh with him. His approach to the Israel-Arab problem was simpler than Count Bernadotte's had been. He readily adjusted his views to plain facts instead of trying to adjust plain facts to his views. Perhaps unfortunately, the Israelis tended to praise his qualities too much, and so provoked among the Arabs the suspicion that Doctor Bunche was just another American pro-Zionist.

4

On the Arab side there was, of course, a succession of delegates to Rhodes. Throughout the whole period of negotiation the chief Israel delegate was Walter Eytan, then Director General of the Israel Foreign Ministry and now Israel's Ambassador to France. He was an agile negotiator, a clever organizer, a man with whom foreign diplomats could talk easily, and whom their ladies were always pleased to entertain at dinner. He was alert and witty. His experience as a don at Oxford had blessed him with a certain cheerful cynicism. He did not pretend that Israel was always right and the Arab or the Gentile always wrong. He had an easy, half-humorous debating manner, which said, in effect:

'Come now, you know very well that I'm right this time. Why not admit it and then let us have a cigar?'

He is not tall. A tendency to roundness makes him look shorter than he is. His hair fluffs about his large head and gives to his plump face a certain puckishness. He smokes a pipe, except on special occasions when he smokes a cigar. His desk at the Foreign Ministry took on a certain distinction from its rack of handsome pipes and its bronze tobacco bowl. There was always a bowl of flowers at one end of the desk. In the afternoon he took tea in the English fashion.

Eytan has always been, or pretended to be, surprised by the fact that the State of Israel has come about, and that a Jewish Government exercising sovereign authority exists. He once said to me:

95

'It's odd, you know. The British don't like our being here. Not really. The U.S. State Department isn't quite happy about us. Thirty million Arabs would like to drown us in the sea. And yet here we are, back in Palestine where we used to be two thousand years ago. All the odds were against us and yet here we are, going strong.'

'How do you account for it?' I asked.

'I can't account for it. You have to be a mystic to account for it. So let's settle for *ein brera* – no alternative.'

Eleven

THE humiliation of the Arabs was at the same time the humiliation of the British Government. On 30th January 1949 that Government, with Mr. Attlee as Prime Minister and Mr. Bevin as Foreign Secretary, recognized the State of Israel *de facto*. It had to do so. It was following the lead of the U.S.A., Soviet Russia and most States in the West and East, with this difference – that in doing so it was also recognizing the pitiful failure of the Palestine policy of the Labour Government from the beginning.

When the war ended and a Conservative Administration was replaced by a Labour Party Administration, the Jews of Palestine felt uplifted. The night Labour was declared victor there was a high moon in the Holy Land, and a group of Jews, seeking an unusual way of celebrating their delight, piled into motor cars and sped over the hills and down to the Dead Sea. I and two other English observers had been swept into their merriment. We lay upon the strangely buoyant cushion of the Dead Sea and watched the big, round moon balance itself on the ridge of Moab immediately above us. The curious unreality of a sea in which the human body could not sink, left us without the normal convictions of mathematics, so that none of us would have been surprised to see the moon roll down the western slopes of Moab and be extinguished in the Dead Sea. It was that kind of night, especially to the Jews. There was a Labour Government in Britain and that meant the release of the Jews in the displaced persons camps and their coming to Palestine. . . . The moon might well fall from Moab into this deep-riven basin where the Dead Sea flowed.

The moon did not fall into the Dead Sea. It rose from Moab into the sky as it had always done. And the Labour Government proceeded in accordance with established rule. There was no change. The White Paper continued to be British policy and found, in Mr. Ernest Bevin, its most fervent champion.

Heaven knows why. The Balfour Declaration was, of course, something that had happened a long time ago. And when it happened it had been part ideal, part expedient. Labour out of office was impressed by the ideal; in office was contemptuous of the expedient. Jewish influence in Wall Street and the White House may have been important during the First World War; but after the Second World War, Arab oil and the Suez Canal came into their own and Zionism was required to take second place. Mr. Bevin was no fool, of course. But many of his advisers of the Foreign Office less than wise. Having convinced the Secretary of State that Britain must at all costs preserve its paramount influence in Egypt, Palestine, Jordan and Iraq, they went on, with equal success, to convince him that British interests would be secure in the hands of the traditional Arab rulers only as long as the British Government gave evidence of practical sympathy for their anti-Zionist policies.

The White Paper of 1939 had been a means of buying Arab support in the nodal Middle East against Germany. It had not been very successful, of course. Haj Amin el Husseini, leader of Palestine Arabs, had gone to Berlin to serve Adolf Hitler's campaign against Britain in the Middle East. There was Rashid Ali's rebellion in Iraq. And everyone in Egypt knew that the Egyptians wanted General Rommel to defeat the British and come to the Nile. Still, when the war was over the White Paper policy remained in Foreign Office judgement essential to the preservation of an Anglo-Egyptian Treaty, an Anglo-Iraqi Treaty and an Anglo-Jordanian Treaty. Britain seems always to have based its Arab policy on the assumption that the Arabs would for ever go on being content with something like a feudal structure of society and that, except when a leader like Zaghlul Pasha was about, the masses could always be diverted from nationalism to some other hysteria and their rulers be made dependent on Britain for the maintenance of power and private fortune.

Until the end of the Second World War there was much to be said for that point of view. After the war it became evident, not that the Arabs were progressing either socially or politically, but that they were ready to take advantage of a Power situation in which Britain had to take second place, even where it had provided the traditional Power influence, to the United States. What is more, there had dawned the exciting prospect of building up, at the United Nations Organization, an Arab block of votes capable of being put to good use when any Arab State found itself in dispute with one or other of the Powers. What U.N. was able to do for the Arabs was shown in the late autumn of 1956, after the Sinai Campaign and the Suez operations.

Nothing of this kind seems to have been foreseen by Mr. Bevin and his political advisers. Between 1945 and 1948 British Middle East policy, and particularly our Palestine policy, was shaped in accordance with the old notion that in order to preserve Britain's influential position in Egypt, Jordon and Iraq, it was necessary to restrict Jewish expansion in Palestine and to make it clear that Britain would oppose the Jews' claim to independent Statehood as set out in the so-called Biltmore Programme. The Jews are indeed a stiff-necked people and our efforts at putting the Palestine Jews in their place were not successful. What Churchill described as a 'squalid war' developed. Our attempt at repressing the Jews won no gratitude from the Arabs and caused serious criticism throughout the world at large, and particularly in the United States. Mr. Bevin tried to appease the Americans by agreeing to the setting up of an Anglo-American Committee of Inquiry to study the Palestine question on the spot and report back. It did all this but to no purpose. Sharp criticism of the Government's policy in Palestine then found its way into the British Press. Mr. Bevin's answer this time was to hand to U.N. the responsibility for finding a solution.

He and his advisers must have known what they were doing. They must have realized how big was the chance of U.N.'s recommending the partitioning of Palestine between Jew and Arab. But there is evidence to suggest that, whilst knowing these things they knew also that any such recommendation, if the attempt were made to apply it in practice, would lead to violent Arab opposition. Before that should happen, Britain would retire from Palestine. When it should happen, the Jews would certainly be overwhelmed. That, apparently, was the considered opinion of Mr. Bevin's military experts. And when this prophecy had come about, Britain would return to Palestine to save the Jews from extermination and to impose a settlement appropriate to what she considered to be her strategic interests.

Matters worked out pretty much as the Foreign Office had guessed except for one thing: the Jews gave the Arabs a sad beating, not the Arabs the Jews.

Twelve

THERE, then, by the spring of 1949, was the State of Israel, secure behind preposterous frontiers drawn by the accidents of war. Its enemies had slunk back.

'We haven't seen the last of them by any means,' said a young Israeli officer who had negotiated with the Egyptians in Faluja. 'Some of the Egyptians, anyway, are going to find out just why everything went wrong. There will be ructions in Cairo and probably in Jordan. Some of those officers down there feel there is a lot of shame to be wiped out.'

One of the officers 'down there' was a certain Abdul Nasser.

Israel had won the 'first round' but everyone felt that a 'second round' would have to be fought one day and would be a harder battle than the first had been. The Arabs would probably reorganize their armies, and would continue, under current treaties, to receive all the military equipment they needed. Besides, Armistice or no Armistice, the Arabs were in a position to hinder the growth of Israel, every one of whose land borders was not merely a political line but also, for the Israelis, an insurmountable wall to be broken, if that should become necessary, only by guns. There could be no trade by land, no peaceful passageway. Israel, a Middle East country, would have to do its shopping and sell its products in far-away markets. And if the Arabs wished, they could keep much of the Israeli countryside in turmoil. It was easy for a band of Arabs to slip through the frontier wall, burn, kill, loot and dash back again. The U.N. Truce Organization was there, of course, to put a stop to that kind of thing by calling the relevant Mixed Armistice Commission together, which could pronounce guilt and call upon the guilty not to repeat the offence.

Israel had won its war and pushed out its borders and given itself, for the time being, something like peace and security. But would that last? The Israelis were confident of their ability to raise and train a still bigger and more effectively equipped defence force; but in order to do so they would have to use up precious foreign currency, which was urgently needed for development purposes and the absorption of new immigrants. In short, this small country, still with the soft bones of infancy, would have to continue on a war footing probably for years. Small wonder, I suppose, that some observers in London and Washington and other capitals, impressed as they may have been by what the Jews had done to the Arab armies, were doubtful of Israel's capacity to survive as a politically independent and economically viable State.

A newspaper colleague of mine put it this way:

'The Arabs can't let it go at that. There are thirty millions of them pressing against these absurd borders and every one of them hates the Jew. Close on a million Palestine Arab refugees will see to it that their host governments keep the Israelis on the jump. And all these new immigrants coming to a country without natural resources. Most of them will be a charge on the State – or on the Zionist bodies that collect money from the Jews abroad. That's another thing. How long will the Jews of America go on supporting the luxury of a State otherwise without visible means of support?'

That, of course, was an exaggerated comment even in 1949; and events rapidly showed how exaggerated it was. At the same time, one did have doubts. Israel setting off on Statehood was something like an English family setting off on holiday to the seaside. It looked anxiously at the sky each morning, listened anxiously to the weather report on the wireless. Would it remain fine or would everyone get soaking wet?

2

The new State's first conspicuous civil move to adjust itself to the responsibilities and privileges of independence was the election of a Parliament. For a year it had had to be satisfied with a Provisional Government made up from the Zionist bodies that had been constituted in Palestine in accordance with the terms of the Mandate. Obviously that could not go on. General Elections were set to take place throughout the whole country in January 1949. Proportional representation had been decided upon as the electoral system to be applied; and a multiplicity of political parties sprang up. Every adult in the country above eighteen and possessing an identity card was entitled to vote whatever his nationality. That meant that even I, an Anglo-Saxon and a British subject with a British passport, had as much right to contribute my vote to the election of the first democratic Parliament in the history of the Jews, as any Jew in the country. I contributed it.

Election day in Tel Aviv was a remarkable occasion. It was a kind of holiday. Public transport had been increased but many shops had closed, at least for the morning. The sun shone but it was a day of wind. From an early hour the wind, almost contemptuously, swept up spoiled or for some reason unused ballot-papers, election manifestoes and placards, trundling them along the streets and flapping them against walls. Polling-booths had been set up in schools, synagogues and other more or less empty ground-floor premises wherever they could be found. The polling-booth of my choice turned out to be a synagogue. I had my golden spaniel, Kleffie, on a lead, but was politely forbidden to take him inside. The inevitable tiny old lady in black satin and old-fashioned hat was standing by the entrance and offered to hold the dog for me. Evidently, she was still a trifle bemused by the astonishing deed she had just performed, and stood there, watching the people go in and out.

I entered the synagogue. A partition had been put across the big, bare hall, hiding the Ark. I went up to one of the bearded men behind a long table and handed him the slip of paper given me by a registrar who had been going about the city for weeks looking at identity cards and filling in an electoral roll he carried with him. The bearded man looked up my name on the roll, gave me ballot papers, and directed me to another table where I could mark my choice. I chose Mr. Ben Gurion's party as he, at that time, seemed to be all that mattered. Then off I went to a tin box that looked exactly like ballot-boxes the world over and thrust my voting paper through the slot. It was done. I had had the remarkable and surprising privilege of voting for the first elected Parliament of the equally remarkable and surprising State of Israel.

I took my dog from the old lady outside.

'He is very patient,' she said. 'Just sat there watching the door through which you had gone.'

'You seem to be patient, too, and to be watching that door very intently. Why?'

She smiled. It was more of a giggle than a smile, as if she were a trifle embarrassed, as a young girl might have been.

'Oh, it all seems, well, not quite real to me. I suppose I am watching the door until I can really get into my mind what is happening inside. You see, it has never happened before.'

She was, as I have said, a little old woman wearing an old-fashioned hat. She had come from Warsaw some years before and I suspect the hat, like the satin dress, had come with her. Her face shone. She patted the dog and then, perhaps feeling that it was silly to go on watching that door, she moved off smiling to herself and clutching a black leather handbag. She had dressed up for the occasion, of course, as well she might have done. It does not happen often that a people suddenly become independent and elect their first Parliament. Revived sovereignties there have been in plenty: Greece, Poland, Czechoslovakia, Hungary, and so on. But always the Poles had lived in Poland, the Greeks in Greece, the Czechs in Czechoslovakia. Here was a people who had had no country of their own for more than two thousand years, let alone a sovereign Parliament of their own. And now all at once they had both. It was not surprising that many of them thought it to be a miracle.

It was no miracle, of course, and was not so surprising as it first appeared to be. The movement given international emphasis and validity by Theodore Herzl was bound to grow in all three dimensions. Once the Balfour Declaration and the League of Nations had declared Palestine to be a National Home for the Jews, there could be no turning back and no standing still. A national home could not be made into a kind of Russian Pale, as implied in the restrictions of the 1939 White Paper; nor could it have existed in the meaning of the term if it had been subjected to Arab government. A national home could only mean to the Jews a place where they could congregate in any number that might seem proper to them, and be subject to their own laws and standards.

It was natural that out of the fertile opportunities provided by a Palestine in which the Jew lived as of right, there should spring leaders of the stature of David Ben Gurion; and a generation of young, forceful Jews who had not known the humility of submissiveness. The rest was done by Hitler. Before the appearance of that ridiculous fanatic there had been urge enough for the Jew to seek conditions in which he could develop communally and be free of the hostility and contempt of racialists. The excesses of Germany between 1933 and 1945, when Jews were killed off as vermin or subjected to indignities on a scale never before practised by one

103

people on another, left no alternative for Jewish leadership but to strive by every means to bring about a political, social and territorial independence within which as many Jews as might wish could find security and a life of self-respect.

Israel's election day in the spring of 1949 was, therefore, no symbol or miracle. It was an event that had been made inevitable by the enemies of the Jews.

3

One hundred and twenty Deputies representing thirteen different parties were returned to the first Knesset, or Parliament, of the State of Israel. By far the largest of the thirteen parties was Ben Gurion's *Mapai*, or Labour Party, with 46 seats, followed by the Left Wing *Mapam* (United Workers), with 19 seats, and then by the Extreme Right Wing Nationalist party, *Herut*, (Freedom Party), the former terrorist organization *Irgun Zvai Leumi*.

It became necessary then – and has been necessary with each succeeding Parliament – for *Mapai* to form a coalition including some or all of the Parties representing religious orthodoxy. It has never been a happy comradeship and has driven Mr. Ben Gurion to advocacy of a constituency system as in Britain, in place of the List system, and two-party or at most three-party representation in Parliament in place of multi-party representation.

On this issue Ben Gurion has few followers even today. Israel has been in existence only a little over ten years and is still composed of sharply-defined sections. It is not, as in most Democratic countries, the simple division between Capital and Labour, or between Socialists and non-Socialists. The World Zionist bodies including the Jewish Agency were always sectional and rightly so, if only because their support came from a dozen different national groups. I remember discussing this subject with Doctor Bader, the most astute of the *Herut* members of the Knesset.

'We are not a unified nation yet,' he said in his thickish, drawling voice, his eyes half-closed, as they usually were, and his hands opening and closing in a kind of soft, weaving motion.

'We are all kinds of people according to our origin. And according to our origin we are making contribution to the national character of Israel. Ben Gurion thinks the only good Israeli is the one who votes *Mapai*. The Orthodox people think the only good Israeli is the one who is something better still, a good Jew. The *Sephardis* have the Sephardic idea of what constitutes a good Jew and a good Israeli. *Mapam*, still haunted by the Marxist illusions of fifty years ago but dead afraid of Communism, wants to break away from Jewishness and turn the State of Israel into a kind of Tolstoyan youth movement.'

'And you?' I asked.

Doctor Bader gurgled like a baby jangling a rattle.

'We? We want to push the frontiers of Israel to the other side of the Jordan. Very naughty of us, don't you think?'

I said I did think so. But *Herut's* expansionist ideas sound harmless when expressed by the comfortably fat, amused and amusing Doctor Bader.

There was not one but four Orthodox parties in the first Knesset: the moderate Right-wing *Mizrahi* and the *Mizrahi* Workers' Party; the *Agudat* Israel, who are, so to speak, the Fundamentalists of Judaism, and the *Agudat* Israel Workers' Party. Later on the two branches of *Mizrahi* joined together and so did the two *Agudat* Israel groups, so that the number of Orthodox parties was brought down to two. Both wings of political Orthodoxy are a constant exasperation to Mr. Ben Gurion, although, until now, at least one of the wings has been in every coalition formed by him. Neither *Mizrahi* nor *Agudat* Israel is easy to work with and one or the other or both have been the cause of many political crises. The division of the Parliamentary Electorate between the strictly religious and the carelessly so, must, of course, make for conflict; and there are many thoughtful people who are concerned at the prospect of a *kulturkampf* one day.

However all this may be, that first Parliament of Israel, elected in the spring of 1949 while armistice agreements were being negotiated with the Arabs at Rhodes, was a proud accomplishment. The Deputies took their seats in a big, ugly, converted cinema theatre on Tel Aviv's sea-front. Mr. Ben Gurion formed his first, constitutional coalition Government, with himself as Prime Minister and Minister of Defence and Mr. Sharett as Minister for Foreign Affairs. Already Departments had been set up and staffed and were operating extraordinarily well. A few idle Tel Avivians, who had nothing better to do, hung about the entrance pillars of the converted cinema to watch their members of Parliament go in and out. But everyone seemed to take the business of government as a matter of course once the excitement of the elections was over.

Then, in July, the last of the Armistice Agreements was signed. The Hotel des Roses, on the Island of Rhodes, was emptied of its delegations and of Ralph Bunche. Already, in May 1949, Israel had been accepted into the United Nations as a full and equal member.

I took my dog Kleffie for his usual evening walk along the beach of Tel Aviv. So strange and often so incredible had been the events of the previous two years that it would not have surprised me to see a great whale come splashing inshore to spew up Jonah all over again.

Thirteen

IPLOMATIC missions began arriving: Ambassadors, Ministers Plenipotentiary, Counsellors, Attachés, with their wives and children. The diplomats had influence upon the social and even the political life of the country. Embassies and Legations were set up in impressive buildings, and the Ambassadors and Ministers were lodged in handsome villas, usually in Ramat Gan, a little town on its own but in effect a suburb of Tel Aviv, high-pitched to catch the sea-breezes and away from the lively vulgarities of the city below. Simultaneously, at the other end of the social scale, a multitude of new immigrants from Rumania, Bulgaria, North Africa, began tumbling in. The diplomats heightened the social level at their end; the new immigrants lowered it at theirs. But the bulk of Israelis moved to an austerity brought upon them by the need to spend every penny the State could raise on settlement projects to absorb the newcomers, and the building up of what was to become the most efficient defence force in the Middle East.

Britain – and Israel – were fortunate in the first British Ambassador, Alexander Knox Helm, who was knighted towards the end of his term. Knox Helm and his wife had the advantage of being Scots. I suppose it is an advantage anywhere. The Scot has a reputation for being more flexible in his opinions, less a prisoner of bias, quicker to understand and sympathize with principles and standards that have not gone through the Public School mill, than the Englishman is. He is a bit more warmly human. That, at any rate, was the feeling in Israel, where the veterans of the National Home remembered with affection and admiration such Scots as Orde Wingate, and the pre-White Paper High Commissioner, Wauchope. Aside from this, however, the Israelis were genuinely glad to see restored some kind of association with Britain. The United Kingdom remained for these people, even for Ben Gurion, their idea of a well-governed country, its citizens their idea of a wholesome, well-disposed people who had risen, as Ben Gurion has so often declared, to quietly heroic stature during the war. British institutions were admired. Even the British Army, which so often had stood in the

Jews' way during the Mandate, was thought well of, especially by that section of the community that had served with it in North Africa and now had become the cadre of the new Israeli Army.

The Israeli, intelligently and at times angrily and for the most part defiantly critical of Britain's Palestine Policy from 1939 onwards, emotionally preserved a liking for the British and were glad of any opportunity to show it. In a sense the appointment of Alexander Knox Helm, the Scot, to be head of Britain's first Diplomatic Mission to Israel, gave them that opportunity. They liked him. They liked his lady. And they were able, thanks largely to the tact and spontaneity of the Minister, to foresee a period when, once again, the warm feeling of the Jew for the Englishman that had come about with the victories of General Allenby and the issue of the Balfour Declaration, would be natural and proper.

Knox Helm was lean and grey. He would stride into a room with loose, agile gait, a smile on his lively face and an immediate friendly greeting for whomever it might be that awaited him. He was interested in things: in the new immigrants and how they were getting along; in the communal settlements and the State schooling; in the part played by Orthodoxy in the social and political development of the country; in the health of Ben Gurion. It was his duty to be interested in these things and to write despatches about them; but one felt that the interest was personal and would have been there, despatches or no despatches. He liked meeting people and attended social gatherings with apparent enjoyment.

His influence upon the affairs of Mr. Sharett's Foreign Ministry was remarkable. In those early days of the new State his advice was often sought regarding matters outside the direct interests of the United Kingdom. It was an odd state of affairs. The United States Government was of much greater use to Israel than the British. Indeed, if the British Government had had its way there would not have been a State of Israel. President Truman had been a good and consistent friend of the new State. His ambassador, James Macdonald, was known to be an ardent Zionist. But it is safe to say that in those formative years of Israel, it was the British Minister, later Ambassador, and not the pro-Zionist American, who was the most influential and, in official as well as unofficial circles of Israel life, the most appreciated diplomat in the country.

The Russians, who had followed the United States in giving the State of Israel immediate recognition, were represented by a young, gracious Ambassador, much liked in Government circles and even among his Western colleagues. Unfortunately, and in the manner of so many of the heads of Missions from Communist countries, he was remote. One often met him at the kind of gatherings where it is customary to meet such people, but he was usually a listener, never a talker.

At that time relations between Soviet Russia and Israel were friendly. The Israelis had vague hopes of getting some of Russia's Jews into their country, who, from all accounts, were good pioneering material. The Russians for their part probably had hopes of a thoroughly Socialist Israel, at least an Israeli foreign policy based strictly on Sharett's 'non-identification' slogan. Both hopes were vain. 'Non-identification' was a slogan and nothing more. From the outset Israel showed plainly its dependence on the U.S.A. and its intellectual preference for the West over the East; and it was not long before non-identification as a policy label was dropped. As for the Russian Jews which Mr. Ben Gurion, himself a Russian, hankered after, nothing ever came of that except the release by the Soviet of a few score aged and often ailing Jews with families already settled in Israel.

Israel's foreign policy during the first few years of the State was not complicated or onerous. Thanks to Sharett's skill as an organizer and educator, as well as to the capacity of his Director General, the donnish Walter Eytan, to impart knowledge and give intelligent training, the Foreign Ministry soon became one of the most efficient and smooth-working Departments of the State. Its policies were straightforward. Briefly put they were these: Peace and non-aggression pacts with the Arabs or at least something better than Armistice Agreements; no frontier changes; no return of the Arab refugees except within the framework of a freely negotiated peace treaty; no military alliances or bilateral treaties of any kind except those affecting credits, trade and what has come to be called cultural affairs; the freedom of Jews to migrate to Israel. Outside these more or less specific issues, the object of the Foreign Ministry was to create for Israel an atmosphere of friendliness wherever it could.

On the whole this general policy of good relations succeeded. Israel has been well served by its diplomatic representatives abroad. It is surprising that it was able to lay its hands on so many aptly qualified men. Among the Diplomatic Corps few men have been better liked or more respected than Mr. Elath, and none has contributed more towards amiable relationship between his own country and the United Kingdom. Aubrey Eban, in Washington, is another of Israel's highly successful diplomats. He has given up his Embassy (and the leadership of Israel's U.N. Delegation) and entered his country's politics.

Moshé Sharett, who was Foreign Minister in successive governments from 1949 until 1956, conducted his Ministry with the punctiliousness of a schoolmaster conducting his school. Daily he briefed the senior members of the service as he might have briefed a collection of form masters. He took Press conferences as if he were taking a class. I remember one surprising incident at a Press conference Mr. Sharett gave at Ha'kirya, the pleasant, walled enclosure of stone houses, bungalows and gardens on the outskirts of Tel Aviv which housed the Foreign Ministry until its transfer to Jerusalem. There were about fifty newspaper correspondents present, foreign and domestic, and I sat at the rear of the big room with Sydney Gruson of the *New York Times*. It had been arranged that Mr. Sharett, who spoke fluent English, should address the conference in English as well as Hebrew, and answer questions in both languages.

He began, however, with a long statement in Hebrew, which took twenty minutes and sounded of the greatest importance, but from which he moved on to questions and answers without giving the initial statement in English. Gruson and I were a trifle worried, as were other foreign newspaper-men present; and at the first opportunity Gruson stood up and begged the Foreign Minister to say in English the Hebrew statement with which he had opened the conference.

Sharett smiled. He said:

'I don't think you will be interested. The Hebrew newspapers have been using an expression meaning, roughly, what you mean in English by the phrase "in the circumstances" or "under the circumstances". Their syntax has been at fault. My opening statement was a little lecture for the benefit of the Hebrew Press on the correct structure of that and similar phrases.'

He was always neatly dressed, his hair in perfect order and his toothbrush moustache trimmed to a precision consonant with his character. Meeting him in his role as Foreign Minister of an independent State of Israel I could never rid myself of the vision of him I had had in 1946, when, with the rest of the Jewish Agency Executive who had been arrested and taken to Latrun detention camp, he was brought back in a lorry to one of the Agency buildings in Jerusalem. He stepped from the lorry wearing a stained shirt and brief khaki shorts, sandals and knee-high stockings, for all the world like a scoutmaster and not a bit like the future Foreign Minister of a State which, at that time, seemed remote.

But he was the obvious man to take over foreign affairs once the State was established. He had been head of the Agency's Political Department for years and was skilled in the arts and devices of international negotiation. Few men in the State of Israel at that time – or since – could have organized the Ministry or built up its policies as efficiently as he did. He was less politician than civil servant, and it is probable that he lacked vision and the capacity to understand the visionary qualities of his leader, Ben Gurion. For that reason the two men often were in conflict; until in the long run Ben Gurion lost patience and rid himself of a Foreign Minister who dotted too many i's and crossed too many t's for a Prime Minister who saw himself also as prophet and seer. Ben Gurion was not easy to work with, of course. Visionaries never are. Once, when Ben Gurion was threatening to put his foot down in connexion with some international decision he thought damaging to Israel, he was told that the State Department, the Foreign Office, the Quai d'Orsay, and the Kremlin had bigger feet to put down than Israel had.

'In this matter they'll get blistered feet if they do,' said B.G.

It happened that Ben Gurion was proved right in the event more often than Sharett. He was proved right in the first place in his decision to proclaim independence on the day Britain surrendered the Mandate. He was proved right when he transferred Parliament and Government from Tel Aviv to the so-called *corpus separatum*, which was Jerusalem. The Foreign Minister remained in Tel Aviv for some months after that for the convenience of Diplomatic Missions whose Governments would not recognize Israel's right to sovereignty over any part of Jerusalem. But it was not long before Ben Gurion's will was effective in that matter, too, so that the Foreign Ministry had to move from its comfortable quarters at Ha'kirya to pre-fabricated huts on the western slopes of Jerusalem, where it remains to this day.

Frontier incidents and the question of the Arab refugees were the chief concern of Sharett's foreign policy during those first few years. The two were, of course, tangled; and in some respects were one problem, not two. Israel had begun by offering to take back

100,000 Arab refugees as part of a more general settlement between it and its neighbours. But it was clear from the start that no Arab Government had the wit or the courage to agree to anything in the nature of a general settlement with Israel; and, of course, as time went on it became more and more difficult for Israel to contemplate the return of any large number of Arab refugees. There was no place for them. The former Arab towns were crammed with new immigrants. The villages had disappeared or, like the towns, had been filled with immigrants. If these people had been ordered out of their new homes to make way for Arabs, there would have been something like civil war in Israel. It is constantly stated by Western diplomats when urging upon Israel the desirability of a conspicuous gesture, that very few of the 600,000 to 800,000 Arab refugees would elect to return within the borders of Israel if given the chance. That may be true, but it is largely guesswork. No offer could be made on such a risky assumption. It is more than likely that the Arab Governments would have found a way of compelling the return of the refugees once Israel had been opened to those hapless people. It would have been a sure way of embarrassing the Israelis and creating for them a serious security and economic problem.

If the refugees had come into Israel it would have been necessary to re-settle them. They could not have returned to their old towns and villages. In the circumstances, it seems not illogical of Israel to ask why the refugees should not be re-settled in the roomier and often more fertile unoccupied areas of Syria, Iraq and even Jordan. It was reasonable to suppose that the Arabs would be happier under Arab government than in Israel in spite of the higher standards of living enjoyed by the 200,000 Arabs who had remained in Israel or had been allowed back under the scheme for re-uniting families divided during the 1948 war. Why, then, since re-settlement was inevitable even if the refugees should enter Israel, solve the problem in a manner likely to create another? For there should be no doubt in anybody's mind that the return of, say, 400,000 Arab refugees to the lands now within the State of Israel, would have put that State's security in serious jeopardy.

The Arab refugees remain refugees because the Arab Governments concerned are not interested in the social side of the problem. Financially, the refugees continue to be a U.N. responsibility. Politically, they are useful as a stick to lay about Israel's back at U.N.

and in London and Washington. In prospect, they are valuable as a possible means of weakening Israel if that country should be internationally bludgeoned into taking back a tidy number of them. Meanwhile, thanks to U.N., most of the refugees are well-billeted, well-fed and generally well looked after. Naturally, these advantages are no compensation for what the refugees have lost. A *fellah* who worked his own small farm in what is now Israel, cannot be particularly happy twiddling his fingers in even the best of refugee camps. A mechanic who had his own workshop in Jerusalem or Ramle or Jaffa probably yearns in idleness for his own workshop. Even a coddled refugee is an unlucky man.

Fourteen

LIKE it or not, there was Israel. It was Jewish, sovereign, free; its sea frontier open to let in whom it pleased: outside, in Germany, Rumania, North Africa, hundreds of thousands of Jews desperately wanting to be let in. By all conventional calculations there were too many of them wanting to be let in to a country too small, too short of natural resources to provide them with homes and livelihood. But Israel was not a country where conventional calculations of that kind were persuasive.

'The Exodus would never have taken place and the Israelites would never have got to the Promised Land if Moses had listened to the experts,' Ben Gurion once said. That remarkable man had two overweaning priorities – the military security of the State and what he called the 'ingathering of the exiles'.

Throughout 1949 and 1950 shipload after shipload of these 'ingathered exiles' were put down, with their bundles and beards and raucous excitements, at Haifa. Lorries, trucks and omnibuses stood by to carry the wondering newcomers off to 'reception camps'. In the barren Negev, in Galilee, along the Sharon Plain, workmen put up huts, laid down settlements. A new, white, ugly quarter was thrust up on the outskirts of Tel Aviv to take the immigrants who preferred town labour to digging fields. The Army helped where it could. When the building of houses and huts could not keep pace with the arrivals, tents were used. The whole thing looked crazy. From Haifa to Tel Aviv camp followed camp. In the first two years of the State over 300,000 men, women and children were added to the initial population of 600,000 – that is to say, one extra Jew for every two already in the country.

It is often said: 'But it wasn't the State of Israel that paid for all that. It was paid for by the World Zionist Organization.'

Zionist organizations paid for the transport of the new immigrants. But it should be remembered that the funds raised by these organizations were a legitimate and essential income of the State of Israel, which could have used for security and development purposes, if it had so wished, the big amounts that went to bringing in the newcomers. The huge work of settlement, and of absorption of the new immigrants into the economy and social structure of the State, was the State's affair for the most part. As a consequence, funds for the customary needs of a settled national community fell low. An austerity régime was introduced and for several years life in Israel became a matter of queues, ration cards, and parcels from friends and family in Europe or America.

Mass immigration at a time when funds were low anyway, foreign currency scarce, housing projects only just beginning, settlement areas in a virginal condition and without irrigation, cities and towns already overcrowded and the labour market full, was criticized by Western Governments and their representatives in Israel. The fact remains that the newcomers did not starve and did not go without roofs of one kind or another over their heads. Today, most of the more than half million who came in 1948, 1949 and 1950 and the majority of those who followed – about another 400,000 – are self-supporting and have fairly well adjusted themselves to their environment. Most of the camp dwellings put up to receive them on arrival have been done away with. Villages and even small townships have taken their place. The process has been one of trial and error, as one might suppose. A good deal of it has been costly error. But although the rate of increase varied from year to year, the policy of bringing into Israel every Jew who wanted to come has been fairly steadily maintained without any of the social or economic crises that many critics expected. Obviously there is some hardship among the newcomers and a certain amount of complaining. It could not be otherwise. But there is rather less, than more, hardship than will be found in any normal community anywhere.

The important thing is not so much that Jews of middle age and beyond were brought among their own free people and given the opportunity to live out their lives in something like pride and dignity. The important thing is that a great multitude of Jewish children, otherwise restricted to the slum conditions of Europe or the primitive habits of North Africa, and subject to the damaging psychological effects of living among peoples who, at best, tolerated their presence, were given an assured place within society, a high standards of education, and good prospects afterwards.

I have known some of these families. I have seen them come in at Haifa, eager, uncertain, hopeful. I have seen them in dejection on the stoops of roughly-built huts in dreary cantonments. I have seen them labouring to build the township or village that would become their permanent home. And I have seen them begin their little household gardens, add to their domestic effects, meet together to discuss their communal affairs. I have seen their children change from the excessive if picturesque raiment of Kurdistan or Persia or the Atlas Mountains into the light, free clothes of the Israeli child. I have seen their young men and women go doubtfully into the defence forces of their new land and come out after two years as thoroughly Israeli as any *sabra* – the native born.

2

There were the Kempinskis, for example. Afterwards they hebraized the name. But when they landed at Haifa early in 1950 they were Josef and Sarah Kempinski, the father and the mother, and four children, Saul, Miriam, Sophie and Itzhaak, all Kempinskis. They were Poles. When the Nazis entered Poland Josef and his wife, with Saul and Miriam, managed in some fashion to get to Rumania, a safer place for Jews in those days; and there Sophie and Itzhaak had been born. Josef, who was a jeweller by trade, had found work in Varna, the Rumanian Black Sea port, from which, in 1950, when the Communist Government in Bucharest thought it politic to be on good terms with Israel and convenient to get rid of as many of its Jews as it could, he and his family sailed for Israel with twelve hundred other immigrants. They were taken into two small, adjoining huts, one for the children and one for the parents. Less than a year later Sarah bore her fifth child, Esther, who was about eight months old when I first met the family.

Josef was a thin, sombre man of about fifty-two. He was conscious of his grievances and brooded over them, but rarely complained. Like Madeleine and her piano he would recall, wistfully, his jeweller's workshop in Warsaw. 'Some wonderful stones went through my hands,' he would say in his fairly good German. Sarah would smile at that, as if smiling at a deluded child; and I gathered from certain things she said on occasion and inadvertently, that Josef's 'wonderful stones' were never more than a moonstone or a turquoise belonging to some shopkeeper's wife or dressmaker in the ghetto and in need of re-setting. Josef's face always looked askew, probably from long habit with the jeweller's eyeglass, which he still carried in his pocket. I have seen him solemnly fix the eyeglass to his left eye and stare for minutes at a time at the callouses on his hand, caused by the work he did three or at most four days a week as a labourer on one of the new roads Israel was building at that time. The job had been found for him by the Ministry of Labour, which was compelled to ration out its work among tens of thousands of new immigrants. It earned him the equivalent of about four pounds fifteen shillings a week, which is not very much for a family of seven even when there is no rent to pay.

Sarah, his wife, looked much older than Josef but may well have been younger. She was an inexpressibly tired woman, as were so many of the new immigrant women. There is something almost dramatic in the worn, tired, expressions and postures of a group of immigrant women waiting in a queue by the entrance to a camp controller's office. Their passivity is a positive thing. Sarah's tiredness was emphasized by a curiously fixed, almost contented smile, something like the smile, barely noticeable, that is characteristic of many women in pregnancy. Miriam, the eldest of Sarah's daughters, would sometimes watch her mother silently for a few minutes and then she, too, would begin to smile like that, as if she had penetrated to her mother's secret and was pleased by what she had learned. Sarah helped the family budget by doing a few hours' washing of clothes, when she could, for fairly well-to-do people – mainly Germans – who lived in an old-established village on high ground about a mile away from the camp.

But one way and another it was a pretty hard life. On his 18th birthday Saul had to go into the army. Miriam, Sophie and Itzhaak were at school, and with luck Miriam would go on to the Hebrew University in Jerusalem. But Josef was still without proper employment and they were still living in huts two years after their arrival in Israel. That second winter was unusually severe. It began with howling winds. Josef and Sarah gathered some heavy stones and weighted the iron roof with them. The winds were cold and the Kempinskis were given a paraffin stove to warm the hut with. One of the immigrants had managed to get an extra hut, which he made into a café, and on cold evenings Josef would go to the little café and sit there warming himself at a charcoal-burning stove. Sarah usually went to bed soon after dark, and the children would bring the paraffin stove as close to the trestle table as they could and get

117

on with their homework. Already Miriam and Sophie and Itzhaak were speaking good Hebrew. It was the language they used among themselves, talking Yiddish only to their parents.

Then the winds turned to pelting rain. One night a wady coming down from the hills burst its banks and spread a flood through the camp, which overturned some of the huts and damaged all of them. Josef's was overturned. The camp was full of wailing and yelling and nobody knew what to do until the Army came along with lorries carrying water-tight tents, dry blankets, field kitchens and loads of food. Army engineers dammed the wady. Other soldiers went about salvaging what they could of the immigrants' belongings, putting up tents and fitting them with beds, handing hot food around and comforting everyone by their cheerful presence. Then some welfare people came from Tel Aviv to look after babies and the sick, and two doctors appeared.

Next day the rain stopped and the sun came out. Those whose huts were still erect put their things out to dry – bedding, clothing, rugs, old framed photographs, albums, a few books. Workmen came and put the broken huts together again. By nightfall everything was in order, and the army and the welfare people went off. Soon after that I had occasion to visit the camp, and came across Josef and Sarah sitting on upturned packing cases outside the hut. I had first met them and their children about a year earlier, when for journalistic ends I was inquiring into the state of the newcomers to Israel. After that, whenever I was passing in the neighbourhood I would make a point of calling in, and usually, as on this latest occasion when I found them taking the sun on their packing cases, Sarah would make coffee and we would gossip for a time.

'So far the winter has been hard,' Josef said. 'Sarah, now, she has suffered much. Naturally she has been afraid for the children, especially the baby. And you know all about the flood we had, don't you?'

I said I did and that I felt much sympathy for them, and I asked Josef if he was beginning to regret having come to Israel. Sarah looked at me with that fixed smile of hers, but said nothing. Josef had no smile. He looked serious, as if he were working something out in his mind. Then he said:

'No. I don't regret it. Do I Sarah?'

'Of course not. You did. But not now.'

'No, not now. Do you know what made the difference? It is

funny, really. Although not so funny if you have lived our lives. You see, when our hut was carried away and all the water was about, soldiers came – you know, soldiers: men in uniform with rifles and badges. They had an officer with them, too. Well, the soldiers came and helped us, helped all the camp, gave us dry tents, and dry blankets and as much food as we could eat. I tell you. That is what happened. It could not have happened to us anywhere else in the world.'

Josef paused a moment to get his breath, and then he smiled. He was not the kind to smile very often. When he did it was an up-twisting smile on the left side of his mouth in keeping with a face that had somehow got out of alignment altogether.

He went on:

'Me, I have always thought – well, yes, why not go to Palestine? My father was a good Zionist. But with me it was what you call an emotion, a nice idea. I never thought anything would come of it, did I Sarah? And then one day ... well, we were told about Israel, freedom, a good life. So we came to Israel. It is not a very good life in one way. But in another way it is. Yes, it is. I learned that on the night the soldiers came.'

Josef paused. Sarah stared at a hut a few doors away, from which came the sound of two people quarrelling. A bus had drawn up outside the main entrance to the compound.

'That is the school bus,' said Sarah. 'Itzhaak and Sophie will be on it. I shall make some fresh coffee for them.'

Joseph looked towards the bus from which the children had begun descending.

'Yes,' he said, 'I thought it was a mistake, this coming to Israel. But Sarah, she would always say: "Think of the children, Josef, how they will grow up here." And she was right.'

Sophie and Itzhaak came along swinging satchels, calling out greetings to women washing clothes outside their huts, shouting to other children making off towards their own huts. They looked bright and healthy.

'Like *goy* children,' said Josef, proudly. But what he meant was not that they were like the children of Gentiles, but like children the world over who are well cared for and without fear.

Sophie wore light-coloured trousers and a woollen blouse – unheard of among Jews in Eastern Europe. Itzhaak had neat khaki shorts and white open-necked shirt. Both were bare-headed, and the feet of both were shod with sandals. They could have been any Israeli children accustomed to open air and spacious playgrounds. I drank another cup of coffee with the family and then went on my way.

About a year later the building of permanent houses on high ground above the site of the camp began. But it was not until 1955 that I visited the family again. Returning one day from Haifa to Jerusalem, and feeling curious to know what had happened to Josef and Sarah and their children, I turned off the main road and ran up to the village of neat brick houses with red-tiled roofs which had taken the place of the camp where I had first met the Kempinskis. At the co-operative store I was directed to the house I had come to find. It was a small house of perhaps three rooms, with a terrace and about one-quarter of a *dunam* (roughly 300 square yards) of garden. Most of the garden was given over to vegetables but there was a strip of flowering shrubs along the front wall of the house. Only Sarah, her elder son Shaul (Saul) and the baby, Esther, were at home. Josef was working in a Tel Aviv factory where precision instruments were made. Miriam was at the Hebrew University in Jerusalem. Sarah glowed proudly as she told me that, and then, to make sure that I had understood it, she repeated:

'At the university, that is where Miriam is. In Jerusalem.'

Itzhaak had joined an agricultural settlement in the Negev which had been founded by a group of young people, none of them over twenty, from one of the Emek communal settlements. Sophie was at high school.

And Shaul, home on two days' leave, had stayed on in the army as a regular. He had the rank of lieutenant and looked handsome in his uniform. I asked him what it felt like to be in the army.

'Good,' he said. 'It feels Israeli. That is enough.'

I was sorry to have missed Josef. I asked Sarah how he was getting along. She looked at me with that fixed smile of hers.

'Very well,' she said. 'He still talks about the workshop in Warsaw but he does not really mean anything by it.'

'Do you never get homesick for Warsaw?'

Sarah shrugged and said nothing. She served me a second cup of coffee and said she had to run into the kitchen. She had some biscuits in the oven.

3

The Kempinskis were representative of those East Europeans whose coming to Palestine had been characterized by the then Archbishop of York as a shameful thing, likely to turn the Holy Land into a slum. That was before the State of Israel had been founded, at a time when people like the Kempinskis were in D.P. camps in Germany or, if lucky, as the Kempinskis themselves had been, were waiting about in Balkan countries or on the coast of Italy. And what, one wonders, would the Archbishop do with slum-dwellers? – Leave them in the station to which, by the Archbishop's reckoning, God had called them? Or give them the chance Israel had given them? And give it above all in the Holy Land, which surely is a fit place in which to restore human beings to self-respect. The Jew may have rejected Jesus. But not Jesus the Jew.

4

It has to be admitted mournfully that some slum-dwellers did come to Israel and did remain slum-dwellers: not many, but enough to set the new State a hard problem. The National Home had never known such evils as murder, larceny, dope-peddling and prostitution. The State of Israel began encountering them within the first three or four years of its existence. Most of the immigrant scallywags were North Africans. The slum quarter they created was among the dark, narrow lanes of Jaffa. Much of the crime they brought was a matter of vicious temper: stabbings and violent brawls in back-street coffee houses or in some squalid apartment where a wastrel father and a nagging mother could hardly move without falling over a member of their numerous family. Nearly all murders handled by the Israeli police have been of that order, and with nearly all of them the knife has been the weapon used. The rest of Israel's crime has been, in the main, burglary, fraud, dealings in narcotics, illegal gambling and – to veteran Israelis that most horrifying of sins – prostitution.

What the pre-State Jew in Palestine thought of prostitution is shown by an incident with which I became familiar. It took place in

Jerusalem shortly after the first truce had begun. A company of *Palmach* made up exclusively of young men from two of the collective settlements of the north had been sent up to Jerusalem and stationed on the outskirts of the city against any possible breach of the truce by the Arabs. If the breach had occurred and had been sufficiently conspicuous, the *Palmach* company might have had another go at the Old City. Luckily, it did not occur. Something much more serious happened.

After the company had been there a few days a young girl, said to be of Kurdish origin, made her way into the camp and sold her favours to two young soldiers. Other members of *Palmach* realized what had happened and began earnestly discussing what to do about it. A committee was formed, which decided to call in one of the senior officers of the Company. The officer heard the tale and agreed to carry it to the Company Commander, who, when he learned of the incident, resolved to bring it to the attention of *Haganah* Headquarters in Jerusalem and to ask that authority be obtained from Tel Aviv for the disbandment of the Company and the return of its members to their respective settlements. The request was given sympathetic consideration by the Jerusalem Commander, who passed it on to the office of the Chief of Staff, General Dori, in Tel Aviv. There, not surprisingly, the petition was refused. It was pointed out that such things happen, especially in wartime, and that, regrettable as it may be, it could not be permitted to unhinge the intricate structure of army dispositions.

The Company accepted the verdict. The two young men concerned went about with their heads lowered in shame. The little Kurdish prostitute stayed away.

Even when prostitution became a police problem it was confined mainly to Tel Aviv–Jaffa. There were occasional reports of it from Haifa. Now and then, walking at some late hour through the streets of Jerusalem one might come across a loitering woman whose profession was not hard to guess. But for the most part it was Jaffa that staged the melancholy spectacle of organized prostitution. The police, quite properly, were less concerned to harry the girls than to catch the men who lived off them. And catch many of them they did, thanks very often to the fact that the *entrepreneurs* of prostitution were usually connected in some fashion with gambling-dens, which sooner or later were brought to the notice of the police.

The evil-doers, whether burglars or racketeers or for that matter muderers, unheard of in Palestine as they may have been before the setting up of the State of Israel, were not more than a handful of the hundreds of thousands of newcomers, penniless as a rule when they arrived and often with primitive backgrounds. Large numbers of them came from the over-crowded, unhealthy and poverty-stricken quarters of Algiers, Tunis and Casablanca. Many of them had spent years in Displaced Persons Camps, following years in concentration camps. Others had been wandering about, more or less in hiding, from one Balkan country to another. By all fair assumption this multitude had the right to a pretty big proportion of morally stricken persons without much respect for the rules of society. It had no such proportion.

However, an increase of population from 600,000 almost mystically devoted people to more than a million within four years and over 1,700,000 within ten years, is bound to bring social problems. Fortunately, there was a nucleus of a trained police force from the beginning. In spite of the modest budget voted to its needs by the Knesset, this force was built up into a highly efficient organization.

5

At the head of the Force and answerable to a Minister of Police was Inspector-General Yeheskel Zahar. I had known him in Mandatory days as one of Ben Gurion's young men. He acted, then, as a kind of liaison officer pottering between the Zionist organizations in Palestine and the British authorities of Government and Army. I suspect, too, that he had much to do with illegal immigration and that a good deal of his liaison work was a delicate powdering of dust in the eyes of the British. He is a pleasant-looking, pleasant-speaking man with easy manners and a taste for the pictorial arts. He was well thought of by most of the British officials with whom he dealt. These included the head of the Palestine C.I.D. under the Mandate, a certain Colonel Giles to whom, I believe, Israel owes much of the efficient structure of its police system.

That is only one of the many paradoxes that made of Anglo-Israel relations immediately after the Mandate had been surrendered, a confusing mixture of friendliness and enmity. The Mandatory police had suffered many casualties from terrorism. The Jews had suffered a good deal of hardship from the measures of an outraged police force. One could have said that no love was lost between the two sides. But the fact remains that British police officers – many of them former members of the Irish Constabulary – left a surprising number of friends behind, and that their Chief, Colonel Giles, worked out in great detail and as a gift to the new State, a blueprint for the Jewish police system taking over from his own. He did so after he had left Palestine and, I gather, while convalescing from an illness.

And yet I suppose no British official during the last years of the Mandate so personified to the Jews all that they detested in British policy as did Colonel Giles. Of course, all Jews have an instinctive distrust of policemen.

'Can you imagine Jews policed by Jews?' Doctor Weizmann once asked me. 'Can you imagine a Jew taking the slightest notice of Jewish policemen? The idea is preposterous.'

For the first year or two this circumstance caused Inspector-General Zahar and his organization a deal of anxiety. Among Central and East European Jews especially, the policeman had never been a symbol of security; always of hostile authority. The idea of Jewish policemen patrolling Jewish streets and interrogating Jewish citizens was, therefore, as laughable to the majority of Israelis at the beginning of the State as it had been to Doctor Weizmann. Matters were made worse for the Israeli police force by the stubborn refusal of many of the idealistic Jews to believe that crime could exist among the Jews of Israel to an extent justifying a wide network of police, criminal courts and prisons. It was not long before they learned better. Today the Israeli police force is accepted as an essential arm of the State.

Fifteen

IN the summer of 1949 I felt that I should try to find out for myself, as nearly as I could, what was the nature of the Jewish *kibbutz* movement, the communal settlement movement, and what the probabilities for its future. It was easy enough to get details of the movement's structure, and some idea of its social object. What I wanted to know was how intelligent human beings with normal human responses adjusted themselves to the peculiar demands of a collective community and lived day in day out with the same people, even messing with them; as surely serving an ideal as any monastic community stuck away behind walls in the middle of nowhere.

I took leave of my daily work and went to the settlement of Ramat Yochanan, one of a circlet of *kibbutzim* above the Zebulon Valley and about twenty-five miles north of Haifa. And there I remained three months. One has to have some experience of the *kibbutz* movement in order to understand in the first place how it was that Jewish and British experts differed so much on the question of the absorptive capacity of Palestine; and also how it came about that the Jews under the Mandatory régime were able to organize illegal immigration as successfully as they did; how they put together an unlawful militia which, overnight, was turned into an efficient national army; and, again, how it came about that when the State of Israel was founded and had beaten off its enemies, it had at hand the experience and knowledge necessary for the colonization of large, uncultivated areas.

Whatever may be the lesser place now given to the communal settlement in the structure of Israel's economy and society, I believe that that structure could not have existed in the form it does if the *kibbutzim* and co-operative settlements had not first shown the way. For that matter, the speed and relative success with which the Israelis were able to put together a civil service owe much to the settlements. Naturally, the Zionist administrative organizations operating in Palestine under the Mandate were able to pass on to the State a good many apt officials. But a surprisingly large number of senior posts was filled from the *kibbutzim*. And something like half the present membership of the Knesset is made up of settlers from communal, collective or co-operative farming villages.

Until the end of the British Mandate even well-to-do families of Jerusalem, Tel Aviv and Haifa felt it to be a matter of pride, and a proper contribution to the development of the Palestine Jewish community, to have at least one son or daughter in a *kibbutz*. To the Jews of that period it was almost as important to have some near relative in a communal settlement as it has always been for an Irish family to have a son in the Church. The adjectives 'communal' and 'collective' have frightened some observers. They tend to convey visions of Marx and Stalin; true enough, somewhere behind the *kibbutz* movements the ghost of Marx hovers. Where it hovers still to some purpose, and is given a kind of ancestor-worship, as in the collective settlements affiliated to the Left-wing but non-Communist political party, *Mapam*, it is a ghost that rubs its insubstantial shoulders with those of Tolstoy. As for the charge, so often heard in the days of the Mandate, that a community organized on communal lines was a Communist community, it is probably true to say that the *kibbutz* movement in Israel is the most effective anti-Communist block in the country. It is too passionately Zionist to be a breeding centre for Communism.

The *kibbutz* or *kvutza* is a collective group settlement where nobody owns anything and everybody owns everything. The land, the machinery, the flocks and herds and the products of the soil are the property of the settlements as a whole. So are the housing and even the radio-set in the bedroom and for that matter the bed-clothes. Every need of every member of a collective settlement from tooth-brush to wedding-dress and from a movie show to a stay at a Swiss sanatorium, is provided by the settlement. In return, the member gives his labour in such a fashion as may be determined by a committee which details the work of each day, something in the manner of a regimental orderly room. He received no wages. If the settlement has a profitable season and there is money over after meeting the group obligations to banks and institutions, that money is not distributed among the members, who can benefit personally from prosperity only in improving housing or services if the settlement as a whole should decide that such improvements are desirable. Even the children born in collective settlements become the responsibility of the whole group, not of the parents alone. All this may sound harsh and cold and friendless. It is nothing of the kind. In practice the collective settlement has shown itself to be socially constructive as well as economically more efficient (taking into account the peculiar circumstances in which the movement began and operated until 1948) than any other method of settlement tried in Palestine.

In the early days of the communal settlements, members would hire themselves out as labourers and contribute their earnings to the upkeep of the whole group and the development of the infant *kibbutz*. Only by pooling all resources, wherever they might come from, and by setting up communal kitchens and communal dining rooms and at a later stage communal nurseries, could the settlers sustain themselves and their settlements during the first few years of heavy work and small return. Zionist institutions provided them with the land they worked and helped them in the buying of agricultural machinery; but for the most part it was hard work and austere living and the settler's knowledge that where he might succeed as a member of a dedicated collective group he would surely fail if he set out on his own, that turned the settlement movement from a gesture of Zionist idealism into a decisive economic and social arm of Palestine Jewry.

The settlers' ideology – if that it can be called – was to make things grow where they never grew before; and, above all, to restore the Jew to the land: to rid him of the mark of the petty bureaucrat, the tradesman, the moneylender, the pedlar, the lawyer; to turn him into an open-collared, hard-muscled grower of good things and welder of iron and builder of roads and bridges. That fervour remains today, although the founding generation grows old and tired and perhaps disillusioned; and, with the coming of the State and its complicated mechanism of government as well as with the trebling of the population, the shopkeeper, so to speak, has come back into his own. Pioneering remains the chief domestic preoccupation of Mr. Ben Gurion and the chief interest of those parties to the left of his own, which have contributed to the development of the *kibbutz* movement. But where the Left-wing parties still cling to the communal or collective formula as the most effective means of opening up the empty lands of Israel, and notably the Negev, Mr. Ben Gurion and his followers have given their preference to the co-operative system. The *kibbutz* movement seems to have had its day. But it was a good and wholesome day, the light of which must continue to shine over Israel for a long time.

The co-operative system now proudly taking the place of the collective settlements, has several variants. The most popular form is that of the *Moshav Ovdim*, which have been officially described as 'Workers Co-operative Smallholders' settlements based on principles of mutual aid and equal opportunity'. Each member of such a settlement has his own house and his own farm, which he and his family work. However, seed, stock and agricultural machinery are provided by the central co-operative of the village, and the farms' output likewise is marketed by the village co-operative. In the co-operative settlement, unlike the collective, each family is responsible for its own domestic services and for the care of its children and receives a monetary income on the basis of output.

2

Ramat Yochanan is typical of the old-established, well-set-up *kibbutz*, or communal settlement. Its white-walled, red-roofed houses and dark, weather-board huts, lie among gardens, lawns and trees on the crest of Zebulon's western slope, and looking out to where, in the broad valley, are the settlement's fish-ponds and banana plantations. The houses are small and divided, as a rule, into two apartments, each with two rooms and perhaps a small terrace giving separate entrance. Here live married couples. Unattached men and women have to be content with a single room in one of the bigger buildings, or, if lucky, are given one of the timbered huts.

Kitchens are unnecessary in a community relying on the communal kitchen and the communal eating-room; and, until recently, separate bathrooms were thought to be unnecessary. At the end of the day's work one took one's bath in the settlement's bath-house. Nowadays, however, in the new lodgings put up since the State was founded, a bathroom has been added to each apartment. Couples with children have none of the usual problems. There is a communal nursery with qualified children's nurses and a host of comforts and conveniences. The children are restored to their parents daily for about two hours before the evening meal, and, of course, can be visited at any hour of the day by a parent with time on his hands. It is an admirable system in many ways. It differs from that of any well-to-do European or American family able to afford a nanny, a nursemaid and separate quarters for the children only in the fact that these children's quarters are for thirty or forty children, not three of four, and can be as far away as ten minutes' walk from the parents' own quarters.

The system has its disadvantages and I am not sure that I should like it for my own children. Its main fault, it seemed to me when I was at Ramat Yochanan, is in the eager professionalism of those who conduct the nurseries and the tendency of settlers, none of whom has the customary experience of parents in the bringing up of children, to give excessive weight to theory, and particularly to psychiatric theory. The solemn and determined effort to ensure that a child shall be without complexes should be enough, it seems to me, to create complex. Anyway, the psycho-analyst is called in at the slightest provocation; but, first of all, the parents and children's nurses meet with the elders of the settlement in the big dining-room and there seriously discuss the symptons of the affected child, deciding then, by acclamation, what shall be done about it.

While I was at Ramat Yochanan the problem of a bed-wetter, aged five, was discussed in this fashion and long debated at a meeting of the settlers in the dining hall. It was resolved to put the matter before a well-known children's psycho-analyst of Haifa. The psycho-analyst came, subjected the child to the mysterious interrogatory tests proper to psycho-analysis, and, at the end, had only a shrug of his shoulders as diagnosis. He laid down certain rules, of course, and gave comforting advice. But the child continued to wet his bed as before, until, all at once, he stopped doing so. Whether that was a natural development or a delayed consequence of the psycho-analyst's visit, I have no notion; but I suspect the former.

One theory of the communal movement is that its members, owning nothing, own everything. Their resources as a communal body are far, far richer than any one member individually could ever hope to possess. That is true enough, of course. No member of Ramat Yochanan or any other communal settlement had to go short of anything he genuinely needed, whether a new blouse or a new pair of shoes or medical treatment or a picture on the wall. Children's education in the settlement was at high level, and any child showing aptitude and desire could go on, at the settlement's cost, from high school to the Hebrew University in Jerusalem or the Haifa Institute of Technology.

The routine life of a settlement such as Ramat Yochanan was anything but dull. The village had its own well-built swimming-pool. It had an attractive concert hall where leading orchestras performed on occasions and soloists of international rank appeared. The *Habimah* and other theatre companies put on plays at the settlements. There were film performances. And if there was something worth seeing at Haifa, for example, special buses carried the settlers of Ramat Yochanan to see it. At week-ends there were excursions to the seaside. Festivals were celebrated as only the settlements know how to celebrate them.

The dining hall at Ramat Yochanan was used in the evening as a kind of coffee house, as well as a meeting place where counsel was taken on settlement affairs. Everything, from the value of religion in the education of children to the influence of American films and magazines on social behaviour, from the most suitable fodder for Friesland cattle to whether a wireless set should be bought and given to one of the settlers who was growing old, was debated in the dining hall among the assembled members, who thought nothing of keeping up their arguments until well after midnight, fortified by lemon tea and cake.

I had been given one of the timbered huts as my lodging during the months I spent at Ramat Yochanan; and after supper in the dining hall it was my habit to return there to read or write. But scarcely an evening passed without half a dozen or so of the settlers calling upon me and setting a discussion going on some subject with which I was supposed to be intimate. Altogether it was a pleasant, talkative life, that of Ramat Yochanan; and the talk somehow gave meaning to the heavy labours of the settlers' day. There they trudged, men and women, with the sun risen barely a half hour, among the vines or down into the valley meadows with sheep or out among the fruit-trees or clearing stones from land not yet cultivated: hard, sweaty work in the summer heat and performed with extraordinary intensity. But at the end of the day there were warm showers and a swim in the pool and fresh clothing and a meal skilfully prepared by trained cooks; and talk, talk, talk, in the dining hall itself or on the green lawn outside. And perhaps a dance or two if the settlement's accordionist felt like it.

3

The Jewish high festivals were merry occasions at Ramat Yochanan and at most of the settlements. One such, *Lag B'omer*, is a kind of harvest festival and surely derives from Hellenistic sources. Under the moon, the harvested foods – grapes, corn, figs, tomatoes, whatever it might be – are brought in procession by young women garlanded and in white robes, to a grassy platform where young, robed men receive the gifts. Then begins a kind of Portland Vase ballet. The Israelis who came to the country in the 'twenties from Russian and East Europe, and those who are native born, are fond of the expressive movements of ballet, and, as at Ramat Yochanan, can perform with astonishing grace.

But the most surprising of the festivals I witnessed at this communal settlement was that of Passover. Ramat Yochanan, like its fellow *kibbutzim*, was believed to be irreligious and even anti-religious. It was nothing of the kind. The Jew cannot successfully detach himself from his religion and remain consciously a Jew. But religion in the formal sense was not part of the social design of these settlements, which, if not in principle opposed to the fundamentals of religion, were thoroughly opposed to the traditional formulas and proscriptions of Orthodoxy. Those who professed atheism were unconvincing.

Passover was celebrated at Ramat Yochanan with almost as much intensity as at any Orthodox table. The traditional herbs and wine were served, and the youngest boy present was asked, and answered, the ritual question: 'Why is this day different from all other days?' However, the text of the service had been adjusted to give it direct application to the trials and labours of those who, a second time, had 'passed over', and a second time had come to the Promised Land, sojourning there in hardship and harassment under foreign domi-nation, if not for forty years for quite long enough, until at length there had come freedom and the rebirth of Israel. The elders of the settlement read the narrative of this new passing over almost as liturgically as any Orthodox family elder reading that night the hallowed text of centuries.

The occasion at Ramat Yochanan developed into merriment even as Passover does in religious homes; and, of course, at my table into an analysis of the inner meanings of Passover and the genius of Moses as an administrator. The point made over and over again by these serious-minded men and women was that their Bible told the history of the Jews. Its authors were historians and moralists, not deputies of God acting to a divine briefing. In many respects their attitude differed little from that of any intelligent

131

student of the Bible. Some of the settlers were shocked when I suggested that any one of them could pass as a theologian, and with only small adjustments could become Dean of St. Paul's. For that matter, I dare the opinion that Israel, morally and intellectually, owes as much to Christian as to Judaic teachings – fair recompense, of course, for what Christianity owes to Judaism.

Anyway, the difference between these settlers and the intelligently practising Orthodox Jew was largely a matter of form, not of faith. The Jew, whether of the Communal settlement or the Rabbinate, believes profoundly in the unique destiny of his race. Both derive that belief from the same source, the Bible. The settler may justify the Bible as history rather than as the inspired word of God; but the part history plays in his everyday life is, in effect, a religious part.

4

As I have said, the communal and collective settlement has been little favoured by those who came to Israel after 1948; and the supply of young acolytes from the 'Mayflower' families has dried up. Already in 1949 Ramat Yochanan, like many another *kibbutz*, was showing signs of middle age. The majority of its members were into their forties. The young ones born and brought up in the settlement were already planning to move out and set up a new colony in the Negev, which Mr. Ben Gurion's enchanted wand had turned into a mystic land of promise. Gradually *kibbutzim* like those of Ramat Yochanan, founded by dedicated Jews with a mission to perform rather than a grievance to redress, have withdrawn to collective seclusion. Many of the new immigrants have been willing enough to till the land and endure some hardship, but few of them like the idea of going without personal possessions and without some kind of regular income to be spent or saved as they choose. The new type of settler wants to own the land he tills, or at least have it on life tenure, and to be master in his own house. The prospect of getting such land and a house to go with it, at the expense of the responsible official institutions, was, without doubt, a big factor encouraging many penniless Jews to migrate to Israel and a main factor encouraging them to work the soil instead of serving behind a shop counter.

The co-operative system has turned out to be the most

appropriate for these people. Co-operative villages now outnumber the communal and collective settlements and it is safe to say that they must one day replace the communal settlement as the basis of agricultural life in Israel and the main source of the country's food supplies. It is not yet the main source of supply. Although technical experts (many of them from communal settlements) guide the new villages, the acreage production of the communal settlements remains much higher than that of lands cultivated by co-operative settlers who have much to learn. The Left-wing collective settlement movement may continue to flourish a good deal longer than that of the Socialist Right-wing, to which Ramat Yochanan belongs. Although not founded under the compulsions of an ideology with a mainly political motive, it is sustained by an active political Party largely based on the settlements. But Left-wing or Right-wing, the communal system is not to the liking of the newcomers to Israel and cannot for long be kept going by a generation which, so to speak, has no heirs.

5

The settlers of Ramat Yochanan were of varying origin. Most of them had come in their youth from Eastern Europe, where they had been members of Zionist youth organizations. Some had had university training. Many of them had been through one or other European High School. Some were village-born but most of them had been town-bred before coming to Palestine. Settlement life in Palestine had rid them of the peculiar marking of their backgrounds and turned them into a cohesion of ardent men and women living harmoniously, perhaps affectionately, together. And as far as I could gather they never hankered nostalgically after whatever circumstance of life was retained in their memory of youth and Europe, with one possible exception.

I came to know several of the settlers well, and kept in touch with them for years afterwards.

There was Shalom, a man of about fifty, not very tall, dressed for most of the day in the pale khaki shirt and trousers affected by communal settlers, but always with the white open-necked shirt after he had taken his shower at the end of the day's work. He was short-sighted and bookish; desperately eager to acquire knowledge and humorously self-conscious of his stumbling quest. He spoke about it with a shy, almost apologetic nervousness. We were squatting on the grass before the dining hall one day and he said, as he pulled at blades of grass:

'I'm fifty now. Getting old. And I'm only just beginning to realize how much I don't know.'

'I suppose every intelligent man has that feeling when he gets to fifty.'

'Yes. But that's not quite the same. I don't think so. No, it's not the same. An intelligent man, fifty or any other age, knows that he can never learn the half of what he would like to know. It's the beginning of the half that worries me. You see, for the first time in nearly thirty years, – thirty years I've been in Palestine – for the first time – and there's many like me – I'm able to think outside the problems of the settlement and the problems of what is now Israel. And as I do that I see a big, empty gap between me and my student days. And that's what I'm trying to do. Get over that gap. Join up with myself when I was a student in Vienna.'

What Shalom was referring to was the nostalgic exception which I mentioned a little earlier. In repudiating the conventional processes of European Jewish life, and setting out to convince themselves and their fellows that a Jew could till land, build bridges and tend iron furnaces, many of these settlers had untethered themselves not merely from the sources, but also from the need, of learning. That was well enough in the early pioneering years of hard work and conflict. The day then was filled with road-building, stone-clearing, ploughing, draining, putting up housing of sorts; the exhausted evenings with long discussions of means and methods, and whether it was proper or improper for a communal settlement to hire labour. And often of a moonlight night there would be training with arms in some well-hidden clearing. There was no time for learning and none to miss it.

Then, when the settlers grew, as Shalom had done, to middle age, and their settlements to relative comfort, and means and methods to a routine, came leisure. As the community of Jews in Palestine progressed from a few score thousand to half a million and developed, partly thanks to the German influx, a highly cultivated society, there came not a regret and perhaps not even the nostalgia I have called it, but something like a sense of work done and now the tools could be put aside for a while at least and they could all go back to their youth and sit again in the lecture halls and pick up where they left off and so come back to their shortening years in the settlements with the fond treasures they had left behind in Europe thirty years earlier.

I would come upon Shalom in the early morning shouting resentfully at a mule that took hardly any notice of him. The mule would be drawing at any pace it pleased and almost in any direction it pleased, a load of stones gathered by Shalom from a clearing shortly to be put under the plough. For seven hours in the sun Shalom would heave big stones into the mule cart, nagging vainly at the mule as it drew the load of stones by a route of its own choosing to a dump used by the settlement's builders of houses, barns and walls. The stones unloaded, back they would go, Shalom and the mule, to repeat the process.

'I would not mind if the mule would turn around and argue the point with me. I like argument, as you know. But the damn thing just takes no notice of me. It goes its own way and does exactly as if it had not heard a word I'd said to it. Most exasperating.'

They were an earnest people.

One day as I was taking my shower in the communal bath house, Shalom entered with two other settlers. They had finished the day's work and had come to take the customary shower before changing into fresh clothes.

As they soaped themselves under the steaming jets of water a loud discussion began between the three about whether or not the Greek city state, within some form of federation, would have been a good system for the Jews of Palestine. Shalom, calling out at the top of his rather thin voice, as if he were still addressing his contemptuously indifferent mule, said:

'Ramat Yochanan could have been another seven-gated Thebes. We are not just peasants. What Cadmus did we could have done. We're hard workers but we're not heroic enough.'

The two others, splashing away, laughed heartily. I had moved from the shower and was towelling myself. I said to Shalom, above the din of the splashing and hissing water:

'You should not forget what Zeus did in that little matter. Not to mention Amphion.'

'Zeus would do it again if we gave him the chance,' Shalom replied, red in the face from the hot water and the fervour of his notion. 'It's not Zeus that is missing, but Cadmus – and don't forget that Cadmus came from just a few miles north of here. As for Amphion, he's easy enough to find.'

As all four of us moved from the showers to the dressing-room the discussion turned into a warm argument about the relative merits of the Theban legends and the Biblical narratives. Earnest indeed can these people be, who argue from field-mice to Shorthorns and from Sophocles to Ben Gurion all the round of the sun and deep into the starry night.

6

The subject of the Theban legends stirs in my mind the memory of Shoshana, a girl of eighteen when I first met her, who was born in a *kibbutz* of the Emek Valley and who, in 1953 was the prime mover in the founding of a *kibbutz* in one of the more desolate parts of the Negev. Shoshana stood about five feet eleven inches. She was splendidly proportioned, had abundant fair hair, blue eyes and a complexion tanned by the sun. Her features were as far from the conventional notion of the Semitic as they well could be. They were features common to the chisels of Praxiteles and Phidias and made familiar to us by Attic decorators in marble and pigment. Her nose ran straight from between well-spaced, large eyes, and ended in delicate nostrils. Her mouth, ample and perhaps a trifle too full-lipped by some standards, was well shaped. Her chin was round and clearly defined; her neck long. She was full-breasted, narrow-waisted, and long legged: in short, as fair a maiden as I have ever seen.

Like most of these native-born Israelis Shoshana was as bright as a polished shoe-buckle and could hold her own in almost any subject of conversation from insecticide to infant psychology. Her reading was a bit haphazard. She talked excitedly about Colette and had read André Gide's *Journals*. His novels she thought 'unreal'. She had memorized A. A. Milne's Christopher Robin ditties and was always quoting them. She had an extraordinary liking for rhyme and rhythm and was fond of translating such poets as Edgar Allan Poe into a Hebrew that went with much the same swing. She talked Baudelaire in the same breath as Kipling.

I have mentioned this surprising specimen of the native-born Israeli girl because, except in the perfection of her physical appearance she was not unusual. A visit to any settlement nursery will show that a type of Israeli is emerging that has hardly any resembanlce to the Jew as he is normally visualized by non-Jews. I have no notion why this should be so. The physiognomy of the ancient Israelite as shown on bas-reliefs, and particularly those of Karnak, seem Semitic enough. Why, then, the straight delicate noses of these children, the fair hair and blue eyes? There may have been some intermixing during the Hellenistic period. Obviously there has been a good deal of it since.

Not all the native-born Jews of Israel are in Shoshana's mould or coloured as she. I have mentioned another *sabra*, Hannah. Hannah was as delicate featured as any woman could wish to be. But they were the features of a Semitic Nefertiti. Many of her type, also, will you find in the nurseries of the settlements. A third remarkable type is that being born today in the Yemenite communities of Israel: black-haired, dark-eyed, and with features of the most exquisite fineness. In brief, an attractive generation is building in Israel. Give that country another twenty years and it should provide as handsome a community of men and women as can be found in the wide world.

7

And so the summer of 1949 drew to the shortening of days and the yellowing of the vine-leaves; and it came time for me to go back to my customary world. I was sad to go. These settlers were a good and bright people and had given freely of their time, their thought, their kindness, and their goods, to a guest. One knew them all; and it was easy to feel oneself a part of them. One bothered about the accident to Aviva, whose leg had been crushed by a falling boulder as she was loosening soil on the hill-side. One cared whether young Aaron could be admitted to the Herzliya High School in Tel Aviv. One was concerned to know if the cow named, for some reason no one could remember, Lady Hester Stanhope, and which was really too old for such labour, had calved without serious damage to herself.

One moved, almost with an awareness of antiquity, through the heavy vineyards with their amber and purple grapes; and down among the ripened cornfields. One climbed the high hills where the pines were thick, and sauntered down among the plantations in the valley. And at night one stood outside the weatherboard hut and watched the lights of Haifa creeping up Mount Carmel: a pretty sight, the lights hanging there like candles on a Christmas tree.

I promised myself that I would go back to Ramat Yochanan one day. But I never did. One lives like that, as it were from noon to sunset; and it remains a kind of platform separate from the walls that environ one. Every now and then one mounts the platform to look out across a happy memory. There are not very many such rearward vistas. A man's life goes on year after year. One trudges it as a goatherd with his staff trudging up the mountain track and hardly ever looking back. But here and there a man must rest and he is lucky if he has a narrow platform to rest upon, warmed by that distant noon to sunset.

Sixteen

MASS immigration was an act of succour. It would be foolish, however, to ignore the harsh encouragement given to the framers of this policy by the compulsions of security. It was not merely a question of adding manpower to the defence forces. There was also the need to people the frontier areas as a deterrent both to the infiltrator and to the border revisionists of London, Washington and U.N. The strategic Jewish settlement in Palestine was nothing new. Many of the *kibbutzim* put down during the Mandatory régime had no economic justification. They were military outposts and national signposts rather than farming villages.

The new frontier settlements are not military outposts. Unlike the old outposts, their inhabitants are not trained militia and usually resent the efforts made to accustom them to having a rifle in the house.

They are neither trained soldiers nor a people of soldierly bearing. They are not the dedicated spirits of the communal settlement. They came to Israel to be given security, not to fight for it; and if they take up farming in a border area they want to farm and at the end of the day listen to a radio broadcast after supper and then go to bed, not fool around with rifles and grenades or listen to some army fellow lecturing on how to beat off an attack by Arab infiltrators. It is the Army's job to beat off infiltrators and protect the settlers.

And the Army does just that, of course, as far as it can. It has an intensive patrolling system along the whole length of the country's land frontiers. The patrols are described as 'Frontier Police'. Their organization is separate from that of the civil Police Force and their training is that of specialized military units. But the frontiers are long and so are the nights and there can be a big gap in the patrolling system, so that some knowledge of self-defence and the weapons to assist it is essential to the settlers themselves. Sooner or later they accept that melancholy fact.

Israel, as I have said, has grotesquely long land frontiers. Up against every single mile of them is a hostile people, often a rancorous people; and, in many sectors, a people who, provoked by their own governments and by the constant agitation of the radio and the coffee house, believe they have a perfect right to harry and kill Israeli settlers, drive off their cattle and sheep if they can, and generally make the life of the new immigrant a hazard. Israel's border patrols are many and active but there cannot be anything like enough of them to ensure security for the rapidly increasing frontier population for twenty-four hours of every day.

Small wonder, therefore, if from time to time the people of some border village pack their belongings and trudge off to Tel Aviv or Jerusalem or Ramle or Lydda to add to the labour problems of those towns.

I have seen something of the kind happen more than once. It happened to a village known to me in the border area not far from the small Jordanian frontier town of Qalqillya. In this area, as most of the way from Lydda to within a few miles of Haifa, the distance between the frontier and the sea varies from five to ten miles. It is good country for marauding infiltrators. They slip across at night in groups of from four to ten, drive off a few cattle, toss a grenade through a bedroom window, and usually get back to their own side of the fence before anything can be done to stop them.

The village I have in mind had been peopled by immigrants from Morocco. One night, a mother and three of her five children were killed by a bomb pitched through the window of their small house at the end of the village. Next morning the victims were buried, and by nightfall of that day every one of the thirty-five houses had been emptied. On foot or astride mules and here and there packed into a small cart, the village people moved off. They had had enough of it. A wind blew up. Unlatched doors and loose shutters swayed and banged to the wind's pressure. The sun went down on what seemed to be a pitiless commentary on the policy of mass immigration and frontier settlement.

But within a week or two the village was peopled again. Today it has some three hundred souls and nearly eighty houses. There are little gardens and makeshift summer-houses against stunted trees. The slopes of the valley have been neatly terraced and planted with vines and plum-trees. Close as the village is to the frontier I have heard of no incident there since the one that sent its first group of settlers scuttling. Security has been aided, perhaps, by the setting up of two more villages close by.

It does seem that the rate of frontier infiltration and marauding goes down as the frontier settlements multiply in number. Reprisal action, too, has its effect upon infiltration and likewise on the morale of the new immigrants. Whether savage reprisal carried out by the armed forces of the State is morally justified or not, is another matter. It is a subject of much complexity. Meanwhile, under such protection as the Army gives, more and more villages rise up. The new immigrants whose white settlements bead the northern Negev, cluster along terraced slopes on both sides of the Jerusalem Corridor's highway, face Jordan land between Lydda and the Beisan hills and move through Galilee towards Syria and Lebanon, include Bulgarians, Rumanians, Poles, Hungarians, Yemenites and North Africans. Visiting these settlements at an early stage of their development one finds it difficult to imagine their turning into anything characteristically agrarian or remotely economical.

A Rumanian in the Negev would take up, with a gesture of disgust, a handful of sandy soil and, spilling it through his fingers would say to the visitor: 'How can anything be made to grow in that?' Another, characteristically flinging his arm out to encompass the whole sky, would say: 'A sun like that! Hardly any rain even in winter. The sheep will die. It's Beduin country, this.' And a Moroccan in the Jerusalem hill country: 'Stones, stones, stones! Day after day I drag stones away. It's convicts' work.'

A Hungarian woman in a settlement not far from Kibya (later the scene of one of Israel's most spectacular reprisal actions), looked sadly towards the frontier and said: 'I have two small children. Ten times each night I wake up in fear and shake my husband awake because I hear something strange outside or because the dog barks. Usually it is nothing. But it can always be an Arab. Look!' She turned and pointed to iron shutters newly fitted to the window of her cottage. 'They have begun giving us those things now,' she said in rather bitter tones, 'as a protection against bombs flung at the window. What kind of life can this ever be? And to bring up children in it!'

Somehow it became quite a good life and most of the children seem to be getting along very happily.

But from time to time a whole settlement would march off in a dudgeon to the Jewish Agency offices in Tel Aviv or Jerusalem, squat day and night in the courtyard or on the pavement and refuse to budge unless the Agency agreed to set them up in a village somewhere else, where it was safer; or to give them better shopping facilities; or better houses. There was always a proportion of new settlers who yearned for the coffee house and the cinema theatre and the crowded streets of Tel Aviv. Some of these would abandon their village, find cheap back rooms in Jaffa as lodgings for themselves and their families, take to peddling, or drift into an idleness supported by means not always lawful. But these were few.

And the white houses with the red roofs spread hopefully through the land. Some appeared in the barren southern country, towards the Gulf of Akaba, but these were settled by members of a youth organization, which, in effect, was part of the Army, and chose the arduous settlement life in the southern Negev in the place of the normal two years' military service. Not all these young men remained on at such remote settlements once they had served their two years; but many of them did. The new immigrants were not put to that kind of hardship.

Towards the end of Israel's first decade a new system of settling immigrants was introduced. A small market town was first built. Then six or eight villages were laid out around it. Instead of mixing national origins in a single village, as had been the practice before, each of this group of villages was peopled by newcomers from one country. One village would be exclusively Moroccan, another Hungarian, a third would be filled with Persians, and so on. The mixing took place in the shops, coffee houses, concert and cinema hall and the schools of the little central market town: especially the schools. Children from each of the villages would be picked up by bus and carried to the central schools, where Bulgarian, Yemenite, Tunisian, Pole, whatever it might be, sat down together at the school desk and played together in the school playground.

2

In 1958 I was present at one of these villages when about forty Persian families were brought in, who had arrived in Israel from Teheran only the day before. They had been brought to the country by two Constellation aircraft and had spent the night in quarters set up for them at Lydda airport. Their village was in the Adullam hill region, where the Judaean mountains fall away to grassy foothills looking towards Hebron. The frontier was about two miles to the south. Westward, beyond the hillocky country around the site of Gath, could be seen the coastal plain and the pale yellow line of the dunes between Gaza and Tel Aviv.

I turned up at the village a couple of hours before the immigrants. Painters were giving final touches to the doors and window-frames of the houses. Soldiers were moving about in the sunshine, clearing the rubble left by the builders, tidying up outside the houses. Smartly uniformed women soldiers were setting out cups and coffee-pots, re-arranging furniture, plucking wild flowers and fitting them in bowls on the living-room table, checking the goods in the central store to see that everything likely to be needed by the newcomers in the way of food and kitchen goods was there. Presently the three buses, their roofs piled high with baggage, were visible at the turn of the newly-made road where it comes out of the tall, rounded hills and winds along the valley towards Adullam, the unfinished market town, and so up to the village of the Persians. By the time the buses came into view the village and every house in it looked as if it had been left only for a few hours and would be re-entered, soon, by people who knew which door creaked, where the pepper-pot was placed and the clean pillow-slips stored, and where to find the broom.

The three crammed buses drew up at the entrance to the village. An officer of the Frontier Police who was standing beside me said:

'Two weeks ago it was Hungarians – in that village over on the left. Now Persians. I am Polish. Funny people, aren't we?'

Young male soldiers stood ready to help with the immense quantity of bundles, cheap suitcases, here and there an iron-bound trunk; but mainly bundles – bundles of every imaginable size and shape and colour. Girl soldiers, a trifle self-conscious, stood smiling at the bus doors. They helped the women, carried the babies, led the families off to their allotted houses. A Jewish Agency official stood by to check names and give an official if mercifully casual welcome. It was a homely, easy reception, not less so because of the presence of the Army, whose efficient-looking camouflaged jeeps were drawn up by the side of the road fifty metres away.

It was an incredible sight. The sun shone. The sky was without a cloud. A tender breeze blew in from the seaward plains. Round about were low hills with the grass still green on their slopes, and the shrubs bearing blooms. Over against a line of hills hardly more than a stone's throw away ran the frontier. It was a safe guess that somewhere along that ridge were armed Arabs, watching, not with evil intent but out of curiosity and perhaps with envy; knowing that if they had been in the same fix as these Persians, no one would have dreamed of building little three- and four-roomed houses for them with white walls and red roofs, and giving them furniture, initial stores of food, farm machinery and seed for sowing.

The Persians themselves provided the most incredible sight of all as they descended from the buses. The men, except the old ones, were drab enough in their newly-bought suits and cloth caps. But the women were dazzling. They wore long, full gowns of blue and rose and green and crimson; glittering ear-rings, row upon row of gold, silver or bead chains, heavy silver bracelets. They looked like the romantic notion of gypsies. The children – and every woman over eighteen years of age seemed to have at least two – were like coloured illustrations in a book of mediaeval fancy: wrapped in satins and silks, jangling bright amulets; their red mouths and dark eyes fixed in a gesture of wonderment as these unfamiliar girls in smart khaki uniforms rocked them and chortled at them or led them by the hand to heaven knew where.

Family by family the Persians and their bundles were taken each to its own house. Coffee was made for them. Sweetmeats were given to the children. Cigarettes were offered to the men. There was a language difficulty, of course, because none of the Persians spoke Hebrew and none of the Israelis except an interpreter, who was never around when he was wanted, spoke Persian. One of the Persian men spoke some English. He had come from Ispahan, where he had dealt in rugs.

'It is nice village,' he said, looking about him from the door of his new home. 'Everybody very kind.'

Behind him, and being attended to by one of the girl soldiers, were his wife and five children of whom the eldest could not have been more than nine.

I asked him if he thought he would be contented in the village.

'Why not? I do not know. It is dangerous, is it not? Over there the Arabs.'

Two huge bundles, looking like bundles of rugs, were placed inside the door.

'Have you brought some of your rugs with you?'

'No. Just those two, to wrap up things. Inside, in much old clothes and straw, I have ceramics, some very old, very beautiful.'

Many immigrants who had come to Israel from Persia had brought ceramics with them, often of considerable value. Most of the good pieces had gone to the Bezalel Museum in Jerusalem, which, building up from what it had acquired in that way, soon came to have one of the best collections of Persian ceramics in the world.

The immigrant from Ispahan, who had brought ceramics with him wrapped up in old clothes and old rugs, went inside to take coffee, which the little girl soldier had brewed. As the family sat around the deal table with their belongings on the floor and the girl soldier making up the beds, the scene looked, if not homely, at least hopeful. I wandered about the village. All may have been hopeful, and indeed it was, but never did a more bemused, sad-looking community take up new lodgings anywhere in the world. The people, even the children, moved as if in some kind of trance. They did what they were told to do, dumbly obedient. And when they were settled in their houses most of the grown-ups came out and sat on the stoops in the late afternoon light. They said little to each other; merely stared about them and beyond. And the children came together in small groups, talking almost in whispers, watching the strange soldiers moving up and down.

It had all happened a trifle too swiftly. Aside from settling in a strange land among strange people, these simple folk had been in Tehran only twenty-four hours ago. They had made the first air journey of their lives. The rigours of day after day in crowded ships' holds, which made the immigrant passenger from overseas long for land and a house of any kind, anywhere, had not been their experience. Yesterday they were among people they had known all their lives, who spoke the same language, had much the same habits, bought and sold in the same way. Yesterday they were in crowded, familiar streets, among the traffic they knew. Today they were in another world: a world remote, isolated, lonely, and in some mysterious fashion dangerous. And thanks to those magic things that fly through the air, all this had happened between one rising of the sun and the next. They sat and looked about them, smiled wanly at the pretty girl soldiers who spoke to them in unintelligible Hebrew, held their small children close to them, gazed into the rooms of the house that was somehow their house, sat on the stoops and looked out over the valley towards where there was another village, about two miles away, just as brightly shining in the sun as their own. Someone had made them understand that that other village was settled by Hungarians, and another one just visible to the south, by Moroccans. Who were Hungarians? Who Moroccans?

For the Jew is racially and religiously a nation but in habit and background as polyglot as the ships that sail the seas. What has the Hungarian Jew in common with the Persian except a far-away history? What has the Jew from Warsaw in common with the Jew from Casablanca? Or the Jew from Berlin in common with the Jew from Cochin-China? The process of bringing these bewildered and desperate peoples, with their conflicting outlooks and varied up-bringings, into a conscious national unity is surely one of the most arduous and impressive tasks ever undertaken by any leadership or government.

It was much easier to turn people from a dozen different European countries into recognizable and good Americans than it is to turn these Jews from a score of different countries into good and recognizable Israelis. The American immigrant fared for himself in a land richly rewarding to those who fared venturesomely. He was in a big, rich, under-populated, unrestricted land and all about him were people who had become rich and were living in a kind of splendour. He could become rich and live that way if he tried hard enough. Pride grew quickly among the American immigrants. But in Israel, to each immigrant was given at best a few acres of stony or sandy ground: no gold to chase; no oil to speak of; no great forests to hew down and send sliding off on broad, brave rivers; no markets opening up all over the place and calling for shrewd traders; no industries virtually building themselves out of the crying needs of millions; no New York or Philadelphia or Chicago or San Francisco. Binding the Pole, the Moroccan, the Russian, the Persian, the Hungarian, the Yemenite, the German, and the Rumanian, were two things: something that happened two thousand years ago and more and was written down in a Holy Book; and persecution, or the fear of persecution, by those among whom they had lived as a despised minority.

All the same, the process of making a nation in the practical, day-to-day sense is moving along swiftly and even marvellously. It is, in its way, an exalting process. It is a process of the profoundest form of rehabilitation. Here, now, in the twentieth century, the century of atomic power and moon-rockets, of Russia and the United States of America, a whole nation is being built up from scratch. It is as splendid as anything Moses or David did.

Seventeen

THESE people, their lands and their goods, have to be protected. The State and its associated bodies induced them to come and it is the duty of the State to protect them. On the performance of that duty depends the State's own survival. In the first place, Israel must be in a position to protect itself against what may be called formal aggression. Its existence as of right is denied by the neighbouring Arab States, which foresee, or pretend to foresee, the time when, in common justice, they will overrun Israel and drive every Jew from the soil of Palestine. In that respect Israel is like no other State. For eleven years it has been in a condition of suspended warfare. It is safe for only so long as it has an army and armaments big and forceful enough to make extremely hazardous any attempt by its neighbours to invade it. It has no alliances and seeks none and can depend only on its own arms. If it were attacked, U.N., of course, would be 'seized' of the issue and after a time might intervene to halt the attackers if they should make headway, and to halt Israel if they should not.

But in modern warfare, and taking into account the greatly superior armaments of Israel and the Arab States compared with those used during the 1948 war, it needs only the time required to call together the Security Council, debate the matter and publish judgement, for cities to be broken to bits and tens of thousands of people killed. Israel is unwilling to take that risk. Thanks to the crazed hatred of Cairo, Damascus, Amman, and Baghdad, Israel must, therefore, continue to spend far more money than it can afford on its Army and the equipment of that Army. It has spent to good purpose so far. Over a quarter of a million trained soldiers can be put in the field at a few days' notice, fully equipped. Half that number, with all the necessary transport, can be on the march within forty-eight hours. Thanks to friendly governments, and especially successive French Governments, the Israel Army has weapons equal in quality if not yet in quantity to those of the United Arab Republic, Iraq, and Jordan. It has a splendid Air Force and is slowly putting together a small, efficient Navy.

Israel differs from other States in this also – that if it were attacked and overrun that, to all intents and purposes, would be the end of it: the end of Israel as an independent sovereignty within viable frontiers and possibly the end of any Jewish community in Palestine whatsoever. It can be said that the United States, Britain and France would not allow anything of the kind to happen. That is an assumption dependent on all manner of unforeseeable circumstances and policies; and even if there should be intervention by these Powers the question posed by Israel regarding U.N. intervention must again be posed in connexion with big Power intervention: at what stage? With what intention? Would such intervention carry with it, as price, an obligation on Israel's part to revise its frontiers in favour of the Arabs, to give up the southern Negev? Besides, supposing it looked as if radical intervention by the West on Israel's behalf would be followed by Russian intervention on the Arab's behalf. Is Israel worth a world war? By every argument, the risks for Israel are such that she must at any cost sustain her defence forces at a level equal, without outside aid, to any likely attack upon her territories.

All that, however, is but one factor of the Israeli security problem. Guerilla warfare organized from across the frontiers; murderous forays by infiltrators formally or informally encouraged by official Arab bodies, have consistently aimed at the weakening of the State and the creating of despair among newcomers settled in the border areas. One of the Israeli Government's most anxious tasks has been to decide upon effective and reasonable measures to check and, if possible, halt altogether the systematic Arab attempts to make a large part of Israeli territory unsafe for habitation except by armed soldiers or para-military organizations.

2

Reprisal is hateful. Aside from the question of principle, it is hateful because as often as not its victims must be innocent; and because, even if reprisal can be justified in practice, it is almost always bound to be excessive. The attack on Kibya village, which lies between Latrun and Tulkarm, in the summer of 1954, is an example of the excesses to which a company of soldiers is prone when fired with the zeal of avengers. There were other examples.

But Kibya became notorious because the casualties were numerous and all of them civilian and many of them women. It had not been a case of shooting down but of blowing up; and at a time when few menfolk were at home; and almost everyone within the blown-up quarters perished. The majority of Israelis, who are a compassionate people, were shamed by Kibya. Even Mr. Ben Gurion defended the action sullenly, as if he knew very well that he had a bad case. It was freely said that he had permitted the operation, following many acts of murder and marauding in that area, only after the insistent pleading of his Chief of Staff, General Moshé Dayan, who is a brilliant soldier with political ambitions but tends to accept and act upon the dangerous slogan that force is the only language understood by the Arabs.

Reprisals became more severe and more numerous during 1955 and 1956; but were directed less at the civil population across the border than at the armed forces of Jordan, Syria and the Gaza strip. Perhaps that steady increase in the number and intensity of reprisals can be taken as proof of the failure of retaliatory actions, I am not sure that it can. Acts of violence by Arab bands penetrating into Israel usually came to an end, temporarily at least, in sectors where reprisal action had been taken; only to occur, however, in some other sector, which then would become the object of counter-action. The question one had to ask oneself was: how far can this process of violence and counter-violence go? The answer was given in the autumn of 1956. For nearly two years the southern half of Israel had been terrorized by bands of gunmen and saboteurs trained as such by a branch of the Egyptian Army with its headquarters in Gaza. Reprisal action had not stopped the daring raids carried out from the Gaza strip by men who crossed Israel, pillaging and murdering, from the sea-coast to the Hebron hills, and in some cases passed through the closely built-up Ramle-Lydda area to reach the Jordan frontier somewhere in the Latrun neighbourhood. War was the counter-action decided upon then. The Israeli Army marched into Sinai and the Gaza strip. The campaign may have been timed and organized to coincide with the Anglo-French landings at Port Said; but in one form or another it would have taken place anyway.

Throughout the whole dispute about the rights and wrongs of reprisal action Israel claimed, with a good deal of supporting evidence, that the governments of Arab countries from which marauders, saboteurs and gunmen came, were primarily responsible for the acts of violence carried out against Israeli citizens and their property. That was demonstrably so in the case of guerilla operations from the Gaza strip. Even where Arab governments were not directly responsible for forays into Israel, as seems to have been so in the case of the Government of King Hussein, the Israelis held them responsible for allowing a situation to develop along their frontiers with Israel, which made it possible for Arabs under the influence of agitators – often from Egypt or Syria – or goaded by radio exhortations, to band and conspire together, obtain arms, and set out on plundering and often murderous raids.

Perhaps in this matter the Israelis were a trifle unfair. If they, keeping close patrol, were unable to prevent the entry of marauders, how should the smaller Arab Legion have gone about preventing illegal passage? It is true, nevertheless, that when the Arab Legion went about it seriously, infiltration into Israel dropped off impressively. This happened several times along the extensive border sector subject to the Israeli and Jordanian military commands centred upon Jerusalem. It would happen following friendly conversations between the two commands, which have occurred on many occasions since 1949. But Jordan has long frontiers and many internal problems. It has never been in a position to deploy any considerable part of the Legion along its border with Israel, and in certain sectors has been compelled to rely upon the para-military and poorly disciplined National Guard, from which body, it is alleged by the Israelis, many of the marauders came.

3

Infiltration from the Gaza strip was another matter. I have already touched upon it but it needs a few more words. The Egyptian armed forces had set up in Gaza an organization for the recruiting of guerillas and training them in the use of automatic weapons, grenades and high explosives. The Gaza prisons were a steady source of recruits. Their commander was a certain Colonel Mustafa Hafiz (later killed by a bomb contained in a packet he had received through the post), who showed considerable ingenuity in training his men not merely to use their weapons and explosives to good effect but also to evade detection when on their murderous way through the Israeli countryside. During 1955 and 1956 incursions took place with astonishing regularity and success. Bombs were flung into isolated villages. A wedding party at one settlement was interrupted by bursting grenades, and the bride was killed. A bomb was thrown into a synagogue where boys from a religious school were at worship; several of the worshippers were killed. Settlers working in outlying fields were shot dead as the marauders slunk by. Mines were laid on roads travelled by settlement vehicles and by frontier police patrols. Electric pylons, irrigation works and bridges were blown up. Now and then a marauder would be caught, who inevitably confessed to membership of Colonel Hafiz's organization and complained bitterly of having been press-ganged into it. But as a rule the guerillas managed to escape detection and get safely across the border into Jordan. Except in the few instances when, for one reason or another, the gunmen chose to strike towards the frontier east of Lydda, the itinerary of murder lay through sparely-settled ravine and plantation country, where the hiding was good.

In Jordan, agents usually awaited the incoming guerillas, looking after their needs and later sending them off again to repeat their violence on the way back to Gaza. They were a source of embarrassment to the Jordan Government, who were being charged by the Israelis with complicity, and who, spasmodically, rounded up the visitors from Gaza and put them into camps to await repatriation via Cairo. Most of the guerillas, however, were able to mingle with the refugees and townspeople of Hebron and its area until the time came for them to set off again.

In theory, Israel could respond to this serious, systematic and violent breach of the Armistice terms, only by making formal complaint to the U.N. Truce Supervision Organization in Jerusalem, or direct to the Security Council. In neither instance could anything be expected more effective than a pronouncement of guilt and an admonition addressed to the offending government to sin no more. Decisions by the Mixed Armistice Commissions were not even heard of by most of those who did hit-and-run operations against the Jews in the Gaza, Hebron, Latrun and Qalqilya districts. They were ignored by Colonel Hafiz, and to that extent also by the Egyptian Government. It is my belief that the Government of Amman, or at any rate the higher command of the Legion, tried from time to time to reduce frontier tension. But King Hussein and his Ministers were afraid to drop too far behind Cairo and Damascus in vocal and active hostility to Israel. The Government in Cairo, while pretending to the U.N.T.S.O.'s Chief of Staff to be on the side of law and order and the terms of the Armistice Agreement, did nothing to check border violations or to halt the activities of Colonel Hafiz.

Reprisal, therefore, against the Egyptian armed forces stationed in the Gaza Strip, was decided upon. In January 1956 units of the Israeli Army entered the Strip and attacked military positions south of Gaza town. A barracks and other buildings occupied by the Egyptian Army were blown sky high. A number of Egyptian soldiers were killed but only one or two civilians. The Israelis returned to their own side of the line without a scratch, and, of course, were then compelled to face a Security Council session and to take a reprimand. The reprimand was justified and must have been foreseen by the Israeli Government when it resolved upon the attack; but by that time Israel had become almost as cynical towards U.N. scoldings as the Arabs seem always to have been. The reprisals action against the Gaza Strip military forces was as unproductive on that side as the U.N. Security Council's reprimand was unproductive on the Israel side. Incursions into Israel went on. Infiltration from Jordan, with violence, increased. And there was one reprisal after another. The situation grew steadily worse and came to its climax in October 1956, when an Israeli Army marched into Sinai and scattered its numerous and highly-equipped enemy in six astonishing days.

There was violence, too, against Israel's northern border: nothing like so much as along the Jordan and Gaza Strip lines of demarcation; but enough to keep the U.N.T.S.O. active, and now and then to bring the Security Council together. At length, in 1958, permanent U.N. Observer Posts were set up to watch the activities of both sides in the demilitarized area north of Lake Tiberias and taking in the River Jordan where, until the completion of Israel's drainage operations, the swamp-like Lake Huleh spread among thickets of papyrus.

The drainage of the lake has led to many formal complaints by Syria, and to much violence. In the first place, Syria denies the right of Israel to any part of these northern lands and waters, and has opposed the drainage of the malarial Lake Huleh mainly because such work, which would be rewarded with some thousands of acres of cultivable lands, tended to confirm Israel in its sovereign possession of the territory. One specific charge was that the diversion of the River Jordan into a deeper channel in order to prevent floodings, deprived a number of Syrian villages of flood waters that had irrigated their lands on the east bank of the river. In fact, only a handful of *fellahin* were affected, and formal assurances were given by Israel to the U.N.T.S.O. Chief of Staff that a flow of water to the Syrian lands would be maintained. A second charge made by Syria against Israel alleged that the area of reclaimed land as marked out by the Israelis trespassed on Syrian territory. The disputes have gone on throughout almost the whole of Israel's existence as a State. Automatic rifle-fire and on some occasions exploding mortar-bombs have broken into the sound of dredgers. But except for a small tract of water kept as a preserve for the remarkable wild life of the Huleh marshes, the lake has been emptied through the Jordan into Tiberias and its dried-out bed has been made fit for ploughing and sowing.

The second main cause of contention between Israel and Syria has been the north-eastern shore of Lake Tiberias, above which rises a steep range of hills on the summit and in the westward sloping pockets of which the Syrian Army keeps nervous watch. That, as much as anything, seems to be the cause of trouble in this unpeopled corner of the Sea of Galilee, or Lake Tiberias. There sits the Syrian soldier on his high, unseen perch, staring down at Israeli fishing-boats and the casting of nets where once the Syrians fished. Day after day goes by and the Syrian soldier high up does nothing about it. But then a day comes when the temptation is too strong. And one more Israeli fisherman lies dead or wounded in his boat. The Israelis, then, may or may not satisfy themselves with a formal complaint to the Mixed Armistice Commission. On occasion they do not, and there has been sharp counter action.

And here again, as everywhere along these preposterous frontiers, one looks in vain for any effective remedy short of genuinely co-operative effort by the authorities on both sides. What seems clear is that the U.N. Truce Supervision Organization and periodic resort to the Security Council have done little towards the effective pacification of the frontiers.

This is not intended as a belittling of U.N.T.S.O. Heaven knows how much worse the situation would have been if that organization had not been there. Its successive Chiefs of Staff, beginning with General Riley of the U.S. Marine Corps, in periods of tension have worked hard and often successfully to keep the disputants from each other's throats. The organization's Observer system had been impressively useful in a multitude of ways: tracing and arranging for the return of stolen cattle or sheep or other goods; attending to the repatriation of captives; measuring and clarifying boundaries; and, by their investigations on the spot, usually within a few hours of a reported incident, at least determining the facts. Even the system of Mixed Armistice Commissions continues to have some merit. The Commissions' meetings in response to complaint by one side against the other, have been a means of letting off steam; and the judgements of U.N. Chairmen can give judicial sobriety to disputes otherwise left to passionate charge and counter-charge.

The aggrieved party perpares his complaint in the form of a resolution, which, after some discussion at the session called to hear it, is put to the vote. Naturally, if the resolution has been introduced by the Arab delegation, that delegation votes for it and the Israeli against it; and the other way about. The resolution that succeeds is the one voted for by the Chairman. There have been instances of what looked like prejudiced U.N. Chairmen but on the whole the presiding U.N. officer has been fair and just. He forms his judgements as cautiously as he can, not alone from the arguments put forth by the two contending sides but also from the reports of the U.N. Observers who have investigated the incident under discussion by the Commission. But if there has been very little bias among the U.N. Chairmen of Armistice Commissions there has been, perhaps too often, the negative approach of an arbiter whose conscientious objectivity robs his judgement of effect.

I have mentioned the hard work done at higher levels by successive Chiefs of Staff, who have dashed about from Jerusalem to Amman and Cairo and Damascus and back again to Jerusalem in an effort to get some obstinate dispute settled amicably, or at least settled. The U.N. Secretary General himself has made several visits to the area at times of tension. His authority and persuasiveness brought about a temporary truce when the Mount Scopus issue was threatening to develop seriously. On an earlier visit he was able to prevent the Israel-Egyptian dispute over the demilitarized zone of Al Auja (Nitzana), on the edge of Sinai, from working up into violent conflict.

These two issues are typical of the more or less insoluble international problems inherent in the structure of Armistice Agreements that have gone on too long. Mount Scopus lies east of Jerusalem and adjacent to the Mount of Olives. Its broad, easy summit, bearing the monumental buildings of the Hebrew University and the Hadassah Hospital, now deserted except for their police guards, commands, on the west, the Old City of Jerusalem and the road to Ramallah; and on the east, the long descent to Jericho. At the Rhodes Armistice negotiations it was agreed that the Israelis should be permitted to police the Scopus area enclosing the University and the Hospital, and that negotiations between the Israeli and Jordan Governments should be set going as soon as possible with the object of arranging for the free access of Jews to the 'cultural and humanitarian institutions' on the Mount. These negotiations were intended at the same time to lead to the opening to Arabs of the main highway from the Old City to Bethlehem, which ran through the southern quarters of the Jewish city. A third object of the proposed negotiations was the opening of the Latrun section of the Jerusalem-Jaffa highway to Israeli traffic.

The Arabs built a new road to Bethlehem running through their own territory. The Jews improved upon their 'Burma Road', which by-passed Latrun. Both were inconvenient substitutes but at least they made the question of the two traditional highways one of little urgency. Scopus, on the other hand, became a source of mounting discontent and at times the scene of minor battles. The Israelis, taking their stand on Article XVIII of the Armistice Agreement with Jordan, which called for the 'free access' negotiations, and pointing to the grand edifices of hospital and university visible from the New City, at this stage cannot be expected to surrender their legally acknowledged rights on Scopus. Regularly every fortnight (except, as has often happened, when the Jordanians refuse passage and so set the tension spinning again) convoys of Israeli police set out from the Mandelbaum Gate at the edge of the Arab city to relieve the garrison on Mount Scopus and to replenish supplies. Medical men and university librarians are frequently included in the convoy. Their object is to attend to the valuable apparatus still in the Hadassah laboratories and to the much-prized library in the university. The search of the convoy's supplies, carried out under U.N. supervision by Arab Legion soldiers, is always a tense occasion; the passage through Arab territory in vehicles built to prevent the passengers from seeing out and from being seen has the quality of hazard. The whole business of this fortnightly venture is an anxiety and a risk.

Where Scopus is concerned the Jews have a good case. So have the Arabs. The Israeli garrison on the mount is supposed to consist of civil police. It can hardly be doubted that they are trained and in some instances specialized members of the armed forces. The Israeli Government consistently denies that anything in the nature of fortifications has been built about Scopus. The Jordanians as consistently charge the Israelis with building fortifications in the area. The charge has never been properly investigated, mainly because U.N. Observers have not been permitted to make anything like a free scrutiny. The Israelis also deny the presence on their sector of Mount Scopus of big supplies of weapons and ammunition; but that, too, has not been fairly investigated.

Obviously, it cannot be comforting for the Jordanians to know that what amounts to an enemy stronghold, dominating the most populous of their cities and the most important of their western strategic roads, exists as an enclave in the midst of Jordan territory. Their suspicion that the Mount gradually is being turned into a military base may be nothing more than suspicion. But in the present state of Israel-Arab relations the suspicion is bound to be there. And the consequence has been endless dispute, sharp tension, trifling, perhaps, but blood-letting battles, in one of which the then Chairman of the Israel-Jordan Mixed Armistice Commission, on an errand of mediation, was killed.

But if Jordan has a good case and the Israelis not such a very good one over this issue, the Jordanians have to be blamed for the fact that nothing positive can be done about it. It has always seemed to me that under conditions of peace Israel could well do without Mount Scopus; and would benefit from being quit of a constant source of bitter enmity. A new and handsome university has arisen on the western hills. A huge new Hadassah Hospital is rising in the same quarter. Israel could do without the buildings on Mount Scopus and might be able to make with the Jordanians a deal by which the Scopus buildings would compensate for some of the abandoned Arab property now held by the Israelis. But it is grotesque to expect any unilateral gesture of goodwill from Israel as long as conditions between the two countries are those of belligerents.

Eighteen

ALL was not infiltration, ambush and reprisal in the Israel of the first twelve years. All was not bemused and penniless new immigrants crouched in melancholy on the stoops of their little houses or squatting in protest about the courtyard of the Jewish Agency building. All was not rancour and bitterness and disappointment. It is the object of a foreign newspaper correspondent to report and comment upon those events likely to tease the dramatic instincts of readers. For the most part, therefore, what was read of Israel in Britain and the United States must have given the impression of a country harassed by infiltrators from across its border; setting out on savage reprisals, stuffing the land with hundreds of thousands of poor and mostly primitive immigrants who must, in the long run, bring about the slum conditions that had been feared by Dr. Garbett, the last Archbishop of York; arming itself to the teeth and doing so at the cost of housing and development and, worse still, with the object of one day pushing out its frontiers to the Jordan River; provoking the Egyptians by trying to run a ship through the Suez Canal, and the Jordanians by building up the Red Sea port of Eilat, and the Syrians by turning a swamp into cultivable land; worrying London and Washington by asking for things which, if given, would upset Cairo, Damascus, Amman and Baghdad; teetering between the nationalist extremism of Menahem Begin's *Herut* Party and the Left-wing 'neutralism' of *Mapam*: all in all, a provocative, nagging, know-all little country that got in everybody's hair and the existence of which had brought about more problems that it had solved.

There may have been something in some of these impressions. A new and sovereign nation can hardly come into being without incident or without giving a great deal of trouble all round. It could hardly come into being in a region that had belonged to others for some two thousand years, and where regional nationalisms were bursting frenziedly through the dried crusts of dead and gone imperialism, without resentment and violence. Nor could it come into being as a Jewish sovereign nation without aggravating racial prejudices and provoking a tendency on the part of the object of such prejudice to poke out its tongue and become more difficult, on occasion, than was necessary or wise. In short, when you come to think of it it is astonishing that Israel has turned out so well, so amiable and so normal.

For, despite all the periodic flurries, Israel throughout the first twelve years has been an agreeable place to be in. It has prospered. Its central and local governing bodies have been, on the whole, efficient. In Israel, things worked: taps ran water; electric lights went on; the garbage was regularly collected; bus services kept to schedule; the plumber knew his job; letters were delivered promptly; the urban and inter-urban automatic telephone services never to my knowledge broke down; a locally-made commodity usually was an effective substitute for the imported one. Not everything was as good as it should have been, of course; but is there any country where it is? And the point I am trying to make is that Israel was a comfortable, convenient country for anyone but the most fastidious to live in.

Its one big city, Tel Aviv, in the course of the State's first ten years acquired most of the attributes of a modern, well-set-up and efficiently organized European-style city. Jerusalem has progressed to the level where it is almost self-supporting. In spite of the fact that many of its streets are cut along their eastern course by rolls of barbed-wire, tank-traps, and stone-built screens to mark the beginning of hostile country, and that the back-windows of some eastern quarters are targets for stones flung from the Old City walls, the New City has become a gracious habitation. It has excellent shopping facilities, good restaurants, good coffee houses. Its street lighting has improved. Modern sewage is being put down. The water-supply is plentiful and pure. Many new and roomy schools have been built. The entrance to the city by the Jaffa-Tel Aviv road, long an eyesore, has been brightened up with trees and paint and the widening of the road. There are plenty of comfortable cinema theatres, and thanks to the munificence of an Argentinian who has built himself a grand villa in one of the suburbs, it will soon have a concert hall that should rival the Mann Auditorium in Tel Aviv.

Handsome buildings are going up as fast as builders can be found to build them. The broad-backed western hills, which were nothing but slopes of rock and scrub a few years ago, are beginning to take on the impressive dignity of a modern acropolis. Ministries are building there. A site has been laid out to take the Knesset, or House of Parliament. The Hebrew University rises impressively from the saddle of its long hill. The whole western skyline is being lifted monumentally.

The new quarters are in country where, on many a spring day, I have scratched my arms and barked my shins plucking irises and scarlet anemones. And have met not a soul on these idle excursions with my dog. Today, a fine road runs through it. There is a national stadium where the best anemones grew. The road runs by the big new Ministry of Finance, on by the spaced-out buildings of the Hebrew University and so to the pine-shaded suburb of Beit Hakerem and new, well-built residential quarters west of that. There is building everywhere in these western hills. The chip-chip of the stone-mason, that most characteristic of Jerusalem sounds, is heard where only a few years ago there was no sound except of the cicada, the pigeon, the grating of grouse-wings and the rolling of a dislodged stone.

It is indeed a good city, New Jerusalem, for all the charges of stuffy provincialism flicked at it by the lighter-built, lighter-headed Tel Aviv. In fact, Jerusalem's social life, although perhaps a trifle solemn, is active enough and, goodness knows, sufficiently in accord with the formulas of cultivated middle-class communities the world over. But the design of social life is determined to a very big extent by physical environment. Tel Aviv lies in flat country against the sea. Its houses are lightly built of concrete and plaster: all doors and balconies, so that one is never more than half inside or half outside. Not only does one look into the street from the house; one can look into the house from the street. And from one house into another. But Jerusalem's houses are built of solid, thick and beautiful stone, and have an air of indestructibility about them. Obviously, a party given in the high-ceilinged, carpeted and dignified drawing-room of a Jerusalem home cannot be the same as a party given in one of Tel Aviv's low-ceilinged, wide-windowed, balconied and tile-floored sitting-rooms, connected through broad, doorless openings with other rooms.

Both cities have their social high level. In Tel Aviv it is provided by the Diplomatic Corps and those hostesses who entertain the Diplomatic Corps. In Jerusalem it is the Consular Corps that sets the tone. Government plays very small part in society. It must not be thought that the Diplomatic Corps in Tel Aviv is any better, socially or otherwise, than the Consular Corps in Jerusalem. Some of the Consular rankings in Jerusalem are quite as high, in effect, as the Diplomatic rankings in Tel Aviv; for the Holy City, with its enchanted status as *corpus separatum*, and the Consular representatives of foreign countries with the wrappings of Ottoman tradition, is peculiar. There can be nothing else in the world like the Jerusalem Consular Corps. Its members do, of course, issue a visa now and then; legalize a document; perform a marriage if there is no risk of its running foul of the Rabbinate. The French and Italian Consulates General have a good deal of work to do in connexion with properties owned by Church Orders. The American and British Consuls write reports and take part in the magnificently uniformed procession to Bethlehem for Midnight Mass at Christmas.

On the whole, however, it is not easy to discover what purpose the fairly elaborate consular staffs in Jerusalem serve. They move freely between the Jewish and Arab cities and keep in fairly close touch with U.N.T.S.O. On arrival in the Holy City they are given no formal *exequator* and in relation to the Governments of Israel and Jordan have no customary status. They are accredited to the *corpus separatum* that is not there. Their hosts are the City Commissioner on the Jewish side and the Governor on the Jordan side, not Government or President or King.

Perhaps one main purpose of the Consular Corps is to act as a kind of branch office of the relevant Embassy in Tel Aviv and Amman. All Diplomatic Missions except those of the Netherlands and Uruguay, are at Tel Aviv; and, just as the British or American or French Consul-General in Jerusalem has no business beyond the Municipal boundaries of the city, so the Ambassadors of the United States, Britain and France in Tel Aviv strictly speaking have no business within the Municipal boundaries of Jerusalem, where, by their reckoning, the Israeli Government itself has no business to be. But the rules are not strictly kept. An absurd situation would be made doubly absurd if they were. Heads of Missions (as quietly as possible) often go up to Jerusalem to consult with the Prime Minister or his Foreign Minister. But they attend no official functions in Jerusalem and give none.

The Jerusalem anomaly is, of course, one of many such ridiculous legacies left by the U.N. Partition Resolution. Clearly, Jewish Jeruselem will remain the seat of the Israeli Government as long as

Israel lasts; and Arab Jerusalem will continue under Jordan sovereignty as long as Jordan lasts. There is precious little chance of re-uniting the two halves of the city under an international administration (or any other), and perhaps no compelling reason for doing so. Sooner or later the two sovereignties exercised in practice over the Holy City will have to be recognized internationally, and the Diplomatic Corps be given the right to move from Tel Aviv, which is about ninety minutes' drive away, to Jerusalem. One day, let it be hoped, unless war takes matters into its own insolent hands and is able to retain its spoils, Israel and the Arab Government controlling Eastern Palestine will come to some co-operative agreement. The city of Jerusalem, still with two sovereignties, then will open all its gates to the inhabitants of both sides and some kind of economic union, as foreshadowed in the Partition Resolution, will come into being.

2

And then there is Haifa. Haifa, with about 160,000 citizens, is as unlike Jerusalem or Tel Aviv as those two cities are unlike each other. It is beautifully situated and better built than Tel Aviv. By my thinking, it is one of the most beautiful cities of the Mediterranean. Most of its residential quarters climb the fairly steep western slope of Mount Carmel and look out to the splendid Bay of Acre. It has an active harbour, much expanded over the past ten years under the pressure of Israel's growing merchant fleet and the driving force of that most remarkable of City Mayors, Aba Khoushy, who seems to be modelled on what one imagines the American City Boss to be. He is a little man. It is odd how often I have to write those words of the Israelis who stand out conspicuously, small as they are, among a people not by any means small in physique.

This little man has been cudgelling the fortunes of the Jews in what has now become Israel since the early days of the British Mandate. Curiously, perhaps, he was admired by many Arabs of those days. When sought after by the Mandatory Police and the British Army who were then rounding up 'dangerous men', Aba Khoushy was given sanctuary in a Druse village north of Haifa, and remained there in hiding until the scare was over.

His city is kept as clean as a Dutch doorstep. Its entrances have been turned into broad, tree-planted avenues. Its public facilities are efficient. Its civic buildings have a certain grandeur. Business quarters in the lower city, close to the port, are functional rather than beautiful but have a worthy solidity about them. Its shopping streets glitter brightly. They do not approach the smart and over-loaded shopping streets of Tel Aviv but serve modestly a population of relatively modest needs; as, of course, is right and proper in a city of staunch trade-unionists. The residential quarters of the city, clambering to the top of Carmel and then spreading themselves over the easy, far-seeing summit, are shady and homely looking.

Haifa exerts the fascination common to international ports: ships of all maritime nations come and go; sailors stroll the streets and fill the small bars; odours – I had almost said of frankincense and myrrh, but anyway of cargoes from Accra, Dakar, Somaliland and the customary western ports, float to one's nostrils and provoke dreams of distant voyages. There are ships' chandlers with their big, magic stores; great bonded warehouses; truckloads of goods moving in and out of customs sheds; grain elevators; the perpetual crank and wrangle of windlasses and swinging cranes; disembarking passengers from half the world, passport in hand – or those without passport, clutching bundles, shepherding children, half frightened, half wondering as they shuffle their way past Jewish guards into Jewish buses waiting to take them along Jewish roads to Jewish villages.

The great thing about Haifa is, of course, Mount Carmel. If I were a Jew and were approaching for the first time Koestler's 'Twice Promised Land', and the approach were towards Haifa, surely the sight of Carmel against the sky would send me to my knees. It is a massive rampart, pale blue as the sun rises behind it and translucent rose and violet as the sun speeds into the sea – and speed swiftly it does in these parts at the end of day. Carmel is a rising up of the land at its sea-edge as though to say: Here am I: I am your welcome and your shield and behind me is your livelihood and your peace of mind. Like so many of Palestine's mountain masses, Carmel has been grandly composed; its line and balance are impressive. And about its pedestal flows the blue, swinging bay of Acre, with the ancient, cool, tranquil town of Acre hoarding its memories by the bay's northern curve.

Much of the shipping in Haifa harbour is Haifa-registered. The development of Israel's merchant fleet is one of the most spectacular examples of the nation's venturesomeness. In 1947 the Jews owned and sailed four vessels aggregating 6,000 tons displacement. The ships were second-hand craft used for the carrying of immigrants, often illegally, and some cargo. Today, Israel's fleet of 34 ships totals 192,613 tons and includes passenger ships, some of which ply the course between Haifa and New York. Its oil-driven cargo vessels and tankers are as efficient as any that sail the seas, and, with the passenger traffic, contribute an important foreign currency income to the earnings of the State. The most surprising things about it all is the fact that this tidy little fleet, which is rapidly expanding, is manned by Israelis. Not very long ago one would have laughed at the idea of a transatlantic vessel captained by a Jew and manned in every department by Jews. But it is a laughing matter no longer. Palestine and then Israel have made the Jew into a contradiction of what most of us expect him to be.

As a shipping and industrial centre, Haifa has a powerful community of workers. Between Haifa and Acre, and against the base of Carmel, are some of the biggest and most valuable industrial concerns in Israel, or for that matter in the Middle East. They include iron foundries, cement works, plant for the manufacture of household goods and electrical appliances, big works for the production of chemicals and fertilizers from raw materials mined in the Negev, and, of course, the Haifa refineries, which today refine only the local requirements of the State of Israel. The most important of these industrial plants are the property of the Trade Union Confederation, *Histadrut*, which exercises on the affairs of Israel an influence only slightly less than that of the Government itself.

The fact that Tel Aviv-Jaffa is a city of 370,000 people, with all the agitation and appurtenances of big, modern cities; that Jerusalem, as befits a house built upon rock, is a town of dignity and quiet grace; and that Haifa is a rapidly developing shipping and industrial centre: – none of this is particularly surprising. It is when you come to places like the Beersheba of today, or the Red Sea port of Eilat, on the Gulf of Akaba, or to Askalon, just this side of Gaza, that surprise is fitting. Beersheba and all around it, like Eilat and all around it, and indeed like almost the whole of Israel south of Tel Aviv, are examples of highly successful colonization: successful socially as well as economically; and likely, as the years go by and there is the dispensation of peace, to become populous and productive, although much of the region until a few years ago was given over exclusively to Beduin tribes with their goats and melon-patches and their shifting hair-tents.

3

Those who remember Beersheba when it was wholly an Arab town will spare that memory a romantically regretful sigh. It was a kind of Beduin market town; and in the course of a brief visit on the way through to Sinai and down to Suez, quite enchanting. It lay there in the dry hot sun, nothing else but desert or apparent desert for miles. Its one long, dusty street smelled of camel harness and freshly-brewed coffee and shone with brass and copper vessels and the clasping silver of bracelets and anklets on dark women. Wares to attract the Bedu hung from white and yellow walls under plaited straw awnings. Embroidered saddle-cloths were spread to catch the eye. Every third shop was a grain merchant's. The street was noisy with the jangle of bells from the necks of lead-camels; the braying of overloaded asses; the tinkle of beads worn by scarred and often jet-black Bedu women and their children; the cursing of caravan men and the shrill bartering in the grain and harness shops. Every now and then a Bedu horseman would plunge his steed down the street, raising a fine dust unless the water-cart had just gone through. Only rarely did the steed look like what we fondly visualize as the desert nomad's mount. Usually it was small in size, and, although undoubtedly Arab in origin, betrayed humble breeding and a lifetime of diligent cropping at salty herbs. But the average Bedu will ride even a listless ass with something of spectacle. He sits his beast proudly and gives to it a measure of his own pride.

And then there was war. The Egyptians occupied Beersheba for a time in 1948. Yigal Alon with his daring *Palamch* chased them out of the town and swept them and all their army into Sinai and against the sea at Gaza. When the Egyptians fled, the settled inhabitants of Beersheba fled with them. When the Israelis entered Beersheba there was not an Arab to be seen, not a camel or an ass; and presently the whole Negev region, of which Beersheba was the centre, lay open to the victorious Jews. The Armistice Agreement left the Israelis in possession and nothing short of military conquest will ever

164

persuade them to give it up. It is the heart and soul of the southern lands that stir in the Israeli, and especially in Ben Gurion, a mystical fervour owing little to the fact that Abraham sojourned there and Hagar suckled Ishmael beside its wells; and much to the promise of a spacious region at one time able to support a chain of Nabataean settlements whose inhabitants irrigated the land from rock-hewn water-cisterns and, apparently, grew abundant food.

What the Nabataeans did, says Ben Gurion, the Israelis can do better. Big irrigation projects dependent on the waters of the River Jordan have been planned and they will come about one day. Meanwhile, parts of the northern Negev are getting water piped from the Yarkon River, which runs into the sea near Tel Aviv; and the sparse rains are put to good purpose. The straight, white lines of settlement after settlement mark the tawny triangle with its base between Beersheba and the Gaza Strip and its apex just south of Rehovot. There are one or two settlements in the central Negev, which graze sheep and cattle. Here and there hydroponic stations have been set up. Scientists engaged by the State are actively experimenting with food-plants that may favour the soil and climate of the southern Negev, and new means of de-salting these long-neglected acres are being tried out. Where plant growth is improbable there is diligent search for minerals: phosphates in abundant quantities have been found; Solomon's copper mines are being worked at; clays of high industrial value are being pulled from the earth. No oil has been found but the fascination of looking for it in a region where, according to some geologists, it should be, preserves the oil-rig as an occasional feature of the landscape from Beersheba to Eilat.

How far the Negev is really capable of economic exploitation and of supporting the hundreds of thousands of colonists foreshadowed by Mr. Ben Gurion and the enthusiasts of the Ministry of Development, I cannot tell. The Israelis are confident. For my own part, the place looks drained of almost everything likely to be needed for the sustenance of human beings. In appearance it is a yellow desert with theatrical mountain ridges flung across it. How the Nabataeans or anyone else could have made a fair living out of it I have no notion, in spite of the much-publicized findings of that handsome and fervent American archaeologist, Doctor Nelson Gluck, by whose testimony the Negev must have been not merely inhabited but even overcrowded during the first few centuries of this era. However that may be, of one thing we can be sure: if it is possible to settle the Negev and make it fruitful, the Israelis will do it.

What they have done at Beersheba perhaps is a token of what they can do in the whole region. At its best, Arab Beersheba never had more than two thousand settled inhabitants. Today there are something like thirty thousand Jews resident in the town and earning their keep at a pretty high standard. Where there were harness shops there are now book stores. Where there were grain sheds there are now pharmacies. Where there were hitching-posts there are now petrol stations. The built-up area is at least three times what it was. There is a hospital, an up-to-date and extremely comfortable rest-house for visitors. There is a fair hotel and several good coffee houses; and all the retail shops a man and his family with a European background are likely to need. Instead of the jangle of camel-bells and the jingle of beads, there is the sound of hammering from one bustling workshop after another. Tractors and agricultural machinery from Canada, America and Britain are drawn up where a few years ago camels sprawled and snorted and asses chewed straw. The romantic has made way for the progressive. It has done so the world over. Beersheba could not evade the process.

But every Thursday some of the errant romance is brought back. Thursday is market day at Beersheba. Beduin from the several tribes that came back to the Negev in the years immediately following the Armistice Agreements, and which have been as loyal to the Israelis as Beduin ever have been to lordly masters exercising authority from a distance, crowd into town with their animals and produce, buy and sell among themselves and the Jews, and turn the occasion into something like a carnival, with good humour on all sides and story-tellers squatting in the shade of an acacia, and the gayest little children in the world running wild, and Sheikh Muhammed, acknowledged leader of the Beduin of south Israel, moving about grandly in his rich robes for all the world like a Sheikh out of Hollywood. Alas! He mounts no charger. He comes and goes in a handsome Buick.

Israel's Beduin policy, like that of the late Ibn Saud, is to transform the nomad into a fixture. On the whole, the policy has worked well. The tribes around Beersheba now cultivate wide lands and pasture their herds in areas reckoned to be their rightful property. Power-driven agricultural machinery has been loaned them by the State and, perhaps for the first time anywhere in Arabia, a Bedu in gown and *Kefiya* can now be seen in the driving seat of a tractor-drawn plough or Massey-Harris harvester. It is an odd and surprising spectacle. But in many ways not more so than the spectacle of a former Jewish tradesman from Warsaw or Casablanca in open-necked shirt and khaki trousers digging irrigation ditches on land adjoining that of the Beduin.

Jewish settlers from surrounding villages and especially from the long-established settlements over against the Gaza Strip, turn to Beersheba for many of their needs and for the agreeable excitement of a day's outing. Askalon is closer but is less of a market town and more a kind of colonial garden city. In the old days, settlements of the south looked to Tel Aviv as the source of their supplies, just as settlements of the north looked to Haifa. Efforts were made to turn Rishon le Zion and Rehovot into southern market towns; and an artificial centre, Afuleh, with opera house and all, was built to serve the settlements between Carmel and the hills lifting towards Lake Tiberias. But decentralization has been a slow process. Beersheba has helped it forward in the south, and the town has developed at such a rate that today it gives the impression of bursting at the seams.

Its air of bustle and growth is due in part to the fact that it has become an important road junction. The main highway from the north to Eilat, on the Gulf of Akaba, passes through it. From it runs the paved road to the Potash Works at Sdom (Sodom) on the Dead Sea, and west to the new port of Ashdod, the terminus of the oil pipeline running from the Eilat tanks by way of Beersheba.

4

The road from Beersheba to Eilat is a smooth-surfaced highway that can be used by any kind of motor vehicle from the regular Tel-Aviv–Eilat passenger buses and the jeeps of the frontier police to the low-slung cars of the tourist. It is a road worth travelling whatever its beginning and whatever its end. I have done the journey three times. The first one took nine hours from Beersheba to Eilat; the second took eight hours; the third took five. It can be done easily nowadays in a matter of five hours. The way sets off by wady slope and volcanic crater country with scarcely a sign of vegetation. Then it rises through stark hills to the lean, thrusting ridge that walls the great Wady Araba cutting down from the Dead Sea to the Red Sea.

It is moon-country. Dry, soaring ridges crested with pinnacles that look like poised spears against the sky – on and on they go, desolate, lifeless, in colours of purple, tawny, steel, and rose according to the hour of the day and the intensity of shadow. The colours lie flatly upon it, cover it like the pigmentation of a tightly-drawn skin ready to tear apart from the hidden muscular effort underneath. So indeed the earth must have looked when the oceans were rolled back and the sun shone upon the first day. These lean ranges, cutting and twisting their way to the Red Sea, have a kind of tormented rigidity as if within them were chained forces capable, once their bonds were broken, of splitting the whole land all over again and bringing back the oceans that had been rolled away in the Beginning.

The road comes down to the Araba steeply. One feels acutely the sense of being on the other side of things. It goes on through scrub country. The scrub gives way at one place to fields of tomatoes, pale but hopeful outcome of a small settlement over on the right, in the direction of King Solomon's copper mines. This side the great wady is Israel, the other side Jordan. The sea glitters from its narrow gulf and then in a few minutes comes Eilat, fifteen minutes' sculling distance across the head of the gulf from Jordan's port of Akaba; and over there, where the hills are low, is Saudi Arabia; and straight down from Elath on the western side of the gulf, there where hills mount to the sky, is Egypt. And from behind the gaunt stockade of stone flows Sinai south and west, with the law-giving Mount somewhere away over the gleaming edge of the cliffs.

It is incredible country all the way from Beersheba to Eilat and beyond. One feels that just such an environment did God create for man on the first day and for the handing down of His Law; and through such a land was it proper that the Israelites should pass in humility and awe and with a reasonable amount of grumbling on their way to Canaan. And here, as might have been expected, did that remarkable and insufficiently documented lady, the Queen of Sheba, land from her royal vessel and proceed on her way to do homage to Solomon the King. That is the kind of country it is. It is the kind of country that gives validity to myth and drives home starkly, as it drove it home to Abraham and Moses, the uniqueness and solitariness of God.

Here, then, against the coral shore of the Red Sea, is the new, white-and-red, Israeli port and township of Eilat. It is a conspicuous example of Israel's gift for colonization. Eilat, now with three thousand souls in permanent residence, is a bright, proud, eager little place with, as far as I could make out from talks with harbour-men, shopkeepers, rug-weavers, fishermen and teachers, no hankering after the northern fleshpots and no doubt about Eilat's brave destiny. A young, sturdy, freckled woman, who had come from Tel Aviv to teach in the school, told me she had chosen to go to Eilat because the place seemed to her to be 'full of imagination'. I asked her what she meant by that expression, and she said:

'Well, between Abraham and Eilat there is nothing much, is there? Only time. It is like starting all over again, where the Israelites began, not where they left off.'

She said it in the natural way these young Israelis have, of saying things like that. While she said it she was pinning back her hair against the north wind that blows too consistently in these parts. The Jews have an acute sense of history; of their own anyway. And I suppose that is what the freckled schoolteacher meant by saying that Eilat was full of imagination. I would not have said that the Israelites 'began' anywhere in this neighbourhood; but it is easy to believe that they did; and certainly there has been as good as nothing between Abraham and this small fervent Israeli township at the head of the Gulf of Akaba.

The harbour provides the reason for Eilat's existence; but it is not yet a busy harbour. Small ships usually on charter from a Greek line run between Eilat and East African ports. Tankers fetch Iranian oil, which is pumped into storage tanks and then piped by way of Beersheba to Ashdod, where Israeli tankers pick it up and carry it to Haifa for refining. Several corvettes of the Israeli navy, brought overland from Haifa, lie moored at one of the new quays. Fishing vessels and glass-bottomed boats through which tourists can look at the coral of the gulf's bed, clutter the small basin. When a ship of some size comes in, the occasion for an hour or two becomes a kind of holiday: all who can get away from workshop, store, office, and schoolroom crowd to the water's edge to watch and shout greetings. Part of the excitement may be due to the fact that every ship coming up the gulf was compelled, until the Sinai campaign, to run the gauntlet of Egypt's batteries at Ras Nasrani, which dominates the narrow channel giving entrance to the Gulf. Ras Nasrani was occupied by the Israelis in the first days of the Sinai campaign. When U.N. compelled the Israelis to pull out, a U.N. force took over, which has been there ever since. It is almost due to give the place back to the Egyptians; and when that happens it will be interesting to see whether Egypt reverts to the harassing of ships bound for Eilat. If it does, said Mr. Ben Gurion at the township's tenth anniversary celebrations, Israel will give a sharp answer.

But it is seldom that ships of any distinction come here. They will one day. The new harbour, south of the old, should be completed soon and will be fit, they tell me, to take vessels up to 6,000 tons. When the projected railway from the Potash Works at Sdom has been built, cargoes of potash for ports eastwards will go from Eilat instead of from Haifa. The Israeli Government is convinced that a valuable trade can be worked up between Eilat and Far Eastern countries, especially Japan. The development of Israel's trade with the Far East has been hampered in the past by the obstinate refusal of the Egyptian Government to allow Israeli vessels, or for that matter Israeli cargoes in ships of other flags, to pass through the Suez Canal.

A minor Eilat industry is the polishing of semi-precious stonex. I mention it because of the curious means by which I first learned of the existence of these stones in the cliffs, and saw what was, I suppose, the birth of the industry.

I had travelled to Eilat with the then Minister of Development, Doctor Dov Joseph, of whom I have written in connexion with his governorship of Jerusalem during the 1948 siege. Israel's Development Ministry breeds an extraordinary enthusiasm among those who conduct its fortunes; or perhaps attracts the enthusiast. At any rate, it is an optimistic and enterprising Ministry. Given the chance and the budget, it would build harbours, railways and roads all over the country, put down industries, dig for oil, mine for almost every known metal, and have the Negev give up riches no one else ever dreamed of its possessing. Doctor Joseph, as Minister, was as eager and enthusiastic as any of his young advisers. As we travelled down from Beersheba, every now and then he would turn excitedly, point to a conical hill or something of the kind, and say:

'Look at that! Almost certain to be valuable minerals there. Phosphates or something. All it needs is a railway.'

And a little farther along:

'See? The railway could run through there. Easy country. Open all this area. Give work to thousands.'

At Elath, the day following our arrival, we were seated at the back of a command car ready to be taken on a visit to some granite quarries. A bronzed man in his forties, carrying a Gladstone bag, came up and begged leave to talk to the Minister. The Minister gave him leave and then heard a quiet account of how, for the taking, there were showers of semi-precious stones in the cliff-sides of narrow wadies, or ravines, running laterally from the Eilat shore and beginning about three or four miles from the town.

The Minister smiled as he repeated the tale to me. But the quiet bronzed man in his loose shirt and khaki trousers stood patiently by. He said something to the Minister in Hebrew and then, balancing himself on the step that gave access to the command car from the back, opened his Gladstone bag and spilled the contents to the floor of the car: topazes, amethysts, turquoises all manner of softly-coloured jewels fell in a heap. Without knowing anything about the value of the stones, we were impressed; and when the quiet man suggested our going out there with him to one of the cliffs to see for ourselves, the Minister agreed. The man jumped in beside us. Away we went.

Some four or five miles along the road skirting the Gulf we turned right, into a wady. At a signal from our guide with the Gladstone bag, the truck was halted. We all got out and followed the man, who carried with him an ordinary hammer. He hardly spoke. Once, looking up the wady, he turned to me and said in English:

'Pretty country.'

It is the last thing I would have said of this harsh, bare landscape.

When we came to the cliff-side the quiet man took his hammer and tapped gently at the russet-streaked and yellow wall of stone. The stone flaked away at his tapping, like the outside crust of well-baked bread. And there, sure enough, in among the crumbling flakes were amethysts, topazes, turquoises, and goodness knows what else. The Minister was impressed and so was I. It was like digging up a treasure chest from the palm-fringed sands of some far-away, fairy-tale island, and running one's fingers through jewels hidden here half a thousand years ago.

When the Minister returned to Jerusalem a few days later, he saw to it that the quiet man should be given the necessary licence and credits to start a workshop in Eilat for the polishing of the stones. The workshop prospers, I am told, but is unlikely to develop into anything much. Export markets have no need of Eilat's semi-precious stones, and, from all accounts, have little need of such stones anyway, because the imitation jewels look as well and, in some instances, better, and are equally suitable for the decorative requirements of modern women. The main thing is that the quiet man with the Gladstone bag is thoroughly happy, and doing well enough for himself and his family.

Nineteen

THE State grew. You could watch it grow over all of its nearly eight thousand square miles. A journey through the northern Negev; or down the Jerusalem corridor; or into the Lachish area that spreads from ancient Gath to where a lonely frontier runs under the Hebron hills; or along the green and dune-gold plain of Sharon; or through the Vale of Esdraelon and down to Lake Tiberias; or upwards into the purple of northern Galilee: – no matter where, every such journey became a surprise because always there was so much there that was not there before: new settlements, new villages, new townships, newly terraced slopes, newly planted valleys, broad acres of food and industrial crops, new factories, new roads.

Statistics enough can be had for the asking, which indicate the pace at which this exultant, thrusting little country has moved. The national income has more than doubled since 1950. So, of course, has the national Budget. One cannot argue prosperity from this especially as more than half of the State's hard-currency income comes from German reparations, U.S. Grants-in-Aid, and from the contributions of international Jewry. Reparations will come to an end in 1964 so that the State's foreign income will be docked of about 70 million dollars annually, and there must always be the risk of a cut in U.S. grants and a falling-off in Diaspora contributions. On the other hand, enormous sums derived from these funds have been shrewdly spent and are beginning to show steadily increasing returns. The trade gap still yawns crazily for such a small country, but exports have gone up from 28 million dollars in 1949 to 245.6 million dollars in 1958. Land under cultivation in 1949 was reckoned at 412,500 acres. Now it runs to over one million acres, with an irrigated area more than four times what it was in 1949. Seventy-five per cent of the nation's food consumption is grown locally – something of an achievement for a population that has expanded from between six and seven hundred thousand to over two million during the same period.

The agitation of growth up and down this sunlit land was a

heartening thing. It shocked economists of course. Israel's whole existence and survival are a shock to conventional calculations. And it is true, for that matter, that chances were taken recklessly. At first the people waiting in Germany, Rumania, along the Adriatic, in North Africa, were brought in too quickly. But somehow, after a year or two, they were settled in and now most of them are happy and doing well for themselves and the State. And after a while the tempo of immigration was revised to bring it nearer to absorptive capacity at all ranges.

But what is absorptive capacity? Here is a country relatively poor in natural resources. In 1948 it declared its independence and at once had a war on its hands. It fought and won the war and then loaded itself up with penniless new immigrants until the population it started out with had become more than trebled. In spite of war and the continued hostility of all its neighbours, the State had to set about creating absorptive capacity at the same time as it was organizing itself into the complicated patterns and functions of a modern State. That organization was just as much a part of absorptive capacity as housing and land cultivation. Government was not merely a matter of holding elections and forming a Ministry. It had to be made to work and to work efficiently. Local Government was less of a problem but that, too, had to be built up over the years to meet the pressure of phenomenal immigration.

An intricate Judiciary had to be formed. It was formed, and today is something for the State to be proud of. I have already referred to the building up of a police force. All these institutions of State could be watched as they grew just as the housing and the land cultivation and the road building and the afforestation and the laying down of irrigation pipes could be watched if one were quick enough to keep pace with it. But these things were not all. Absorptive capacity meant also an astonishing expansion of scientific research, of which some of the main and immediate objects have been the fertilization of arid zones, the de-salination of water, the provision of solar power. Surprising progress has been made in all three directions.

Side by side with these urgent developments were two others of immense importance, the need of which grew year by year at a rate out of all proportion to that of such annual expansion in other countries. These were health and education facilities.

Luckily, Israel had a highly efficient health system to start off with.

This was thanks to the so-called Workers' Sick Fund set up by the Trade Union Confederation, or *Histadrut*, during the period of the British Mandate, and to the *Hadassah*, an organization of American Zionist women who founded hospitals in Jerusalem and Tel Aviv. Today, the Workers' Sick Fund, with 16 hospitals, 910 clinics, 15 convalescent homes, 198 mother-and-child welfare stations, employing one-third of the nation's medical practitioners and serving a membership covering two-thirds of the total population, has a budget more than double that of the Ministry of Health, which in its turn has 17 hospitals and a nation-wide system of welfare clinics. But these figures mean little, except as evidence of the national effort over the past ten years to keep up with the population increase.

But the effort covers enormously more than that.

Pretty well half the present population of Israel came to the country in need of rehabilitation, physical as well as economic and in many instances psychological, too. As fast as the new immigrants entered and were disposed in villages, towns and city suburbs, the health and welfare oganizations of the State had to scurry around in search of qualified staff and then set up new clinics and special help stations. Multitudes arrived either under-nourished or badly nourished or a bundle of nerves or, worse still, a bundle of super-stitions. Many of them were ignorant of the elementary rules of hygiene and had no notion of pre-natal and post-natal care. The first four hundred thousand to come in after 1948 raised the child mortality rate of Palestine Jews from an estimated 20 per thousand to over 50 per thousand. That has been got down to 30 per thousand and will fall still lower in a year or two.

It is not merely a question of providing adequate doctors, nurses, and other qualified helpers, or of setting up the required number of clinics and advice stations and fitting them out. Most of the new-comers had no liking for medical and welfare busybodies, who wanted to stick needles into their children or subject them to devilish contrivances like X-ray.

'I've borne thirteen children,' said one woman to me. 'I've lost five but I've brought up eight. Do these people think they can teach me anything about being a mother?'

I saw much of that woman and her surviving children, which have been reduced from eight to six. But she has changed her mind about the special clinics and child welfare stations. The older children persuaded her to change her mind. And by one means and another most of these people from backward countries were persuaded in the long run to accept the health and welfare organizations as at least on the level of the post office: a facility for their benefit, not a tedious and suspect interference in their domestic affairs.

Doctor Fritz Yekutiel, chief of the Health Ministry's Department of Epidemology, believes that tens of thousands of young lives have been saved from death or crippling disease during the past few years thanks to the presence of clinics and mother-and-child welfare stations within the new communities set up all over the country.

'Running to the doctor when there was obvious sickness would not have been enough,' he said. 'We have had to concentrate on preventive measures and that has meant what amounts to a house-to-house educational campaign. It has taken a lot of time and a lot of patience but we've got a lot to show for it already.'

Doctor Yekutiel, who has worked himself as thin as a papyrus-reed, lives in a modest Jerusalem house on a salary that would horrify an American or even a British G.P., let alone a specialist. The State of Israel depends a great deal on the public spirit of dedicated men and women: too much so. But the public spirit is there, and as long as it lasts Israel will continue to be the exhilarating country it is.

2

Good health and good education for the children – these are the intense objectives of Israel, which is not merely consolidating a political and social conception known as a sovereign State but is, indeed, creating something very like a new race.

Whether the educational standards are as good as they pretend to be, I cannot judge. There are good schools and less good schools as in every country and, as in most countries, a shortage of qualified teachers. But the Israeli at every age is keen to acquire knowledge, and, to this common urge among the children passing into secondary schools is added the encouragement of example given by their leaders from Ben Gurion down. The Prime Minister, who has also held the portfolio of Defence, somehow has found time to master ancient Greek over the past ten years. The first Chief of Staff of the armed forces, General Dori, has become Principal of the Israeli Institute of Technology, one of the main seats of Higher Learning in Israel. The next Chief of Staff, General Yadin, resigned so that he could take up post-graduate studies at Oxford. General Moshé Dayan, Chief of Staff at the time of the Sinai Campaign, resigned in 1957 to become a student of the Hebrew University.

That kind of thing seems to be going on among Israelis at all levels. Recently I wanted to talk certain matters over with the Military Attaché at the Israel Embassy in London, Colonel Neuman. I called him up on the telephone. His secretary apologized for Colonel Neuman's absence, saying: 'He's sitting for his degree in physics at London University.'

Over 350,000 Israeli children attend elementary or secondary schools and there are something like 7,500 students at the three main institutions of higher learning – the Hebrew University in Jerusalem, the Institute of Technology in Haifa, and the School of Law and Economics in Tel Aviv. These figures are roughly four times what they were in 1949, and it should not be difficult to imagine what this has meant in terms of school accommodation and staff. One result of the expansion is that the highest single allocation, after Defence, in recent national Budgets has gone to the Ministry of Education and Culture.

The Israeli youth is a good youth, physically and mentally. He matures, perhaps, a trifle too soon, and is more tempted than the youth of other countries to feel himself a cut above his elders. That is due, I think, to the fact that he speaks the national language better than most of his elders, and feels himself more profoundly an Israeli than they are. One of the most devoted of Mr. Ben Gurion's followers was a certain English Jew, Harry Beilin. I knew him well, admired and liked him. He had come to Palestine during the period of the British Mandate, working in the cause of Zionism and working hard; and had brought with him a delightful and remarkably intelligent English wife, a Gentile. He died recently, although only in his forties; and on hearing the news of his death I remembered a conversation with him, in his pleasant home in the German Colony. We had been discussing the progress made by the State in a matter of ten years, and I said to Beilin:

'You know, Israel owes you and people like you a very great deal.'

'What for? If I have done anything for Israel it is exactly the same as every other parent in the country has done – in my case much less than most parents. I've contributed a daughter. A damned good-looking and clever young woman, too, even if I do say so myself. But we, I mean people even of my generation, are not Israel, not really. The true Israel will come when most of us who worked hard to put up the framework of the State are dead and the new generation has taken over. Our children are Israelis willy-nilly. The rest of us have elected to be called Israelis and are as loyal as hell but we can't help still being English, American, German, Polish, Russian, North African, and God knows what.'

3

Well, there it was, the outcome of a few crammed years of solid building: the building of hospitals, schools, homes, farms, harbours, factories, roads, railways; the building of a healthy, competent, proud people, an economy to support them and a national administration appropriate to a free, aspiring community. And the building of security, physical security, which cost too much money and took too much time but without which the whole thing that had been built up could have been made to topple to bits in as many days as it had taken years to raise up. In the building up of this people and the environment proper to any civilized nation of our day there had been mistakes, failures, even shameful things. The fact remains that something like a miracle was done: done overnight if one relates it to the growth of even the youngest of the established nations among which Israel now sits at U.N.

But in one thing affecting the stability and even the survival of all this, Israel had failed; or the Big Powers had failed; or U.N. had failed. The enemies of 1948, when the State was founded, were still enemies. What had been formal war in 1948 had continued year after year and in defiance of Armistice Agreements, Security Council warnings and the earnest endeavours of the U.N. Secretary General, Dag Hammarskjold, in person and on the spot, as frontier warfare, diplomatic warfare, and psychological warfare. What, said the new immigrant, is the good of a home if its windows have to be covered with steel netting to keep out grenades? What comfort can we get from schools and clinics that every now and then get blown to bits by Egyptian or Jordanian explosives? Reprisal action was all very well and did indeed bring periods of tranquillity in areas directly affected but then at once there was an outcry at U.N. and in the world's Press, and the Powers who had done nothing to help Israel pacify its frontiers immediately increased their arms supplies to the Arabs; not, of course, as an encouragement to attack Israel, perhaps even under the impression that the Israelis wanted to attack the Arabs. The one thing certain is that the consistent flow of armaments to the Arab countries without any balancing supply to Israel, did not serve the cause of Middle East peace. And, as Israel was considered by all the Arab States to be their common enemy, and the violent destruction of that country their common and loudly avowed purpose, small wonder that Israeli anxiety could not be allayed by soothing words from London, Washington and U.N., and that it became acute when, early in 1956, shiploads of heavy armaments as well as jet-powered bomber and fighter aircraft began to reach Egypt from Soviet Russia.

Israel at that time had nothing remotely approaching the quality, let alone the quantity, of the tanks, artillery and aircraft now streaming into Colonel Nasser's reorganized and expanded Egyptian Army. Egypt had enough, at least by paper calculations, to make short work of all that Israel had built up in the absurdly narrow space between its frontiers and the sea.

Israel had every right to be anxious. In fact, the anxiety was largely official. The average Israeli had become accustomed to scares especially if he lived in the well-settled areas and could sleep peacefully at night instead of waking fearfully every time a dog barked. Every season had had its crises, which, somehow, had passed. War had seemed likely a dozen times during the past five years. Tension had been the rule, not the exception. War would come one day but the general impression was that the Arabs were not yet ready, and that Colonel Nasser, even taking into account his Soviet arms and aircraft, would not move against Israel until he was doubly certain of himself.

To be sure, Nasser's *Feyadeen* were asking for trouble. These organized commando-type gangs, recruited by a special unit of the Egyptian Army Intelligence, trained at the military base of Nakhl, in Sinai, and in the Gaza Strip, from which they operated under regular army briefing, represented a big advance in determined hostility and ruthless technique over the marauding gangs armed with rifles and grenades that had terrorized the frontier areas ever since the signing of the Armistice Agreements. The *Feyadeen* penetrated deep into southern Israel.

According to Israeli military experts these operations were intended by Colonel Nasser to 'soften up' the civilian population of the south and retard settlement, especially in those areas through which the Egyptian and Jordanian armies would make junction in the event of war. On March 11th of 1956 Israel cited before the Security Council 180 *Feyadeen* and other 'acts of aggression' against its people and territory carried out from the Gaza Strip. At the same time, Israel complained of the massive build-up of Egyptian troop concentrations along her southern borders. Then, in May, Mr. Hammarskjold came out and, as usually happened after his soothing ministrations, there was something akin to tranquillity for a couple of months. There were occasional raids from over the borders, of course, and by mid-August it looked as if the *Feyadeen* were starting up again. But nobody outside the inner political and military circles seemed to think that war was on its way. For one thing, Colonel Nasser, in July, had announced his intention to nationalize the Suez Canal (which Israel officially decided was a quite reasonable thing to do). He was busy making fun of the angry British and French; fending off international mediation; conferring with the Russians. He had enough on his hands, or so it seemed that midsummer and early autumn, without provoking Israel.

And it was hot. September is a bad month in these parts. The *khamseen* came greyly out of the desert to blow a hot, oleaginous grit into our faces. We were tired. Everyone was tired. Obviously matters would quieten down now. Nasser would keep close to his Suez Canal and let Israel wait. Israel would realize that it was no use doing anything dramatic at a time when the world was interested only in what Nasser was going to do about Anglo-French interests in the Canal and what England and France were going to do about whatever it was that he did do.

In October I decided to take a holiday. Cautiously, I paid to a situation no worse than usual the compliment of acknowledging its capacity to get very much worse than usual. Instead of taking home-leave, which was my due, I went to the pleasant seaside resort of Herzlia, only twenty minutes' run from the Ministry of Defence, the Public Information office, the Censorship Department and the cable-head at Tel Aviv.

Twenty

I ARRIVED at my rented cottage in Herzlia on 17th October. For the first few days all went well. The *khamseens* had ended and the sun, although it hit hard, was tempered by a breeze out of the west. The sea rolled in at leisurely pace, creamy petticoats showing from under the blue as it sprawled in a succession of arcs along one of the finest beaches of the eastern Mediterranean. There was good swimming, good undersea fishing up where the rocks were that had formed in antiquity the harbour of Apollonia; and good, firm, pale-yellow sand to lie upon.

Occasionally, one of the new *Mystère* fighter planes streaked over the sea: noisy things, which frightened the children on the beach. But there was nothing in that. Israel is a small, narrow country. It is difficult in such a small country to keep out of the way of the Security forces; and the jets had to be flown along the coast or risk the charge of overflying into a neighbour's air space within a few seconds of the take-off. The *Mystères* came by and meant, to me, nothing more sinister than a nuisance. I was glad the Israelis had them, wondered how many they had and how long it would take them to train pilots.

I listened to the news on the wireless and now and then telephoned newspaper friends or the Public Information Office. Nothing much was happening. There had been some damaging raids from across the Jordanian frontier in the Qalqilya area. That was nothing new. What was new was a reprisal action in which the Israeli avengers came up against the Arab Legion and suffered casualties. It was unusual for the attackers in a reprisal action to get badly hurt and some of us who, whilst accepting the reprisal policy as unavoidable, had come to think that the Army reacted too readily and too heavily to what in many instances were bandit raids for which only the bandits themselves could be held responsible, felt that the lesson of Qalqilya might have healthy consequences. The incident required a run into Tel Aviv, a talk with the Army people and the despatch of a couple of cables. Then all was quiet again and I went back to my beach.

A few days later, on the 25th October, it was announced that Egypt, Jordan and Syria had concluded secret military talks with a decision to unify the armed forces of the three countries under Egyptian supreme command. That was bad. Clearly, it was a move directed against Israel, which now would have co-ordinated Arab armies up against all its land frontiers and waiting only for the word *go* from Cairo. What was Colonel Nasser up to? For that matter, what was Soviet Russia up to?

In 1947 the Russians had eloquently supported the establishment of a Jewish State in Palestine and in 1948 had approved of the despatch of Czechoslovak arms to the embattled new State they had helped to sponsor. Why, then, the conspicuous right-about-turn less than ten years later? I suppose Israel had disappointed the Soviet. It had shown that collectivism in agriculture could be far removed from Communism and that Marxism in the Socialist Left-wing groups could be national, that is to say Zionist, instead of international. Israel began by giving to its foreign policy the label 'Non-Identification with West or East', but before very long it realized that its interests were bound up with the West willy-nilly; and so it dropped the label. Israel did its best to keep up amiable relations with Russia, from whom it hoped, one day, to receive the kind of Jew the country needed badly – technicians, farmers and the like.

It is probable that in Soviet calculations the Israelis had served their purpose by defeating the combined Arab armies in 1948 and thus providing the motive or provocation for the Neguib-Nasser *coup*, from which followed intensified Egyptian nationalism and its team-mate, anti-Western Imperialism. The big opportunity for Moscow came when the United States and Britain turned down Nasser's appeal for money with which to build the new Aswan Dam. Moscow offered to pay and the offer was accepted. Moscow also offered to equip the Egyptian Army, Navy and Air Force; and did so massively. Thus Nasser had found a way of throwing off the 'yoke of Western Imperialism' without his being left out in the cold; and by doing so had become something of a hero to thirty million Arabs. The Russians had bought a much better bargain than Israel ever could have been; and the bargain went up in value when Nasser turned Britain and France out of the Suez Canal. From then on, the foes of the Arabs became the foes of the Soviet Union; and Israel, in Russian propaganda broadcasts as in the broadcasts of the

'Voice of the Arabs' from Cairo, became a 'tool of Western Imperialism'.

That was the state of affairs in the summer of 1956. Probably it was the state of affairs that encouraged Nasser to unify his army with the armies of Jordan and Syria and to feel tempted to lead a new *Jehad*, a Holy War, for the recovery of all Palestine and the extirpation of the usurping State of Israel.

What, if anything, did Ben Gurion intend to do about it?

2

I ran into Tel Aviv to see if I could get an answer to that question; talked with the right people; telephoned the Foreign Ministry in Jerusalem. I scratched my head and tried to analyse the situation as shaped by this latest and most threatening Arab move against Israel. Then I wrote the required despatches.

That was that. War might come, but not in a matter of days. Tension had not touched ceiling and anyway there must surely be a gap between a decision announced from Cairo, Amman and Damascus and the putting of the decision into practice. As for the Israelis, there was no evidence of their readiness to take the field preventively. I went back to the beach at Herzlia and re-settled myself into a mood of holiday.

Next morning, 26th October, the milkman wakened me. I went to the door and the milkman said:

'What do you suppose all those lorries and trucks and things are doing parked over there?'

'Over where?'

'In the vacant plot just across the lane.'

'I thought I had heard a devil of a noise during the night. And up there, too,' I said, pointing to the wooded park on rising ground about a quarter of a mile away.

'Do you think it is mobilization?' I asked.

'How would I know? I'm too old anyway. But let's ask.'

There were trucks, vans, and even city buses coming along the sandy road that led off the main Tel Aviv–Natanya–Haifa road, and moving up among the trees of the park. We went into the lane and stared at the parked vehicles opposite. Mechanics were fussing about among the engines. There were a few men in uniform. We asked what it was all about and were told:

'Mobilization. . . . '

I took the car and ran along the main highway. Strings of heavy vehicles, without loads, were moving along the highway and obviously making for specified assembly points. Here and there, at pick-up stations, were groups of young men in uniform carrying kit and in some instances a weapon, waiting for the first military transport that should pass and have room for them. There was nothing particularly dramatic about the scene: no haste, no visible concentrations of armed soldiers, no unusual movement, as far as I could see, of military armour, half-tracks, command cars; nothing much except the steady assembly of civilian vehicles among trees and in vacant lots, and the idle, waiting groups of uniformed men, never more than seven or eight at a time, at pick-up stations. For the rest, traffic and people were going about their business in the sunlight just as on any other day.

But something was afoot. I went into Tel Aviv. The city looked normal enough but one felt a difference, a certain tightness, almost as if the people in the streets were holding themselves a little straighter, striding more firmly than usual. At the appropriate official source I was told:

'Oh! It's nothing to get excited about. Just a partial mobilization test. Never know what may happen nowadays so the Army thought it a good idea to have a test call-up. After all, ours is ninety-five per cent a reserves army. We have to try out organizational methods every now and then just to see how they work.'

There was nothing more than that to be squeezed from the military or political spokesmen or even from my more exclusive sources: nothing to do, indeed, except report the quote test unquote mobilization of Israel's reserves and then go back to Herzlia, change into bathing things and go swimming.

But something was about to happen. I knew that.

3

It did happen.

It happened three days later. In the early hours of 30th October my telephone rang and I was told of an official communiqué announcing that Israeli armed forces had entered the Sinai Peninsula and were advancing westwards. That was about all the communique told.

So much for the 'test' mobilization. It had been a mobilization for war and had been astonishingly smooth, swift and effective. How complete it had been there was no telling. One knew that the Army could collect about a quarter of a million trained men and women in a few days but it was reasonable to suppose that any such rapid call-up would dislocate the daily routine of national life and bring with it conspicuous spectacle. The mobilization that had begun on October 25th and had been as good as completed by October 29th had brought little apparent dislocation and no remarkable spectacle. It had been a quiet, brilliant piece of organization, as creditable to the loyalty of the Reservists as to the quiet skill of those responsible for bringing them together in a matter of a couple of days as an army ready to march.

But October 30th was a frustrating day for foreign newspaper correspondents and, I suppose, for the Israelis themselves. The military and political authorities would add nothing to the early communiqué. We learned that a Paratroop Brigade was in action westward through Sinai in the direction of the Suez Canal at its southern end, where it flows into the Gulf of Suez. One Battalion of the Brigade had been air-dropped just east of the decisive Mitla Pass. That was about 150 miles from the Israeli frontier and not more than forty miles from the Canal at Port Tewfiq. The rest of the Brigade was pushing westwards by land, in vehicles if the vehicles could manage the sand, the stony wady-beds, the roadless cliffs; and on foot if they could not. They had to clear the Egyptian fortified positions at Kuntilla, Themed and Nakhl, directly in the rear of Mitla, and put a force at the Nakhl crossroads to meet any Egyptian column that might come down from the big northern bases. And if all that went well, and the units of the Paratroop Brigade that had been given an infantry job to do, joining up with the Battalion which had been dropped just east of Mitla, and which sat there fighting off Egyptian columns coming up from the Canal and down from Bir Hasne, to the north, then the assault on the Pass itself would be made.

We came by this information in a fragmentary way but could not use it. Censorship stood firmly between us and our newspapers. What bothered some of us was to know whether it was war or a particularly elaborate raid. There had been much talk about the *Feyadeen* training base at Nakhl, and such as we could learn of the operations carried out between the late afternoon of the 29th and the morning of the 30th put the Israelis on both sides of the Nakhl position. We knew nothing of the moves farther north, against the main Egyptian concentrations around Quseima, el Arish and Rafa. And what were the British and the French about? And why was the U.S. Government evacuating its nationals?

I was received that morning of the 30th by our Ambassador, the astute and courteous Jack Nicholls. He seemed, as we talked, to be as much in the dark as I was and to have been as much surprised by the outcome of the 'test' mobilization as I had been. But he was not in the dark, of course, and probably had not been greatly surprised. He made this remark:

'It looks as if the Israelis are making for the Canal. We can't have an Israeli-Egyptian war going on along the banks of the Canal and I wouldn't be surprised if we and the French decided to do something to keep the two sides apart.'

And, of course, we had so decided. At four o'clock that afternoon the Anglo-French ultimatum was handed to the Egyptian and Israeli Governments. It required that the Egyptians should withdraw their forces ten kilometres west of the Canal and that the Israelis should halt their advance ten kilometres east. The Israelis accepted, the Egyptians, who had no alternative, refused. There was no longer any question about whether the Israeli operations represented an elaborate raid or full-scale war. It was war. And by all the tokens, Israel was going to war against the Egyptians in the company of Britain and France. No one in authority would admit it. Indeed, the Israelis were saying that they disapproved of Anglo-French intervention and for that matter had thought well of Nasser's decision to nationalize the Suez Canal. It was all a trifle confusing and gave every promise of remaining so.

But the Israelis on that day seemed curiously at ease. They are not a fidgety people and have remarkable self-assurance. Their Army system is such that it has become an integral part of the citizen's daily, domestic affairs. Someone comes along, knocks at the door and leaves a note behind, or a post office messenger leaves a telegram behind, and then a husband or a son and perhaps a daughter as well packs a kitbag, slips an automatic rifle over the shoulder, bids good-bye and sets off, a thoroughly trained soldier, to the assigned task. And it is not as if that task or the grand and fearful strategy of war were being designed in some unapproachable, mysterious place where sits a lordly Supreme Command whose personages are known to the people only through the newspapers. Moshé, Haim, Ezra – men everyone has seen about, men like themselves, men they greet in the streets, men who could be anybody's neighbour and who knew half the Reservists by their first name: these, under Ben Gurion, were the leaders. One way and another, therefore, the Israeli Army has remained an intimate affair, intimate within itself and in relation to the people as a whole, so that the confidence, that day, of the Israeli citizen going about his customary tasks was the confidence a man feels in his own household.

The unusual and exciting factor was that Israel seemed to have powerful friends at this critical moment. What else could the Anglo-French ultimatum mean? That evening it was taken for granted that the Israeli invasion of Sinai and what clearly was an imminent Anglo-French military assault on the Suez Canal, had been co-ordinated. The horrid word 'collusion' cropped up only the next day.

In Tel Aviv there was not much evidence of a country at war except at the big, luxury-type Dan Hotel on the seashore. Suddenly, it was emptied of its American visitors, who were being evacuated by air along with the women and children of the U.S. Embassy and Consulates, and whose places at the Dan were being taken by newspaper correspondents flying in from all over the world. One noticed, also, a marked reduction in Tel Aviv's bus services, and in heavy traffic generally. Most of the absent vehicles were far away to the south. One had seen them parked among the trees and in vacant plots off the main road and then all at once they had vanished. Now, one supposed, they were out in the Sinai Desert; many of them, no doubt, held fast by sand drifts, or heeled over among the boulders of some serpentine wady-bed.

My hairdresser, 'Yosh' – a nickname for Josef – was down there, too. An elderly Jew from Rumania had taken his place at the little saloon in Ben Yehuda Street.

'Yosh is on holiday,' said the old man. 'He's making the trip to Cairo in an Egged bus.'

'I hope he gets there.'

'Don't worry. He'll get wherever they tell him to go. He'll be back in a few days.'

The impression that it would be a swift campaign was a common one. That surprised me in view of the newspaper build-up given to Egypt's Russian equipment, and to the strength of the fortified bases in northern Sinai, which, according to reports, had been designed by German military experts. Where confidence hesitated was on the question of the respective air forces. Would Israel be able to protect its cities and towns, from Eilat to Beersheba and Askalon and on by Tel Aviv and Haifa, from the attacks of the Ilyushin bombers in Colonel Nasser's possession?

Nobody knew. The night of that disturbing, venturesome day fell. There was an air-raid alarm somewhere around midnight but nothing happened. We went down to the Dan Hotel's basement shelter but after about twenty minutes went back to the bar, which quickly filled up. A group of young men entered wearing the uniform of the French Air Force.

4

And that same night, at about ten-thirty, the earth-bound, sand-clogged, worn-out paratroopers who had battled overland to join up with their airborne comrades east of the Mitla Pass, made junction. It must have been an exciting re-union. One has been puzzled to know why the bulk of a paratroop brigade had been set an infantry operation when there were infantry regiments enough. The Army, in a paper written by Lt.-Col. Benzion Tehan, has given this explanation:

'It may have seemed wasteful to commit a Paratroop Brigade in the role of an Infantry Brigade on the ground instead of keeping it to the function for which it had been trained. But there were sound reasons for the decision. The overland route to the forward position, known as Parker's Memorial, east of the Mitla Pass, was hard and hazardous. The distance is 125 miles and the track could not be expected to take the weight of the number of vehicles, many of them tracked, needed to move an Infantry Brigade to schedule. Taking all this into account it was considered desirable, as a means of making doubly sure of the junction with the Paratroop Battalion dropped at Parker's Memorial, that a special psychological link should exist between the Column moving overland and the Battalion towards which it was moving, a link that would accentuate the urge to surmount all obstacles, expected and unexpected: the bond of a mother-formation with one of its own units.'

It was a correct assumption and one characteristic of the Israeli High Command's reasoning. All obstacles, 'expected and unexpected', were indeed surmounted; and they had been many. The job had taken thirty hours and cost many vehicles. Luckily, casualties among the men had been few in spite of minefields and the absence of adequate artillery to support the attackers at Themed and Nakhl. And now, ahead of them, rose the decisive Mitla Pass, likely to offer sharp encounter. Behind it, the first of Colonel Nasser's shining new MIG's were preparing to take off, and an armoured column had crossed the Canal and was making in the direction of Parker's Memorial.

None of this did we know on that night of 30th to 31st October. Nor did we know that well to the north an infantry brigade had advanced upon and occupied the key road junction at Quseima. It mopped up the Egyptian outposts along the Kuntilla and Nakhl tracks and took 250 bewildered prisoners. At noon on the 30th the Chief of Staff himself, Major-General Dayan, his black eye-patch covered with dust, turned up at Quseima and ordered the brigade to send a column down the seventy miles of track and drift-sand to join up with the paratroop unit which had been left to defend the Nakhl road junction. That night, as we in Tel Aviv went to our beds puzzled to know what was keeping Nasser's *Ilyushin* bombers grounded, the column from Quseima, using city buses for transport, and supported by a platoon of tanks, pushed, rode, scrambled down through the sand towards Nakhl.

The Quseima intervention of General Dayan was typical of the man and of his Army. That kind of thing happened over and over again during the campaign. Dayan, his cap on one side, his shirt open, his good eye glittering, several times appeared at forward battle positions to urge on the attack or swiftly to shift an operation's emphasis if he thought it necessary. He expected his officers 'to lead, not to push', and was ready himself, if the need should arise, to lead instead of pushing. The Israeli soldier expected no less of his officer and was splendidly equal to such leadership.

We did not know of these several developments that night,

and did not know that an armoured brigade was in action south of Um Gataf and that its reconnaissance unit had slipped through the Dyka Defile to reach the Abu Ageila-Jebel Livni road; and that the main forces of the Israeli Field Army were already poised for the break-through to Ismailya and the daring assault on Nasser's major concentrations against El Arish and Rafa, east of the Gaza Strip.

We knew of none of these things and slept soundly. No bombers came over. But next morning, at breakfast, we learned that a reckless Egyptian destroyer, the *Ibrahim el-Awal*, had made stealthy way to the approaches into Haifa, had lobbed a few shells into the startled waters of the bay without hurt to anything, and then, as it turned tail, had been intercepted by an Israeli naval vessel, boarded and taken into Haifa. The *Ibrahim el-Awal* was the first conspicuous prize of the war; and the crowds came down Mount Carmel to look at it and cheer. There have been published reports to the effect that the Egyptian destroyer surrendered after taking heavy punishment from the guns of the French cruiser *Kersaint*. The reports appear to have been inaccurate. It is true that the *Kersaint* picked up the *Ibrahim el-Awal* on its radar and, although the Eypgtian was well out of range, fired in her direction. But the *Kersaint* at that time was on its way to Cyprus and confidently left the handling of the *Ibrahim el-Awal* to the Israelis.

That was the news we had for breakfast. For lunch, nothing less than British bomber raids on Egyptian airfields was our topic – that and, of course, *collusion*!

5

The word 'collusion' wrapped itself about with sinister meanings, thanks chiefly to London's horrified denials of its existence. There had to be collusion. Nasser's Suez Canal policy had brought him into bitter conflict with Britain and France and as early as mid-September Mr. Ben Gurion knew perfectly well that if he were to set out on a military campaign intended, in the words of his Chief of Staff, 'to create a military threat to the Suez Canal by the seizure of objectives close to it; to capture the Egyptian positions dominating the entrance to the Gulf of Akaba; and to bring about a disintegration of the Egyptian Order of Battle in the Sinai Peninsula' – if he were to set out on such a campaign, he would be unlikely to run into opposition from the British and French Governments and might very well receive their support.

There were, however, two grave objections to any large-scale Israeli operation in Sinai; and these could only be overcome if France were told of the planned offensive and were ready to help. The first objection was the inadequacy of Israel's armaments in relation to the heavy Soviet equipment piled up at the Egyptian bases in Sinai; the second was the plain fact that the Israeli Air Force, even if France were to supply it with additional jet-propelled aircraft, would be in no position to give support to its attacking forces in Sinai and at the same time protect Tel Aviv and Haifa, which together held one-quarter of the total population of Israel, from disastrous bombing raids which, it might be supposed, Nasser's MIG-screened *Ilyushins* would launch instantly. Mr. Ben Gurion's Cabinet gave approval to the Sinai offensive only on condition that the French Government should be persuaded to provide fighter protection against Egyptian bombing raids directed at the civil population and especially at Tel Aviv and Haifa. The French Government were so persuaded; and in that development above all, collusion may be said to have begun in earnest.

The urgent delivery to Israel of certain indispensable arms and equipment, and the French agreement to give Israel air cover against likely Egyptian bomber raids on the civil population, were arranged somewhere about the middle of October. The planned Israeli offensive then became definite. Obviously the French Government advised the British Government of the Israeli intention; and obviously, therefore, the Israeli offensive when it began on October 29th did not surprise Sir Anthony Eden or M. Mollet or the advisers of either, nor did the armed intervention of Britain and France surprise Mr. Ben Gurion. It is difficult to estimate the extent of the co-ordination between the three attacking forces. Clearly, according to my inquiries and observations, the two operations – those of the Israelis in Sinai and those of the Anglo-French forces based on Cyprus – were separately planned. Neither was in any way dependent on the other except in the measure of Israel's reliance on French protective air support in the event of attempted massive air bombardment of its towns and cities.

There is no evidence of French air support given directly to the Israeli forces in action. French military aircraft based on Cyprus used Lydda airport. They carried, slung underneath their wings, special emergency fuel containers shaped like napalm bombs, and this resemblance inspired certain foreign newspaper correspondents to report active French participation in the Sinai offensive. French pilots and technicians were present also at some of Israel's military airfields. They were there not to fly but to advise the Israelis regarding the use of equipment which had arrived from France only a few days before the campaign began. Certain parachute equipment, never before used by the Israelis, arrived on the morning of 29th October for use that very afternoon. Nothing could have been done with it if the French had not been there to show the Israelis how.

It would be foolish and ungenerous to suggest that the Israelis were not greatly aided by the French. They were: and the Israelis have not forgotten it. But it would be equally foolish and ungenerous to suggest that such aid in any way decisively affected the course of military operations in Sinai. The credit for those unexampled operations should go exclusively to the Israeli armed forces. A competent U.S. military analyst, Brigadier-General S. L. A. Marshall, in his book *Sinai Victory*, has written:

'My conclusion while in Sinai – and it stays unchanged – is that Israel's Army did it by extending the limits of military daring. Hitting forces travelled farther over more formidable country in less time than any other combat body in history. Decision was won in three days. By the fourth day some of the brigades were mopping up two hundred miles beyond their assembly points.
'This alone is a feat at which to marvel. A fortified area about half the size of Nevada and far more repellent than the harshest wastes in that state was conquered by a small field army fighting as it drove forward almost at the rate of an unopposed motor caravan.'

But let it be said that there was collusion: the charge hurts only those who deny it.

6

The 31st October was a bright day, not too hot. Some of us dawdled about the streets of Tel Aviv looking for the signs and effects of war but there were none. At one end there was the clamour of iron against iron in a dozen workshops. At the other there was the cool swirl of water-sprinklers on the lawns of big, new, white apartment houses. In between, the smart little shops were piled with their customary goods: the shoppers were there with their baskets and, surprisingly, met with hardly any shortage; the broad pavements were crowded with men and women about their normal business. Only the Dan Hotel, where newspaper correspondents chewed their pencils, wasted money on telephone calls, and gazed apologetically at their typewriters, kept up a grimace of war.

At Haifa, at least there was the *Ibrahim el-Awal* to look at. In Jerusalem there was the knowledge that on the other side of barbed wire and old tank-traps set across eastward-running streets was a potential enemy which less than one week earlier had concluded an agreement placing its army, together with that of Egypt and Syria under Egyptian command, the agreement to come into force, presumably, in the event of conflict with Israel. But Jordan, very sensibly, manned its border defences and there stood still. So did Syria.

In between Jerusalem and Tel Aviv, and between Tel Aviv and Beersheba on the one side, and Tel Aviv and Haifa on the other, and up into Galilee, fields were being sown; for it was sowing time. In some parts there were not enough sowers because the farmers were down south. There was a notable absence of men from the fields west and north of Haifa. They had been mobilized on Friday 26th October and given forty-eight hours to draw equipment and make their way to an assembly point at Kfar Yeroham some forty miles south-east of Beersheba. Their transport had been anything the brigade could lay hands on. Their Commander was the bulky, six-feet tall Colonel Avraham Yoffe, a veteran, by Israeli standards, in his mid-forties. His nickname, Gideon, was appropriate to the brilliant daring he had shown during the 1948 war and was to show again in what was perhaps the toughest operation assigned to any of the Israeli formations during the Sinai Campaign.

He was to take his brigade overland through trackless eastern Sinai where as good as nobody had been since the tablets were handed down to Moses. He was to get men and supplies and vehicles and some artillery up ascending sands and over shadeless ridges stretched tautly between three and four thousand feet towards the sky and through narrow defiles blocked by huge boulders. They would come down through this kind of country to

Dahab, on the Gulf of Akaba, and probably have a battle of sorts there and then would push on through more of this bitter lunar geography to what should be a big battle at Ras Nasrani, which had in its grip the Narrows through which ships could pass from the Red Sea into the Gulf of Akaba and so to the Jordanian port of Akaba and the Israeli port of Eilat, at the head of the Gulf.

But I am getting ahead of things. It is still the 31st October and on that day Gideon's brigade of northern farmers was pushing doggedly over the dust track to Kuntilla. Colonel Sharon's paratroopers had cleared that initial way two days earlier and now were ready to advance into the Hitan and Mitla Passes and come out opposite the southern end of the Suez Canal. For that matter, the Abu Agheila, Rafa and El Arish defences in the north-east had yet to be smashed so that the way would be opened to the Canal at El Kantara and Ismailya and to the Gaza Stip at the back. And these decisive, big-scale operations had to be carried out while Gideon's men were clambering through sand and over rock to their objectives at the southern tip of the peninsula, which were at least five and probably six days' haul and march away.

The battle for the Mitla Pass began at noon on the 31st. It was, in fact, a battle for the Hitan Pass, slightly to the east, the possession of which would give the brigade possession of the whole Mitla area and the road to Suez. Not much resistance was expected because enemy convoys moving up from the Canal had been intercepted by Israeli bombers and had had most of their vehicles and motorized armament destroyed. It was a fair assumption that the survivors among the men had turned back towards Suez.

But they had not. They had moved into the Mitla defile, which is bow-shaped, cliff-walled and something less than four miles long; and there had set themselves up in positions of ambush along the cliffs and in concealed caves. In the dry, harsh light of early afternoon the Israelis entered the pass and came under devastating fire from positions they could not see. Four MIG fighter planes roared over, adding to casualties and confusion. Then two Israeli fighters appeared, drove the MIG's off and brought all four of them down. The brigade at the pass took what cover there was and its commanding officer thought hard about what to do next. The decision was characteristic. It was to work up the sides and along the ridges – difficult enough even without an enemy to fight at the same time – and then down to the caves.

The battle lasted seven hours. In some ways it was the hardest fought battle of the whole Sinai Campaign. Almost everywhere else the Egyptians, fearing they could not sustain the obstinate Israeli attack, had broken while there yet remained a way out for them. At the Hitan–Mitla positions there was no way out. Some of the defenders are believed to have got away to the desolate terrain stretching northwards, but the rest were taken prisoner or killed. There were 200 Egyptian dead at the end of those uncanny seven hours. The whole of the southern axis of the main Israeli offensive into Sinai was now secure and the big northern assaults could plunge on without risk of having to divert part of their slender and precious air support to Mitla.

Next morning, November 1st, found Gideon and his farmer Reservists at Ras en Nakb, west of Eilat at the head of the Gulf, and facing south. He was ordered by the High Command to stay there for twenty-four hours and let the battle for Rafa, away to the north, go forward. And glad enough the brigade was to stay there and rest a while before setting off, with meagre supplies and a minimum of drinking water and without artillery because there were ten chances to one that artillery would get stuck in the sand or blocked in narrow passes – glad enough they were to rest before setting off into the unknown, imperfectly mapped, forbidding topography rising from the western shores of the Gulf of Akaba.

The decisive northern offensive began with the attack on Rafa's fortified approaches at 0400 hours. In that attack, says an Israeli military report, 'we suffered heavy losses, with some of our officers and men killed and the wounded running into several scores'. Almost the overriding consideration of the Israeli High Command during the Sinai Campaign was the necessity to keep casualties down to the lowest possible. It is easy to imagine Ben Gurion, striding up and down at Staff Headquarters in Tel Aviv, pressing that point home. Therefore, 'some of our officers and men killed and the wounded running into several scores' as a result of the battle which opened the way to the most strongly defended of Egypt's Sinai bases, could be described as 'heavy losses'.

After the first break-through towards Rafa, the Chief of Staff, Major-General Dayan, appeared at the front line and ordered the final attack. It began at three o'clock in the afternoon and was over by nightfall. The Israelis were in Rafa, one part of them turning towards El Kantara and the Suez Canal, and another part towards

Khan Yunis and the Gaza Strip. By that night the whole of the Egyptian chain of command had broken down. From Eastern Command Headquarters on the Canal had gone out the message, *Sauve qui peut*. Vast stores of petrol, food and clothing and a massive booty of Russian tanks, guns, vehicles and electronic equipment had been left to the Israelis. The number of prisoners taken was so great as to be a serious embarrassment, but even so the desert swarmed with pitiful fugitives plodding southward through the dunes and coastal lagoons.

Next morning, 2nd November, El Arish was taken with hardly more than a shot. Later that day the Egyptian Commander of the Gaza Strip surrendered. Israeli columns moved west along the coast road to within sight of El Kantara and ten miles from the Canal. Other columns swung down the main desert highway from Abu Agheila to within ten miles of the Canal and facing Ismailya. Colonel Sharon's brigade was through the Mitla Pass and up against Port Suez. Israel was bivouacked along the whole length of the Canal and all Sinai was in its possession except the southern tip, the peninsula proper.

But Gideon and his men were on their way to sweep clean that corner. The account of their expedition through pitiless sand and ascending rock, even as told in the curt phrases of unit and formation report, has a quality of antique heroism. Colonel Sharon's brigade had had it tough enough in all conscience on the grievous track to victory at Mitla. Gideon's brigade had been given an even tougher job; and quietly had gone about it, day after day, pushing through sand that gathered around them like ocean tides, clambering up steep, rock mountains where no tree or shrub grew and no track had been cut since they were thrown up out of the molten earth and left to cool.

At one stage a Dakota appeared above them, black against a starlit sky. In it was the Chief of Staff, General Dayan. He spoke on his radio telephone to Gideon:

'Is everything O.K.?'

'Yes, everything is O.K.'

'Then push on.'

They pushed on. On the evening of 3rd November the brigade came down from the heights to Dahab on the shore of the Gulf. They fought a brief battle there and sustained a few casualties. An MTB which had been carried overland from Haifa to Eilat's harbour brought them supplies of petrol to Dahab. Then they moved up again and on towards Ras Nasrani. Ras Nasrani comes down in sharp, jutting rock, on which four powerful naval guns had been mounted to give emphasis to its authority. Almost a regiment can be lodged in the fortress hewn from the rock, and round about are concrete bunkers, wire entanglements and a broad apron of minefields. The Gulf at this point has a narrow passage between coral reefs and the island of Tiran and there is no other way to the head of the Gulf so that even a battleship would be in sad plight if it tried to get by against the will of the garrison and the fire of the four naval guns, let alone a merchant ship making for Eilat. With this garrison and these guns, therefore, Egypt had been able to keep ships away from Israel's port of Eilat.

Gideon's Brigade should have come up against a big battle at Ras Nasrani. Instead, the great fortress was a walkover. The Egyptians had withdrawn their garrison, spiked their guns, and concentrated at the much weaker position of Sharm es-Sheikh, the administrative centre farther south. So the brigade moved on. They had an asphalt road to go along. They reached Sharm es-Sheikh on the 5th November and at once broke through the Egyptian lines. In a few hours the last of the Egyptian Sinai defences fell and the last of the Egyptian garrisons on Sinai surrendered. Gideon's brigade rested thirty hours at Sharm es-Sheikh and then, under orders from the High Command, went home. The men were needed to sow the winter crops and pick the ripened fruit. They had travelled fourteen hundred miles there and back and had covered territory that would have tried the ingenuity of an experienced, intrepid and well-equipped party of explorers with plenty of time on their hands and no enemy to obstruct their course. They had shaken the Egyptians because it was against all reason that a hostile force should descend upon them from a land barrier that was their own natural defence.

It had been an expedition without precedent in military history and at the end of it the men who did it went back to their farms and groves. And so the Sinai Campaign ended. Israel's Army, in seven days, had captured from an enemy greatly superior in numbers and equipment a territory two and a half times the size of Israel itself.

Twenty-one

THERE were no victory displays. There was no marching through proud avenues of waving arms. It had not been that kind of war. All at once an army had been got together and put into action, and all at once it was brought out of action and dispersed. The delegates of 57 nations assembled at U.N. Headquarters had told the conquerors of Sinai to turn about and go back, leaving their conquest to the guardianship of an international force under the command of the Canadian, Major-General E. L. M. Burns, who had been Chief of Staff of the U.N. Truce Organization set up in Jerusalem after the 1948 war. Something like that was bound to happen once the United States Government set its face against the Anglo-French landing at Port Said and had beside it the Soviet Government with its face set even more grimly. Probably it would have happened to the Israelis anyway, even if their campaign had not coincided with the Anglo-French operations and there had been no 'collusion'.

But the Israelis got where they wanted to go before Washington or Moscow could reach the U.N. megaphone and shout *Halt!* The British and French did not. Their offensive had dilly-dallied and was abortive. Whether or not it deserved better I shall leave to the political moralists. I suppose nothing of that kind is likely to succeed nowadays if Washington resolves that it shall not; and much less so if, as in this instance, Moscow backs up Washington. At one time there was even the fear that the Russians might take a direct hand in the hostilities; and for a few days in early November the Israelis pondered the risk of Soviet-manned bomber aircraft coming down from Syria. It did not happen but it could have happened and that may have been one of the reasons why the U.S. Government took the firm stand it did and forced swift acceptance of the Cease Fire from Port Said to Gaza.

The Anglo-French failure, whatever its reasons, slightly blunted the edge of Israel's victory and gave Colonel Nasser the opportunity, fairly taken, to weave for himself garlands of triumph out of the embarrassment of France and Britain. In that way he may have

deceived the Cairo crowds, who are easily deceived; but not the
Arab States that had been looking on, and whose political and
military leaders knew well enough that Nasser's armies had been
thoroughly whipped and put to flight by the Israelis. These political
and military leaders would continue to talk, as would Colonel
Nasser and his Army Commanders, of the day when they would
drive the Israelis into the sea; but it would be a day pushed well away
from realistic intention.

On 9th November the Government of Israel accepted the U.N.
terms and agreed to withdraw its forces from Sinai as soon as the
international force was ready to take over. Announcing this in the
Knesset, Mr. Ben Gurion was able to say:

'The main outcome of the Sinai Campaign has been the
strengthening of Israel's security by the destruction of Egypt's
Sinai armies and the consequent removal of the threat to our
southern borders. . . . We have broken through to the Red Sea
and ensured the free passage of shipping to and from our port of
Eilat. . . . The Egyptian dictator's stature in the eyes of Middle
East peoples is no longer what it was. . . .'

He may have hoped for more. He cannot have hoped for much
more, in territories the destiny of which is the business of competing
Powers. The war had not been visualized as a war of territorial
conquest except, perhaps, where the Gaza Strip was concerned. That
narrow, nerve-racking Strip was within the boundaries of Palestine
and isolated from the rest of the Arab world. As an Egyptian
outpost it had done no good for itself and much hurt to Israel, and
its cooped-up refugees from the 1948 war, about 200,000 of them,
must continue to be a source of tension unless re-settled. Israel would
have been willing to re-settle them and had even worked out elaborate settlement plans. Whether these plans have been torn up or
merely shelved against some future chance, I do not know.

It is probable, also, that Ben Gurion and his colleagues would
have liked to keep garrisons at Ras Nasrani and Sharm es-Sheikh,
which command the entrance to the Gulf of Akaba and the only
navigable passage from the Red Sea to Israel's port of Eilat. But
that, like the Gaza Strip, was not to be. Ben Gurion made no fuss
about these disappointments. He knows when to give up as surely as
he knows when to take. Public opinion supported him and there
were few signs of dismay.

'The Israelis have shown that 1948 was not an accident,' said a

Western diplomat in Tel Aviv. 'If the Arabs have learned that lesson, the Sinai Campaign has been well worth while.'

Of course, the lesson was not merely a re-emphasizing of the fact that the Israeli makes a good soldier. He does. His exceptional morale, his confidence in a leadership that is always near at hand, and the reinforcement of these conditions by the principle of *ein brera* – no alternative to victory – are enough to make a first-class soldier. But the phenomenal success of the Israeli forces against the Egyptians in 1956 – as against the combined Arab armies of 1948 – is due also in some measure to fatal defects of training and leadership in all Arab armies except the Jordanian.

The Egyptian soldier is not a coward. Nations who live fatalistically, as the Arabs do, often are capable of an amazing courage. But fatalism is not proof against fear or panic in a unit under heavy attack and with no notion what to do about it. There is no sense, even for a fatalist, in getting killed instead of running away. Over and over again during the Sinai Campaign units were left without leadership. They were left to meet an attack, do what they could against it, and run when they had to. The result was that a system of highly-fortified positions was not made full use of; while vast stores were left behind because no one in the Egyptian Command seemed able to foresee probable attack or to measure a unit's capacity to hold the attack.

Colonel Nasser's main contribution to the Egyptian Army since 1948 has been to stamp out corruption and to ensure effective supplies. That means a good deal. No army of comparable numbers could have been better armed and fitted out than were the Egyptian Sinai forces in 1956. But not until social conditions in Egypt have been enormously improved will any Egyptian army equal in training, initiative or moral resource, men accustomed to advanced social conditions and able to understand the complicated craft of modern soldiering.

2

As fast as the U.N. forces moved into Sinai, the Israelis moved out. That was not as fast as General Burns would have liked, mainly because the Israelis had seen to it that no single strategic road or track in the Peninsula should remain passable. But the U.N. was

200

up as far as El Arish, Rafa and the Abu Agheila cross-roads by January 1957, and on 8th March moved into the Gaza Strip. By dusk of that day not one Israeli soldier was left on Egyptian territory or in the Strip.

One of the last to come out and be demobilized was Yosh, my hairdresser of Ben Yehuda Street in Tel Aviv. He was back with his scissors on 12th March.

'It was nothing,' he said, twirling the scissors and staring at my reflection in the looking-glass, 'just movement, movement. I tell you, that war was a funny thing. You fought a bit and then on you went, fought another bit and then on you went again. And the worst part of it was the moving. Nightmare country.' He smiled. 'But look how brown I am! Pretty good, eh?'

And that was all Yosh had to say on the subject of the astonishing Sinai Campaign.

Israel went back to work: Yosh to his scissors; Yehuda to his workshop; Mordechai to his farm. You could see the whole country settling back quietly to its accustomed ways. But the settling back was a special thing in the border settlements and villages: one almost heard the sigh that went up; saw the smile; and felt the relief. The dogs at night could rattle their chains and bark their heads off. No matter. Turn over and go to sleep again. The children could play in the groves until well after dusk. Let them be; they can come to no harm. The village truck could set off along the sandy road at dawn. It will be back, safe and sound: no road mines have been laid during the night. The night-guards were withdrawn and now could do a decent day's work in the fields: a single watchman, instead of ten or a dozen prowling the village or settlement boundaries, was enough. Nobody said it was peace but it was better than anything that had gone before.

'For years we've felt like a listening-post between our own lines and those of the enemy,' said a young girl settler of Nahal Oz, up against the Gaza Strip. 'Now we can get up and walk about and go to bed at night. It's such a different feeling. Oh, it's made a big difference to us down here.'

Tel Aviv could not be expected to feel the difference; nor could Haifa. The lights and the crowds were there and the *Fayadeen* had never dared to strike that far and so dangerously for themselves. But in the lands fanning out from Beersheba, and up around Lachish, and even along the Jordanian border where it follows the Wady

Araba and where, in the centre, it runs only a few paces from the Tel Aviv–Haifa railway tracks, the day had been made almost safe and the night almost as safe as the day.

Of course, it would not last. Nobody expected it to. But it would be a year or two before U.N.'s international force moved out of Sinai and Gaza and the Egyptians moved back and the *Feyadeen* could be reorganized and trouble began all over again. Meanwhile, Colonel Nasser would have to be satisfied with holding up Israeli ships in the Suez Canal or confiscating Israeli cargoes carried in foreign bottoms. The Jordanians might start something on Mount Scopus: that would always be a sore point. But none of the likely events would hinder a man from sowing his fields or a woman from getting a night's sleep or a child from playing in the dusk. The terror raids had been a different matter, just as the massing of Colonel Nasser's Soviet-armed forces against the southern frontier had been a different matter.

By Middle East standards then, the first post-Sinai year was reasonably tranquil. In an official summary of national events during 1957, published in the spring of 1958, the following main headlines occur:

> Anti-Polio Vaccination Campaign Begins.
> Withdrawal from Sinai and Gaza Strip Completed.
> First large Ocean-going Vessel puts in at Eilat.
> Knesset Approves Eisenhower Doctrine.
> International Nuclear Science Conference opens at Weizmann Institute, Rehovot.
> President Ben Zvi begins Second Term of Office.
> Arid Zone Research Institute opened at Beersheba.
> Lake Huleh Drainage Scheme Completed.

It was a quiet and profitable record for the year. The last of the headlines given by the official summary calls for an unquiet footnote. When the waters of Lake Huleh had been drained off and 15,000 new-won acres lay shining in the sun, the Syrians grew restive and there was some shooting in the area. Along went U.N. Observers and land surveyors to keep the disputants apart and to measure the boundaries of the reclaimed land, which the Syrians said lapped over into what properly was their territory. Thanks to the U.N. intervention, no serious trouble developed. As I write these words it occurs to me that one could very often write such words. Anyone who cared to go to the trouble could work up an impressive account of the border conflicts between Israel and her neighbours that have remained minor ones thanks to the intervention of U.N.'s Truce Organization.

But the Sinai Campaign in the Autumn of 1956 undoubtedly contributed, above all other influences, to the relative tranquillity along Israel's borders during 1957 and throughout the State's joyous Tenth Anniversary Year, 1958. The Mount Scopus dispute cropped up again in the summer of 1958 and this time U.N. felt it necessary to intervene at a higher level than usual. First of all Mr. Hammarskjold's assistant, Doctor Urrutia, came out; and then Mr. Hammarskjold himself; but before the tension could be ended quite a little battle had to be fought on the Mount, in which several lives, including that of a U.N. officer trying to mediate between the two sides, were lost. Scopus will work up into dispute again, we may be sure of that. Like so much that has been left over from the Armistice Agreements, it is bound to remain as a dangerous irritant until such time as the two sides can be brought together to work out a logical settlement. When all is said and done, Israel's basic weakness, which has been carried over into its second decade, is unchanged: the hostility of every neighbour with the possible exception of Lebanon; and the survival, under a system of Armistice Agreements, of frontier anomalies likely from time to time to stir that smouldering hostility into something like frenzy.

Twenty-two

THE future? Who can tell? Of the Land of Prophecy perhaps it is wise not to prophesy.

I do not doubt that it will survive. It's people are venturesome, courageous, and hardy. The young ones are growing up into men and women at least the equal of their elders, who brought the State into being. But as the State develops its problems multiply at all three of the most vivid and impatient levels – security, social, and economic; of which the economic is likely to be the most immediate if only because German reparations payments, which have been a major source of foreign currency income, are coming to an end. More and more the cost of new immigrant settlement, industrial and agricultural expansion, and national defence will have to be met from the earnings of the State and the value internationally put upon its credit. But they are a hard-working, shrewd people who have not been wasting their time; and it is fair to assume that the money and labour invested during the past twelve years will soon bring in returns capable of balancing such losses as may be caused by the withdrawal of special funds.

But the proper development of Israel's economy, like the solution of more than one of its social problems, is dependent in the main on a solution of the security problem. That must continue to be the chief preoccupation of the generation now ready to provide the country's leadership, as it has been of the leaders who are approaching the end of their public service. And the question of security is, of course, the question of peace. By one means or another the four Arab States bordering Israel must be persuaded to give up harassing their neighbour and threatening its extermination. The prospect hardly encourages optimism. It may improve when, on the Arab side, some kind of social stability has been reached and inter-State rivalries have become less fierce. Before that time has been reached, Israel should have new leaders, not wiser than the old ones but, having inherited a State already economically sound, and with an Army that has proved itself to be the most effective in the Middle East, better able to dare generously in the cause of peace.

I take Major-General Moshé Dayan as an example of the kind of man now entering Israeli politics and likely to venture into gestures of peace once the Arabs show some sign of willingness to respond. Dayan, victor of Sinai and former Chief of Staff, in his military capacity was known as a ruthless 'activist'. His answer to Arab raids into Israel was to mount heavy reprisal actions, which, approved as they may have been by Mr. Ben Gurion, often were impolitic to say the least. Their adverse effect on Israel's relations with the Western Powers – and for that matter with the Soviet Union, too – often outweighed the temporary good that may have been done in the border area concerned.

Dayan resigned from leadership of the Defence Forces in 1957 and became a student of the Hebrew University. In 1959 he took his degree and, at his own wish, was removed from the active list in order to take part in the political campaign leading up to General Elections in the winter of that same year. He is a warm supporter of Ben Gurion who, in turn, is a warm and almost paternal supporter of Dayan. He is a loyal member of the dominant Labour Party, or *Mapai*, which placed him high up on its electoral list, but is by no means a blindly subservient party man and has already caused a great deal of heart-fluttering and head-shaking among his party elders. The evidence suggests that he will be as unconventional and daring in politics as he has been in war, and that his clear-cut, intelligent, and imaginative approach to Israel's problems will win him wide public support, especially among the young men and women of the country.

Dayan realizes that Israel wants peace and that however good its army may be, it is not an army of conquest, but of defence. Activist as he has shown himself to be when the Arabs were terrorizing the Israeli countryside, he is realist enough to know that peace is worth a price: not a price involving substantial territorial concessions, which no Israeli of any political group would tolerate, but nevertheless likely to be tempting to Arab leaders serving national interests and accepting the plain fact that Israel is there to stay and had better be put up with. One such concession, which I believe Dayan thinks logical, would be the granting to Jordan of a free zone from its border through Israeli territory to free-port facilities at Haifa. That is only one example of the profit the Arabs, as well as Israeli, could make out of some working agreement aimed, in the first place, at putting an end to border tension and a state of suspended war.

205

I do not suggest for a minute that Dayan and his like in the new Knesset or the next will accomplish or attempt to accomplish anything dramatic. In the first place, before any radical change in Israeli–Arab relations can take place, there must be a radical change in the internal affairs of the Arab countries. That change, I suspect, may be on its way. Meanwhile, it is idle to accuse the Israelis of being stiff-necked and uncompromising in their attitude to the Arab complaints. Israel recognizes the existence of an Arab case, and over and over again Mr. Ben Gurion has offered to sit down with Arab leaders to talk matters over. But no Israeli Government dare offer to take back the 800,000 refugees. There is nowhere to put them. The security problem likely to develop if only half that number came, must be obvious to anyone. But there is no doubt that Israel could help in a joint re-settlement scheme for the refugees. Then again, there are such questions as the adjustment of the borders for the benefit of villages cut off at present from their lands or water source; compensation for abandoned property; the Mount Scopus enclave and the El Auja (Nizana) zone in the south.

None of these or any other of the sore questions outstanding between Israel and her neighbours can be satisfactorily settled as long as those neighbours insist, as Egypt does officially, on preserving belligerent status and acting belligerently, again as Egypt continues to do, and on stating in so many words that the only settlement possible between Israel and the Arabs is a violent one to be brought about by the extermination of Israel. Of course, that may only be talk. But it is talk backed by big armies and big concentrations of modern armament; and who is to guarantee that it is only talk? It is hardly logical to expect the Israelis to take Whitehall's or Washington's word for it, especially at a time when the Soviet Union seems ready to support Colonel Nasser's Egypt and General Kassem's Iraq and to do so to the accompaniment of anti-Israeli propaganda.

Arab nationalism, of course, is nothing of the kind. It was not nationalism that brought Colonel Nasser to power and it is not nationalism that has brought General Kassem to rulership of Iraq. Nearly all the violent and so-called violent nationalist upheavals in Arab countries since the fall of the Ottomans, in any other part of the world would have been social revolutionary movements brought about by poverty, ill-health and dreary hardship. But the illiterate Arab of populous Middle East areas has not the habit of analysing socially the griefs that are his and were his forefathers'. The resentment he feels is resentment not directed at his rulers or exploiters or at anything to which he can point a finger until along comes some agitator to work up resentment into hysteria and to point the finger at France in Syria, at the British in Egypt or Iraq, at anything handy and, at last, at Israel.

The process has worked equally well for opposition movements, like the Moslem Brotherhood, and for Governments feeling the need to cover up social failures by diverting popular discontent. British Imperialism has served Colonel Nasser well but there is not much of it left in Egypt, Jordan or Iraq, although it still does his ambitions good service on the eastern periphery of the Empire he covets. But Israel is there in conspicuous measure, right up against Lebanon, Syria, Jordan and Egyptian Sinai and, so to speak, under the very noses of the Arab masses. What more natural than that he should earn the applause of the Cairo crowds with threats to annihilate the Israeli armies and exterminate their State? And what more natural than that he should try to work up the Jordanians against their rulers and the Iraqis against theirs by proving to them, through the radio and the paid agitator, that he alone has the will and the might to exterminate the Jews? And, as if it were not enough that the Israelis should be Jews, and therefore without any right in the Middle East, the good old anti-British anti-French and even anti-American line can be brought in to tease mounting resentment by describing the Israelis as 'tools of Western Imperialism'.

Probably Colonel Nasser and those other Arab rulers who compete with him have not the slightest intention of trying to exterminate Israel. The Israeli Defence Forces have been shown to be a peculiarly tough proposition. Neither Colonel Nasser nor General Kassem nor any other Arab leader taking part in such a war of 'extermination' could survive defeat. And even if they were strong enough to stand a fair chance of pushing back the Israelis by weight of number and armaments, what would the Western Powers and U.N. say – or do? And would Soviet Russia risk a world war in order to expand its already surprising influence in the Arab Middle East?

Unfortunately, most Arab countries quickly lose patience with logic and common sense, and are easily driven towards their own disaster. Colonel Nasser and other Arab leaders cannot go on working up the passions of their people with anti-Israel threats and boasts and leave it at that. One day they will be expected to make good the threats and to justify the boasts. The question then will be whether they can divert such expectations to some other object. And the question now is whether they will have the good sense to rest on their anti-Israeli anti-Imperialist oars and set about improving the social conditions of their people to a standard at which peace will be something worth enjoying and hysterical animosities will have lost all political profit. It is the question asked by the Israelis, who, until it is answered hopefully, will have to take account of the Arab threats and prepare to meet them.